Challenging Social Exclusion

Multi-Sectoral Approaches to Realising Social Justice in East Africa

Editors

H. Hintjens, J. M. Maguru,
F. Nyakaisiki, J. Odong

FOUNTAIN PUBLISHERS
www.fountainpublishers.co.ug

Fountain Publishers
P.O. Box 488
Kampala
E-mail: sales@fountainpublishers.co.ug
publishing@fountainpublishers.co.ug
Website: www.fountainpublishers.co.ug

First published 2015

ISBN: 978-9970-25-887-1

Contents

Preface v
Editors viii
Bio Notes x
Acknowledgements xiv
Abstracts of chapters xvi

1: Introduction: From Bird's Eye View to Worm's Eye View? Social Justice, Human Rights and JLOS in Uganda and East Africa 1
Jimmy M. Maguru, Florence Nyakaisiki, Jackson Odong and Helen Hintjens

Part One: Historical and Restorative Justice in East Africa 31

2: Social Justice: Recognition and Reparation: Connecting Kenyan *Mungiki* 'gangs' with the Mau Mau Legal Case 32
Nancy Muigei

3: Justice on the Radio? An Assessment of Justice Frames in 'Facing Justice', an NGO-supported Radio Programme 62
Jackson Odong

Part Two: Land Justice in East Africa 93

4: Law and Land Justice in Urban Tanzania: The Case of Mbeya 94
Thomas Munzerere

5: Beyond Rights Awareness: Women, Men and Land Rights: A Case Study from Eastern Uganda................. 138
Clare Cheremoi

6: Land Rights in the Context of Post-War Northern Uganda: The Case of Amuru District, Uganda............ 181
Grace Angeline Chelimo

Part Three: Health Justice and Disability Rights in Uganda...221

7: Health Justice and Gender Justice: the Role of Traditional Birth Attendants (TBAs) in Uganda....... 222
Florence Nyakaisiki

8: Disability and social justice: The Role of Refugee Leaders in Enhancing Access to Social Justice by Refugees with Disability... 250
Jimmy Mugisha Maguru

Part Four: Legal Justice and Social Justice in East Africa.283

9: 'Street-level' Bureaucrats in Rwanda: Working for more just outcomes of Judicial Reforms 284
Gervais Twahirwa

10: No Justice? Mob Violence, Community Policing and Crime Control in Uganda's Urban Markets.................. 322
Joshua Mugambwa and Helen Hintjens

11: Conclusion: The Future of Social Justice across the JLOS Institutions in East Africa 357
Freda Joyce Apio

Appendix 1 381
Index 384

Preface

Social justice has been used by various scholars as a very general concept to refer to ideals as well as aims and outcomes of policies and practices. However, it has not been used continuously; it has gone in and out of fashion. Social justice implies that the activities of government, social actors and other institutions should be geared towards ensuring equality, responsible, dignified and socially acceptable behaviour in society, and that the weakest and most socially excluded in society should be able to express their needs. For sustained social and economic development to take root in any country, professionals in NGOs, JLOS sector institutions, health and education sectors should desist from considering citizens as simply 'clients', 'offenders' or 'patients'. They should be viewed as full participants and beneficiaries. This will enhance the advancement of justice for all.

As the authors of this volume recognize, social justice has to include economic justice for the poor, respect for the capacities of the disabled, and acknowledgement of the critical roles played by minority groups, poor households, children and non-citizens, and other vulnerable people in all spheres of life. The needs and rights of those considered 'marginal' is unlikely to be a priority for most policy-makers and officials, and yet to make them a priority is what social justice requires, as articulated in this volume.

This volume challenges the perceptions of professionals in the JLOS sector and beyond. The problem across East African

Countries is how such professionals relate with ordinary members of the public, especially the minorities, socially excluded or those in vulnerable positions. In 2011, studies carried out by Nsamizi Training Institute for Social Development, in four pilot Districts in Uganda, Bugiri, Mpigi, Sheema and Oyam, identified problems faced at community-level in relation to justice, law and order services and local people. These problems included: negative attitudes and behaviour of professionals due to lack of skills needed to administer justice by formal and informal courts, probation and social welfare officers, state prosecutors, police and prison officers at community level. These problems arose especially when dealing with complaints of women, children and other vulnerable people. The sentencing and punishment regime was viewed as mechanical and devoid of special or social considerations critical to effective rehabilitation of offenders and avoiding the negative effects of sentencing for children and communities. There was also inadequate knowledge of human rights and of professional procedures, and generally inadequate documentation.

This volume will be useful to academicians and social justice practitioners in East Africa as it argues for a socially just and human rights-based approach to public policy implementation in the JLOS sector and beyond. This implies that policy-makers and practicing professionals should be prepared to listen to ordinary people expressing their own needs and priorities. The case studies tackle current and emerging issues such as congestion in courts in East African countries, increasing case backlogs, homosexuality and minority rights, the case of women resorting to TBAs, 'mob justice', informal justice and crime control, bribery and corruption and charging of illegal fees, land rights and land justice, refugee and disability rights.

I take this opportunity to thank each and every individual who has made it possible for this book to be published. This especially goes to the tireless efforts and sacrifices of time and energy put in by the editors Ms Florence Nyakaisiki, Mr Jimmy Maguru, Mr Jackson Odong and Dr Helen Hintjens. I thank the editors and staff at Fountain Publishers for their thorough job in the editing of this volume, given its considerable length. The contributors of the various chapters are strongly commended for the great job. Last but not least, I sincerely thank the Royal Netherlands Government, through their funding body NUFFIC, for the financial support in the production of this work.

For God and my Country

Dr Charles Kanyesigye
Principal

Editors

Helen Hintjens ISS Staff

Helen Hintjens is senior lecturer in Development and Social Justice at the International Institute of Social Studies, based in The Hague in The Netherlands, a constituent part of Erasmus University Rotterdam. She is interested and publishes on the post-genocide politics of the Great Lakes region, and on the politics of refugee and asylum advocacy between Europe and Africa. She has an emerging interest in the politics of restitution, starting with the Kenyan Mau Mau compensation case currently going through the UK courts. Her contact is hintjens@iss.nl.

Jimmy Mugisha Maguru NTISD

Jimmy Maguru has a BA (SS) (Hons), PGDCBR, MA (Development Studies) and MPHL. He has been involved in community development oriented programmes in Uganda and has a lot of experience in research, training, project management and evaluation. His research interest is in disability and development, refugees and development, public health and social protection. He is a senior lecturer at Nsamizi Training Institute of Social Development and also manages a refugee' outreach programme of the Institute in collaboration with UNHCR Uganda. His contact is magurujimmy@gmail.com

Florence Nyakaisiki NTISD and ISS

Florence Nyakaisiki is a senior lecturer at Nsamizi Training Institute of Social Development. She graduated with a BA (Social Work and Social Administration) degree from Makerere University in 2008, and a Masters of Arts in Development Studies degree in 2012 (majoring in Human Rights, Development and Social Justice) from the International Institute of Social Studies, Erasmus University, Hague, Netherlands. Key areas of research interest include Women's Rights, Children's Rights and Welfare, Community Development and Gender and Development. Her contact is flo.nyakaisiki@yahoo.com

Jackson Odong RLP and ISS

Jackson Odong has worked with the Refugee Law Project, School of Law, Makerere University from 2010 and has since then been engaged in research and advocacy on conflict, peace building, and post-war development in northern Uganda. His research interests include media, gender, human rights, transitional justice, and youth unemployment. His contact is jackodong2009@gmail.com

Bio Notes

Joyce Freda Apio is a human rights lawyer and a democracy practitioner. She holds a Master of Laws (LLM) Degree in Human Rights and Democratisation from the University of Pretoria, South Africa. She is the Programme Manager at Kituo Cha Katiba (KcK), a regional think tank on constitutionalism, good governance and democratic development. Previously, Joyce worked with various NGOs including Parliamentarians for Global Action (PGA), The Ugandan Coalition for International Criminal Court and Human Rights Network-Uganda. Outside KcK, Joyce lectures at the Centre for Social Justice of Nsamizi Training Institute for Social Development, and the College of Humanities and Social Sciences, Makerere University. Joyce's areas of interest include socio-economic rights, international criminal justice and constitutionalism. Her contact is fredaapio@gmail.com

Grace Angeline Chelimo is an experienced Ugandan lawyer and fellow of the International Institute of Social Studies of Erasmus University in Rotterdam from where she graduated with a specialisation in Human Rights, Development and Social Justice. She is currently working as the Resource Person for Land Justice at the Justice Law and Order Sector Secretariat in Uganda. She previously worked for the Justice for Children Programme and the Uganda Human Rights Commission. She is passionate about securing the rights of the marginalised, poor and vulnerable. Her contact is angelinechelimo@gmail.com

Clare Cheromoi is a lecturer and researcher at Uganda Christian University, Mukono. Clare holds a Master's Degree from Erasmus University, of the International Institute of social studies. She majored in Human Rights Development and social justice. Her professional and research work focuses on problems undermining the development of economies in Africa, with a particular interest in human rights abuses, poverty, anti-corruption practices and development. She works hard to promote the rights of girls from disadvantaged regions of the country. Her contact is cheroclare@yahoo.com

Joshua Mugambwa holds a Master's in Governance and Development (University of Antwerp, Belgium) and a Master's in Management Studies (Uganda Management Institute, Uganda). He is a PhD student at Makerere University. His professional and research interests include Governance and Development in Sub-Saharan Africa, with a particular interest in innovation in local governance mechanisms and practices. He is especially concerned with innovations in practices that have potential to improve Human Development indicators in the Sub-Sahara African region. His contact is mugambwaj@yahoo.com

Nancy C. Muigei is a human rights practitioner, focused on the Horn of Africa and East Africa. Her research interests include: Youth, Militias, Transitional Justice, Media and Conflict. Nancy has been a recipient of various awards such as the NORAD scholarship at the University of Oslo (2009) and the Netherlands Fellowship Programme (Nuffic) in 2011-2012. She holds a Master's in Development having specialised in Conflict, Reconstruction and Human Security at the International Institute of Social Studies (ISS) of the Erasmus University, Rotterdam. Nancy is also a published poet. Nancy currently works in the Development Sector with a focus on Human Rights. Her contact is muigei.nancy@gmail.com

Thomas Munzerere joined the Judiciary in Tanzania as a Resident Magistrate in 2007. In 2009 he was appointed as an Assistant Registrar of The District Land and Housing Tribunals where he currently works. He holds a Master's degree in Development Studies with emphasis in Human Rights, Gender and Conflict Studies from The Institute of Social Studies of Erasmus University Rotterdam in The Netherlands. He also holds a Bachelor's in Law (LLB) from The University of Dar es Salaam in Tanzania. In 2005 he worked as an Assistant Protection Officer with the United Nation High Commission for Refugees, and his present post involves him in justice administration in relation to land disputes in Tanzania.

Gervais Twahirwa was recently appointed Director General of Corporate Services in the Ministry of Justice. After working for some years with NGOs like ADRA International, German Agro Action, and World Relief, Gervais joined the public justice sector in 2006. He went to the National University of Rwanda and graduated in the Faculty of Economics, Social Sciences and Management in 2003. In 2010, he went to the Netherlands for further studies where his Master's was in Development

Studies, majoring in Public Policy and Management from the International Institute of Social Studies (ISS), Erasmus University, Rotterdam. His Master's thesis was about the Impact of Judicial Reforms on the Motivation of Street-Level Bureaucrats: The Case of the Supreme Court of Rwanda. His contact is twahiger@yahoo.fr

Acknowledgements

The editors wish to thank all the staff and students of the two 'sister' institutions who were involved in this study from the start and who are too numerous to mention. The two institutions are Nsamizi Training Institute for Social Development in Mpigi, Uganda and the International Institute of Social Studies (ISS), of Erasmus University Rotterdam, the ISS being based in The Hague in The Netherlands. Through relationships between their two institutions, the idea of a series of books accompanied the process of collaborative partnership building between NTISD and ISS over the past decade or more. This is the second such volume; the first was *Issues in Social Development and Local Governance in Uganda,* edited by Nicholas Awortwi and Auma Okwany, and available on-line (Shaker Press). Especial thanks are due to Nicholas Awortwi, who is now based in Nairobi as Director of Research at the Partnership for African Social and Governance Research (PASGR), and was formerly at ISS. Together with Charles Otim and Okey Ndubueze, Nicholas crafted the project that was funded by Nuffic – the Netherlands higher educational support institution – and which sustained this publishing venture. Thanks to Kristen Cheney and Auma Okwany for their inputs and energy in terms of research capacity building and supporting budding researchers in both institutions. Thanks also to the staff at the Embassy of the Kingdom of The Netherlands in Kampala, where Joyce Ngaiza was particularly supportive, and for giving a push to extend the networks of our researchers. This, plus our contacts through training, made it possible to extend the research beyond Uganda to the wider East African region. Veronika Goussatchenko and her several interns provided support and logistical inputs and oversight that made working on this study a pleasure. Finally, and not least, we thank the staff at Nuffic, especially Armand Gaikema, for their open and yet firm approach to making sure we realised our goals and set up researchers with capacity to continue publishing in future.

Abstracts of chapters

Chapter 1: *From Bird's Eye View to Worm's Eye View? Social Justice, Human Rights and JLOS in East Africa* - Jimmy Maguru, Florence Nyakaisiki, Jackson Odong and Helen Hintjens (Editors)

This chapter draws on four pilot studies on the general public's views about the Justice, Law and Order Sector (JLOS). These studies were carried out by Nsamizi Institute staff in four regions of Uganda: in Mpigi, Oyam, Sheema and Bugiri Districts, in 2011. The key findings of these studies are then related to recent international scholarship, in relation to both formal and informal justice systems. Questions of forms of governance and accountability are also raised. Some implications for the JLOS sector in East Africa, and especially in Uganda, are identified, and each chapter in the book is introduced in terms of its key arguments and themes.

Chapter 2: *Social Justice: Recognition and Reparation: Connecting Kenyan Mungiki 'gangs' with the Mau Mau Legal Case* - Nancy Muigei

This chapter considers how social justice frameworks can help to understand the dilemmas involved in addressing the historical injustices and deep-seated grievances that can be at the root of the political violence of specific social groups within society. This research situates *Mungiki* of Kenya within this broader context. The *Mungiki* (a Kikuyu term meaning 'a multitude of people') remain proscribed, and their illegal status tends to reinforce their criminalisation. The *Mungiki* claim social justice, and redress for a history of land-grabbing, corruption and mistreatment of the Mau Mau. Potentially, these claims are powerful ones, and have been acknowledged in UK courts. However, since the *Mungiki* have become synonymous with violence, this tends to undermine the legal cases now proceeding through UK courts, for violence inflicted on suspected Mau Mau supporters in the late colonial period (1950s to 1960s). The implications are that social justice should also be integral to much wider, and longer-term projects of transitional justice, which combine recognitional and distributive justice claims, sometimes over decades, or even centuries.

Chapter 3: *Justice on the Radio? An Assessment of Justice Frames in 'Facing Justice', an NGO-supported Radio Programme* – Jackson Odong

This chapter presents findings of a study conducted on 'Facing Justice', and the kinds of justice frames that this radio programme includes in its broadcasts. This NGO-funded radio programme was intended to contribute to post-war reconstruction and reconciliation in northern Uganda. The aim of the study on which the chapter is based was to find the different meanings, or frames, used to represent justice on the radio programme, and to link these with different actors involved. The actors are at local, national and international levels; the key question was how their frames differed, and how this might influence the effectiveness of a radio station aimed at promoting justice and reconciliation. Programme content was analysed and a model for understanding justice frames found that there was a connection between justice frames and actors located at various 'levels'.

Chapter 4: *Land Justice in Urban Tanzania: The Case of Mbeya* – Thomas Munzerere

Based on fieldwork in urban Mbeya, and the experience of working in the formal justice sector, this study shows that there are three key problems with land justice in Mbeya. The first is a lack of information and record-keeping concerning land disputes and land cases. The second is that leadership (or governance) is not sufficiently transparent and accountable, including at national level. Finally, a third factor identified was the law itself. Land in Tanzania remains the subject of too many disputes in terms of authority structures, mode of ownership and use, and unresolved lines of authority over land.

Chapter 5: *The Limits of Awareness: Women and Land Rights, a Case Study from Eastern Uganda* - Clare Cheremoi

Ensuring the protection of women's land rights has enabled even the most vulnerable rural women, widows and orphans, to derive a more secure livelihood from farming. This study selected the case of Busia District in Eastern Uganda and focuses on women's awareness of their rights of access and ownership in relation to the JLOS. How can existing legal and institutional frameworks be made more supportive to poor rural women's access to their land rights? Findings revealed that the majority of respondents (around 60%) had experienced land disputes involving gender issues, and that about 90% were aware of the existence of women's land rights as codified and legislated by the law. The study found that local council courts and district land boards were important when it came to settling land disputes in Busia district. Finally, the study found that women's struggles to protect and claim their land rights had been effective in most cases in spite of corruption and patriachal customs.

Chapter 6: *Land Rights in the Context of Post Conflict Northern Uganda: The Case of Amuru District, Uganda*
- Grace Angeline Chelimo

Much academic and policy thinking about post-conflict reconstruction has stressed the importance of resolving land disputes as part of a wider resettlement process of formerly displaced people. For mainly agrarian societies, access and entitlement to land plays a key role in the resettlement process and in enabling vulnerable rural returnees to derive a more secure livelihood. This study selected the case of Amuru sub-county in northern Uganda (formerly part of Gulu district), an area in which land disputes are rampant. This study focuses on how existing legal and institutional frameworks are handling land disputes in the case of post-war Amuru sub-county. Findings revealed that local council courts were vital in resolving land disputes, though the process was characterised by a number of irregularities, which sometimes led to miscarriages of justice. Finally, the study found that the magistrate courts play a vital role, but were slowed by the overwhelming work burden of their staff. In the case of more vulnerable complainants, specific challenges were identified in addressing land disputes; the main one being the high cost of accessing justice. The study concluded that more critical attention needs to be paid in future to specific land tenure arrangements, land boundaries and registration, land ownership and user rights, especially in relation to poorer households, within a post-war district like Amuru and other similar settings.

Chapter 7: *Health Justice and Gender Justice: The Role of Traditional Birth Attendants (TBAs) in Uganda* - Florence Nyakaisiki

In developing countries, especially in rural areas, women seek assistance in childbirth from informally trained helpers. Less than half are assisted by a formally trained and medically qualified health worker or midwife. Approximately 60% of childbirths in Uganda are handled by TBAs. In most cases delivery takes place within the women's homes, and TBAs visit the women before, during and after the birth. Uganda's high maternal mortality rate – at 410/100,000 in 2010, – means many thousands of women die needlessly from childbirth every year. In rural areas there is little or no access to Emergency Obstetric Care (EOC). This study highlights the important contribution of TBAs to a safe, healthy and happy delivery for mothers. Conducted in three sub-counties of Mpigi District, and drawing on perceptions of health workers, rural mothers and TBAs, this study investigates why women still seek TBAs' services rather than relying exclusively on modern health care services. The study is intended to inform public policy makers and other stakeholders about how to design appropriate interventions to provide and improve maternal health care services in Uganda, and foster a conducive environment for TBAs by legalising, registering and monitoring them in order to maintain minimum health standards for the rural mothers.

Chapter 8: *Disability and Social Iustice: The Role of Refugee Leaders in Enhancing Access to Social Justice by Refugees with Disability* - Jimmy Mugisha Maguru

The aim of this study was to find out whether PWDs in a refugee settlement are enjoying their rights, accessing services and participating in all activities in their communities, much like the other refugees. It also aimed at finding out the roles of refugee leaders and stakeholders in the process of making refugees with disability visible as a minority group of the marginalised and in ensuring that they enjoy their rights and access the available services much like other refugees within the settlement. It looks at what has been done to improve the wellbeing of these refugees with disability bearing in mind that they have unique needs and must of neccessity be separated from other categories of persons with special needs. It points out the concerns of this minority group of refugees and gives recommendations as to how they can be empowered through an inclusion strategy in all decisions affecting their lives in the settlement.

Chapter 9: *'Street-level' Bureaucrats in Rwanda: Working for more just Outcomes of Judicial Reforms* - Gervais Twahirwa

This chapter uses the concepts of the 'street-level bureaucrat' to explore the role of those who staff Rwanda's judiciary and deal with the public on a daily basis. It asks how these people can contribute to improving the efficiency of the justice sector's operations in future. It is concluded that the main problems are the huge backlogs, and problems with existing levels of training and professional capacities among 'street-level' bureaucrat staff members. A possible solution is to be found in the intensification of computerisation, which has made recording of details of cases far more efficient. Other solutions include restructuring of the professional tasks of individuals. The overall aim is to enhance the legitimacy of judicial institutions.

Chapter 10: *No Justice? Mob Violence, Community Policing and Crime Control in Uganda's Urban Markets* - Joshua Mugambwa and Helen Hintjens

It seems that the Uganda Police Force's implementation of community policing has yet to have a visible impact in bringing down rates of crime. Community members' training and action, does not seem to prevent collective and violent 'mob justice', which remains entrenched at community level. Lives and property are lost to 'informal justice'. Communities often prefer not to report the crime to the police at all, and instead intervene directly to punish suspected thieves. This study establishes the meanings of 'mob justice' as a form of community-legitimated violence that may or may not be controlled by the state. How can this be understood and handled, especially through community policing strategies? To try and answer this question. the study compared experiences in Owino and Nakulabye markets, both located in Kampala, Uganda. These markets were selected because they varied and they are busy. Stronger bonds in the Nakulabye market vendor community have contributed to relatively better control of mob violence in that market. Respondents were asked about mob violence and which factors made it more or less likely.

The study uses mainly qualitative data to contribute to the literature on how this violent popular response to crime can be understood in relation to poverty and the state institutions of police, judiciary and prisons. For the Ugandan model to become more successful, a few examples from elsewhere in the developing world are explored for insights into what can be done.

Chapter 11: *Conclusion: The Future of Social Justice across the JLOS Institutions in East Africa* - Freda Apio

This concluding chapter gives an overview of key commonalities and differences in the experiences of East African states in integrating social justice considerations into the justice, law and order sector institutions. The sector wide approach (SWAP) to development adopted across the region is examined for its ability to leverage opportunities for greater collaboration and synergies between the different institutions and Non Governmental Organisations (NGOs) involved in legal service provision across the East African Community (EAC). Each member state is discussed in terms of models of best practice for specific social justice issues, including gender, land rights and security sector reform. In the EAC context, the chapter applauds efforts to advance the coordination of legal and judicial affairs, accentuating the need to learn from best practices in the region. Bridging gaps between law and practical justice outcomes remains a challenge, requiring close attention to how best practices can be extended through enforceable legal provisions and a social justice perspective.

Chapter 1

Introduction: From Bird's Eye View to Worm's Eye View? Social Justice, Human Rights and JLOS in Uganda and East Africa

Jimmy M. Maguru, Florence Nyakaisiki, Jackson Odong and Helen Hintjens (Editors)

Introduction

This introductory chapter provides an overview of debates and dilemmas around social justice and what it means for professionals working across different sectors, including the Justice Law and Order Sector (JLOS), social work, health and education. Reflections on local practices are integrated with a review of the latest international scholarship around formal and informal justice systems and the implications of social justice for professional practice. The focus is on East Africa, with special attention paid to local-level cases from Uganda. In this introduction, social justice issues are considered in relation to the JLOS sector and criminal justice, and in relation to 'marginalised' social actors in other sectors, such as social work and health. Cases are placed firmly in their national and regional context, with chapters on Kenya, Tanzania and Rwanda as well as Uganda. Each chapter will be discussed in more detail at the end of this chapter.

The chapters in this study are based on primary research by East African researchers and their collaborators, through work of data collection in the field, through interviews of all kinds, focus group discussions, archival work and observation. The aim is to provide case studies that can be useful for students in a range of areas, including law, social work, social development, social policy and criminology. This chapter draws on four situational analyses around social justice and JLOS, carried out with local populations in Mpigi, Oyam, Sheema and Bugiri Districts in Uganda in 2011. Researchers of Nsamizi Training Institute for Social Development in Mpigi, Uganda, and their research partners from HURINET (Ugandan Human Rights Network) conducted these studies. By providing examples that can be useful for teachers, the hope is also to engender debate among students and practitioners about what 'social justice' looks like in the Justice, Law and Order sector, in Uganda and elsewhere in East Africa.

Without romanticising the 'local', this study tries to reinsert the local dimension back into the study of public policy, through a multi-sectoral approach to social exclusion and disadvantage. How do JLOS institutions, educational institutions and health services operate in relation to the poorest and most vulnerable in society; how can professionals working in these fields take social justice considerations on board in their working practices? Whereas general criteria for efficiency tend to be 'socially blind', and mostly about economic growth, the concept of social justice is based on the premise that truly efficient outcomes need to be socially just as well as based on income growth and more economic output. In terms of gender, disability, refugee status and low-income groups, social justice implies taking consideration of vulnerabilities, uneven opportunities, and structural inequalities, both horizontal (between communities) and vertical (between classes and occupational groups).

Ideally in this study, the 'bird's eye' view of state officials, laws, policies and principles will be combined with the 'worm's eye' view that starts with 'human practice rather than with arguments about the eternal truth' of what social justice means (Harvey, 2009: 15). Social justice is in some ways a quaint term, not that much in fashion, but nonetheless important. As Nancy Fraser points out, social justice is about economic and social, but also about cultural justice. As she puts it: '...once centred on distribution, [social justice demands are]... now increasingly divided between claims for redistribution, on the one hand, and claims for recognition, on the other' (Fraser, 1998:1).

The term social justice has gained growing currency in Uganda, in East Africa and beyond partly because of donor policies, especially those of the Netherlands, which prefers to use the more inclusive term 'social justice', rather than referring explicitly to 'human rights' obligations, which can provoke a backlash from governments resentful at Western meddling. Having social justice in mind means going beyond technical solutions to social problems, and recognising that success depends on making the 'human' element central to how various public sectors implement their policies, including the Justice, Law and Order Sector (JLOS).

Citizens are not only 'clients', or 'offenders', or 'patients', but also participants and beneficiaries. Professionals, whether they work in NGOs, in JLOS sector institutions, in health or in education, need to attend to promoting wider goals, and are asked to contribute to the social and economic development goals of East African governments. The Ugandan National Development Plan of 2010-15, for example, has identified the Justice, Law and Order Sector as a national priority, noting its potential contribution to economic growth, as well as to 'Justice for All'. Social development goals thus need to be linked explicitly to how JLOS institutions and officials operate locally, within rural and urban areas, and on a daily basis within specific localities, as well as to the framework, grids and networks of the formal justice infrastructure and regulatory machinery. These are the worm's and bird's eye views to which this chapter has referred. In practice and in theory, the meaning of social justice – as indeed of human rights - is highly contested, as this chapter will show.

Conceptualising Social Justice

Social justice is a very general concept that conveys general ideals about distributive justice, with the task of government, social actors and institutions being to foster a more equal, socially responsible and dignified set of values and practices across society. It has been used by various scholars to refer to ideals as well as the aim and outcome of policies and practice. Ideals of social justice include genuine equality of citizenship, respect for fairness, respect among peoples, and meeting obligations towards those unable to claim their own rights effectively. Systemic social justice implies that even the weakest and most socially excluded in society can find a means – whether through advocacy or organisation; to express their needs. Social justice, for David Harvey, for example, implies the element of need, the notion of a common good and common ethical standard (Harvey, 2009:101-107).

At transnational level too, social justice can be translated as 'global justice', or international justice, which again involves a notion of distributive justice. The relation between social justice and rights has often been neglected, and yet it is obvious – a rights-based approach to social justice would also need to include some historical component to distributive injustices (Pogge, 2005). In relation to human rights-based approaches and priorities of social justice, as the UN Department of Economic and Social Affairs notes: '...to support the concept of social justice is to argue for a reconciliation of these priorities [i.e. human rights and distributive justice] within the context of a broader social perspective in which individuals endowed with rights and freedoms operate within the framework of the duties and responsibilities attached to living in society' (UN, 2006:13). Social justice is usually agreed to include an international component, but this can be rendered invisible by the assumption that the nation state is the appropriate locus for social justice promotion.

Justice is like security, a 'hybrid' concept, which has both top-down and bottom-up elements (Luckham and Kirk, 2013). Luckham and Kirk analyse three types of problems, which may also be relevant to social justice in relation to the justice, law and order sector: (i) 'Unsecured borderlands', '...where state authority is suspended or violently challenged by alternative claimants to power or providers of security'. This is the case in parts of East Africa, and could remain the case in future. In Uganda, it was characteristic mainly of the Uganda-Sudan cross-border area and the lives of refugees from across the Great Lakes region. (ii) 'Contested Leviathans', is the second type of problem identified and involves governments 'whose authority and capacity to deliver security are weak, disputed or compromised by special interests'. This too can be said to apply at different times to parts of East Africa and lastly, (iii) 'securitised policy spaces'. Here 'international actors collaborate to ensure peace and fulfil their responsibility to protect vulnerable end-users in unsecured regions' (Luckham and Kirk, 2013:1). Achieving social justice in such contested, compromised and securitised contexts can be additionally challenging, since equality and rights may not be viewed as priorities, when human and political insecurity are pervasive.

Another useful way of thinking about social justice in practice is to distinguish between problems of law and policy, systems of governance and management, and wider social attitudes, both among the public and among professionals. A recent study of health sector corruption across 28 EU countries, put it this way: 'What is needed is a combination of effective generic anti-corruption policies and practices (legislation, enforcement), aimed at addressing fundamental health system weaknesses (managerial and financial), a general rejection of corruption by society (including a self-regulation by health sector actors), and specific anti-corruption in healthcare policies and practices' (European Commission, 2013:3). This problem can also be identified in East African countries, but has been less explored so far. However, accountability could be one useful concept to add into our framework for ensuring improved respect for social justice principles across the JLOS sectors (Brinkerhoff, 2004).

In making such distinctions between justice and security, we argue that similar analytical lenses can be turned upon international actors in securitised policy spaces as well as upon state and non-state security actors. However security also refers to simple 'human security', that includes the most basic rights, such as the right to give birth safely, be respected as a refugee, and to have one's status as a disabled person respected. Being poor sometimes means in practice not having access to free government services, which end up being bought and sold instead of being provided freely.

Themes and Questions

How can the most marginalised sectors of society be considered as key informants for justice professionals, including those across all the Justice, Law and Order Sector (JLOS) institutions? Can decentralisation enhance the citizenship rights of marginalised groups in society, such as poor women, disabled people and criminal offenders? Or does focusing on local-level experiences with policy simply mean 'bringing oppression rather than accountability closer to the people' (Sjorgen, 2013: 182, in Mamdani, 1996).

In this volume, social justice has been defined quite broadly, to include criminal justice based on human rights norms, as well as gender justice, respect for rights of social groups usually considered vulnerable, but also powerless. These include minorities, poor households, children and the disabled, as well as non-citizens. Social justice should include economic justice for the poor, respect for the capacities of the disabled, and acknowledgement of the critical roles played by women – and by men – in all spheres of private and public life. The needs and rights of those considered 'marginal' is unlikely to be a priority for most policy-makers and officials; yet to make them a priority is what social justice requires. Those considered 'undesirable' should be given priority, unlikely as that may sound, especially for those who are socially stigmatised as well as deprived of formal rights. Victims of mob lynchings, who are suspected of being thieves, for example, or witches, are a case in point of why those who are the most reviled need to be a priority if improved social justice is to be achieved.

Social exclusion can be defined as the situation in which people, usually groups of people, are prevented from actively taking part in community decisions, on the basis of their identity or social status. Social exclusion can happen around differences of race, gender, religion, sexuality, age and occupation among others. Socially excluded groups are also often blamed for their own exclusion because they are deficient in some ways (Estivill 2003:13). Estivill, J. (2003) Concepts and Strategies for Combating Social Exclusion: An Overview. International Labor Organisation.

This volume challenges the perceptions of professionals in the JLOS sector concerning how they relate with ordinary members of the public, especially those who are minorities, socially excluded or in a vulnerable position. What this volume argues for, overall, is a more socially just and more human rights-based approach to public policy implementation, in the JLOS sector and beyond, implying that policy-makers and practicing professionals should be prepared to listen to ordinary people expressing their own needs and priorities. This is close to being our definition of social justice; the improving of practice so that perceived needs can be met for the local population, with those who experience forms of social exclusion being the main priority.

Bridging social justice and multi-sectoral interventions

In this section, we consider how social justice issues can be understood in relation to a multi-sectoral approach to policy delivery that includes the JLOS sector, as well as others. We reflect on the comparative situation in East African countries. Across the region, the public bodies responsible for monitoring human rights violations are being kept busy. Thus for example, each year the Ugandan Human Rights Commission handles hundreds, and sometimes over a thousand, complaints about the failure of public servants of all kinds, including JLOS officials, to properly and professionally provide services (and justice) for members of the public. Complaints are made mainly about police, specific named corrupt individuals and the army. In the case of Uganda, the complaints are pronounced in two post-war areas of Soroti and Gulu, where complaints about the police are especially high, a shift from the period of the war, when most complaints in the North concerned the army.

Strangely, in 2012 the UHRC reported only one complaint for the whole of Uganda concerning the judiciary (UHRC, 2012:2). The US State Department report on Human Rights in Uganda for 2012, notes that human rights violations declined between 2011 and 2012 (US State Department, 2012). Despite this, in 2012, 'the total amount of compensation awarded to victims of human rights violations was almost 330 million Uganda shillings. The awards made by the Tribunal were mainly for violations of the right to freedom from torture and cruel, inhuman or degrading treatment or punishment and the right to personal liberty' (US State Department, 2012).

However, even if laws are to be adequate, for example as for domestic violence, the report notes that advocates for social justice question whether laws are properly implemented (US State Department, 2012:25). These kinds of problems, where implementation may be a concern, led Nsamizi Training Institute for Social Development in Uganda to carry out four pilot studies in 2011, related to community-level complaints around the Justice, Law and Order services in local areas across Uganda, including Mpigi (near Kampala), Sheema (Western region), Bugiri (Eastern Uganda) and Oyam (Northern Uganda). In all these pilot studies, the main problems identified, included:

a) **Negative attitudes and behavior** among law enforcement officers towards complaints and issues defined as 'social' and having to do with conflicts within families or communities. At local level, this could explain why local formal and informal courts, Probation and Social Welfare Officers, state prosecutors, police and prison officers all lacked the skills needed to administer justice at community level, especially when dealing with complaints by women, children and other vulnerable members of the community.

b) **Inadequate knowledge of human rights and professional procedures**. A lack of awareness was noted among JLOS staff, who lacked awareness of human rights provisions and how their own work could affect local communities seeking justice. This could reinforce, for example, poor handling of witnesses by police and courts, which were noted, but also lack of sensitivity to issues of gender, poverty and social exclusion in general.

c) **Inadequate documentation**. There was lack of information and record taking about cases and decisions. Many policies were poorly documented, and state prosecutors, police or local courts did not always take social issues very seriously. Those who were discussing these issues in the pilot studies felt that neglecting documentation was part and parcel of malpractices which they noted, including early release of suspects and even of convicts without due legal process.

d) **Lack of innovation in approaches**. The sentencing and punishment regime was viewed as mechanical and devoid of special or social considerations critical to effective rehabilitation of offenders and avoiding negative effects of sentencing for children and communities.

Many of the official documents in Uganda sound as if the country had not just ended over two decades of civil war. In fact, a report on the legacies of northern Uganda's violent conflict suggests that the traumas and legacies will be relevant to the JLOS reforms for some time to come. Thus, for example, one study based on a survey with over 2000 respondents suggested the scale of traumas experienced in and around Gulu, Lira, Kitgum and Soroti. According to this study, 40 per cent of respondents had been abducted; 58 per cent had witnessed a child being abducted; 45 per cent had witnessed a family member killed; 33 per cent had carried loads for LRA and 25 per cent had witnessed sexual violence or rape. Finally, 24 per cent were assaulted or injured by a family member (ICTJ & HRC, 2005:22).

Attitudes towards justice institutions are a growing field of study, and show that justice is viewed as a priority particularly for the poor. In Uganda's context, those who have been disadvantaged by decades of war, experience injustice as related to the past violence. Thus, another study of northern Uganda found that respondents defined justice in terms of dignity, freedom of speech, education and a 'life with peace and security and without fear' (Pham, Vinck and Wierda, 2005:22). Ordinary people's concerns in post-war Uganda may have more to do with the search for dignity, economic and social rights (distributive justice) and free movement than with fighting crime or achieving proper punishments, which is how JLOS institutions tend to understand justice (ICTJ & HRC, 2005:22). Each person and group in society feels they have their due, and it may be that criminal justice through the legal system is not the only form of justice solely aimed at. In a survey of post-war respondents in northern Uganda, almost a fifth responded to a question about justice that they did not know what the term meant (ICTJ & HRC, 2005:23). The notion of justice is so vague that it needs to be qualified as criminal justice, legal justice or transitional justice. Social justice is the broadest form of justice of all, and in principle can include all these other forms. Social justice, however, cannot be secured through judicial/legal justice or criminal justice alone. Thus, social justice can include criminal justice, but also includes socio-economic and distributive justice and justice in the broad sense of respect and dignity for human persons.

Administrative competence also needs to be part of ensuring that social justice is pursued across different sectors, including in the JLOS, since waiting lists and case backlogs deny justice as effectively as wrong decisions or professional malpractice. Court systems in most East African countries, including in Uganda, are very congested. They are so congested as to constitute a denial of justice, and to violate people's basic human right to a fair trial, to remedy for victims of crimes. As Twahirwa in Chapter 9 suggests, the problem of backlogs can be tackled, including with sophisticated information systems. However, among the poor, vulnerability to delays is heightened since they cannot use their influence to speed up a case stuck in the backlog. The pilot studies were useful since they identified these gaps in the education of JLOS personnel. Training is vital, and so is JLOS reform.

For example, whilst it is important to reduce crime, what is more important is to reduce crimes that disproportionately affect the poorest in society. Uganda's crime statistics suggest that poor people, including single women, children, and orphans, are often the most affected by crimes. Violence is also endemic in poor households, with 60 per cent of women of 15-49 years of age having experienced domestic violence (Ugandan Demographic Health Survey: 2006). All kinds of other disturbing social problems have increased in the past few years, including child sacrifice, human sacrifice, drug abuse and mob violence. To be compatible with justice for all, the police crackdown on crime needs to protect the rights of the accused, the rights of victims, and needs to pay special attention to social crimes that affect the most marginalised and poorest people most directly, since they have few means to protect themselves from the violence that accompanies growing discontent (MFPED, 2009).

Formal and informal justice: East African contexts

The context in different countries of East Africa is varied and this study, whilst grounded in research in Uganda, reflects on that diversity in various contributions. The extent of state control and centralisation varies, for a start. In some contexts, it is clear that the state is the key actor, and is mainly 'in control' of the way that both formal and even informal institutions operate. This is not always the case, however. Sometimes 'legal pluralism' means there is significant room for manoeuvre by citizens and the way in which 'state law is adapted, ignored or resisted', when it fails to promote and protect people's rights, and social justice goals (Nagy, 2013:83). Nor can we, as Nagy suggests, hope to grasp all 'the variety of legal and normative orders across different socio-legal fields at the international, transnational, state and community levels' (Nagy, 2013:83).

The idea that formal and informal systems for achieving justice should be harmonised is nothing new, and applies across East African countries. So is the idea that policy should be based on evidence from a wide range of sources, including the views of the general population. However, this is not as simple as it looks, for various reasons. What is needed, perhaps, is to: 'open up avenues for the application of human rights principles to the operation of non-formal justice systems' (Nyamu-Musembi, 2003:7) across East Africa. This way, perhaps social justice-oriented reforms that make formal justice sector institutions more accountable, receptive to cooperating and 'reforming' with both researchers and traditional institutions, might work better. Distrust has been identified as a particular problem in the Ugandan context, when compared for instance with how JLOS and related policies work in Tanzania. As a study on the health sector suggested: 'A strong public health research community exists in Uganda, as in Tanzania, but it has more difficulty translating its findings into policy. The research-to-policy transmission mechanism that was so effective in Tanzania was almost completely absent in Uganda' (Croke, 2011:12).

A good example of this problem is the law passed in 2009, which was never implemented concerning TBAs (Traditional Birth Attendants) in Uganda. Recently, the decision in Uganda to ban the work of TBAs created some severe restrictions in the availability of pre-natal and birth health care for rural and poorer urban women in Uganda's context. This is an example considered in the chapter by Florence Nyakaisiki. A later section of this introduction will introduce the contents of each chapter in the volume in more detail.

Already, more than a decade ago, in 2003, Celestine Nyamu-Musembi identified some fundamental obstacles to 'Reforming non-formal justice systems to improve access to justice for poor people and other vulnerable groups in the East Africa region' (Nyamu-Musembi, 2003:3). The main problem, she suggested, was the 'legitimacy and accountability' of informal institutions. Yet, linking with 'the judiciary and other relevant formal institutions' was seen as essential to finding solutions, since in reality, whatever the legal regime in place: 'simultaneous use of formal and non-formal systems is a reality for a significant number of people' in the East African region (Nyamu-Musembi, 2003:4).

The case of women resorting to TBAs is discussed in this volume. In this case, in Uganda, the government strategy has been abolitionist, and illegalisation has been the result. This does not change the local realities, as the chapter by Nyakaisiki shows, which leave women with few choices but to resort to TBAs. Gender justice thus requires more than technical skills or medical services; it requires an awareness of the constraints that women face, and their lack of choices at local level, given their need for moral and health support during birth and pregnancy. The lack of gender inclusiveness of policy makers can be demonstrated through their abolitionist leanings, which view local cultural traditions as mainly misguided, rather than seeking to work with TBAs, who in some regions had already received training to improve their skills. Existing coping strategies can be undermined by a lack of awareness of the vital need for basic, accessible health care. Whilst providing no alternative care, abolition simply worsens the burdens on women by making assisted birth potentially a criminal act. Meanwhile 'the role of extended family support networks in providing social protection [for the most vulnerable women] is declining due to difficult economic conditions and also to shocks brought about by crises such as HIV/AIDS' (Nyamu-Musembi, 2007:204).

It may be claimed that the problem of gender justice has been tackled at least in Tanzania and Uganda, since in both cases the governments have introduced 'quotas for women in state-sponsored forums applying customary law' (Nyamu-Musembi, 2003:4). However, the implications of formalising the informal are not always to promote gender justice; as the same author explains, it can also happen that: 'formal state law... has validated and reinforced structures of inequality that have come to be viewed as resulting from or being dictated by... custom or religion' (Nyamu-Musembi, 2005:46).

Finally, there can be conflicts with human rights principles, both in relation to customary views on gender relations, and issues like 'mob justice'. The same study also suggests that land issues should not be ignored, since although they are rarely considered as part of the formal justice system, they are integral to informal justice, and indeed to social justice for poor people in both rural and urban communities (Nyamu-Musembi, 2003:6).

Governance issues in the JLOS sector: Social justice dimensions

Institutional weaknesses are often blamed on policies being less effective than expected; and yet what does this really mean? In many JLOS-sector institutions, for example, the impact of sector reform has not lived up to its role as a dynamic sector able to stimulate the wider economy of the country. In the Uganda National Plan, mentioned earlier, a great deal of job creation and income generation was expected from JLOS reform. Yet evidence from surveys suggests that the Ugandan public still considers corruption and the lack of professionalism of JLOS-sector staff as serious obstacles to trusting JLOS institutions and processes. Moreover, perhaps with good reason; JLOS experts are seen as more interested in protecting their own interests than serving the public. As one Ministry of Justice and Constitutional Affairs survey, conducted in 2008[1] showed, 41 per cent of Ugandans who were interviewed claimed they had personally observed examples of bribery and corruption. The majority agreed that this was common practice among public officials in their locality. In the same survey, the vast majority of the general public rated formal JLOS institutions as corrupt (85 per cent). They rated the police as the most corrupt of all. Clearly, there is a problem with the informalisation of formal institutions.

Formally, the JLOS process in Uganda is now more than a decade old, having started in 2001. Its goals were to increase: '...communication, coordination and cooperation among several stakeholders who collectively implement reforms that have been drawn from a single policy and expenditure plan, under the leadership of the Government of Uganda. The Sector is composed of 11 institutions'. These institutions include many social departments as well as the Ugandan DPP (Directorate of Public Prosecutions), the judiciary, prisons and police, Ministries of Justice and of Internal Affairs, but also the Uganda Human Rights Commission, the Ministry of Local Government which controls Local Council Courts and the Ministry of Gender, Labour and Social Development, including probation and juvenile justice departments.[2]

The Prisons Services' aims to be 'a centre of excellence in providing human rights based correctional services in

---

1 A National Integrated Baseline Study on Demand, Use and Access to JLOS Services in Uganda, for Ministry of Justice and Constitutional Affairs, 2008. Prepared for JLOS Reform Programme: By Steadman Group, 2008.

2 http://www.prisons.go.ug/index.php/41-projects/36-justice-law-and-order-sector-jlos for more information on JLOS process.

Africa', quite a demanding standard to achieve; and even more demanding should social justice be added into the mission statement too. The core values described in the Prison Services website echo the idea that community involvement is both desirable and cost saving. Economic efficiency and human rights-based correctional services are thus expected to be compatible. Farming in prisons, for instance, gives prisoners vital skills in an alternative way of earning an income, reduces costs and improves the quality of food. In other ways, too, community involvement is emphasised through a preference for non-custodial sentencing, co-operation with the community as well as with the rest of the JLOS institutions, the public right to know and participate in the criminal justice system and finally, the role of the prison system in shaping the future of Uganda as a humane and just society. All this suggests that the reform process has at least had an impact on core values and mission statements. The question this volume asks is what impact JLOS has had on practices in relation to local contexts and specifically some of the more vulnerable groups of people in Ugandan society, including children and youth, poor women, former convicts and those involved in land disputes, for example.

Access to justice for the poor and marginalised is especially difficult because they cannot afford the informal costs of accessing formal justice procedures. Growing disenchantment with the dominant legalistic paradigm for transitional justice regimes in countries like Uganda means that people resort to their own means of seeking justice, sometimes through violence (Nagy, 2013 and also see in this volume Mugambwa and Hintjens on mob killings). As Nagy puts it: '...just as customary law was 'made' through its interaction with colonialism, so too is traditional justice 'made' through its interaction with international transitional justice *as mediated by the state'* (Nagy, 2013: 82 emphasis in original). The relationship between the state and society in East Africa is a matter of perspective. As Sjorgen notes, from the perspective of the state, civil society often looks incoherently divided among itself, unable to organise itself for a common purpose, whilst from a grassroots perspective, the priorities of governance and central state institutions overpower local initiatives and ignore or repress locally-rooted social movements (Sjorgen 2013:26). In this context, informal traditional justice systems continue to have salience for local people, including in terms of land allocation and ownership, dispute resolution and contingency support for emergencies (on traditional institutions and land issues, see chapters in this study by Cheremoi and Chelimo). Alongside these informal systems, national and international forms of legal justice are unable to function according to the logic of formal rules and procedures. This juxtaposition of formal and informal, in part the result of a 'gap' in provision for the most marginalised among the citizenry, is explored in several chapters of this study. Thus in 2008, almost half of Ugandans surveyed – around 47 per cent – were aware of Alternative Dispute Resolution (ADR) mechanisms, and expressed their general confidence in such systems.

Every year, the Human Rights bodies of East African countries, like the Ombudsman's office in Rwanda, and the Human Rights Commission in Uganda and Kenya, handle an overwhelming number of complaints. These can relate to cruel, inhuman and degrading treatment, human rights violations, and denial of personal liberty. They may be about violations of the right to a fair hearing or speedy trial. However, a significant number of complaints concern improper practices, notably charging of illegal fees by public servants. External intervention in the justice sector usually seeks to address these kinds of obstacles to justice, but often with implicit biases for the security sector, so social conflicts that can result from resource misallocation are rarely addressed.

> Because security like other public goods has an almost unmatched symbolic prestige, the power to create new and shape existing security and justice institutions is intimately bound up with the political processes central to state making and state breaking. (Luckham and Kirk, 2013:6).

Bringing improved modes of justice delivery through international aid or other forms of international intervention, is a priority, and comes at a price, especially in post-conflict and post-violence situations like that of contemporary Uganda, Kenya and Rwanda (Baines, 2010). This is particularly salient for a study like this one, which arises in part from a Nuffic-funded project of Capacity Development between the ISS (International Institute of Social Studies) in The Netherlands, and a Ugandan Higher Education institution, Nsamizi Institute of Social Development Training. This very project is part of the supposed concern of the Global North for the well-being of higher education in the Global South. Most international justice interventions tend to ignore traditional justice mechanisms, turning them into a sort of folkloric spectacle for the transitional justice industry. On the other hand, researchers have started to take informal social protection systems, traditional forms of justice and alternative forms of health care more seriously in recent years. This is because the hope has emerged that such informal institutions can prove more able than formal ones to enable the poorest sectors in society to achieve greater social, gender, criminal and distributional justice than formal governance structures (Nagy, 2013).

Themes in the chapters

In Uganda, Kenya, Rwanda and legacies of conflict and violence are an important dimension of any 'transitional justice' process, and affect all sectors from primary health care to the work of the judiciary. In northern Uganda following civil war, and in Kenya after post-election violence, hybrid forms of justice that combine formal and informal justice systems have become more evident, as also in Gacaca courts in Rwanda. Combining neo-traditional institutions with 'modern' and formal state institutions is not always the favoured approach. However, recourse to justice and remedies for the poorest and most disadvantaged can sometimes be supported through hybrid forms of redress. Combining acknowledgement of past wrongs with recompense for violence and harm can mean intervening in the politics of memory, a highly contentious issue in the contemporary post-colonial, post-war era.

How do poor women, vulnerable young people, criminal suspects, the disabled, refugees and sexual minorities frame their own demands for rights and social justice? If they voice their concerns, are the staff and policies of JLOS institutions in East Africa receptive to these expressions of the priorities of socially excluded groups? How might staff working across the Justice, Law and Order Sector institutions, social work, refugee rights and disability for example, become more attuned to, social justice priorities in their daily work with marginalised groups? These are central questions explored in this study through a range of case study chapters drawing on experience from different sectors, including policing, health, refugee protection, education and land justice systems.

The volume is divided into four parts. The first reflects on a number of examples that explore fundamental and contextual issues in relation to historical and reparational justice. The second chapter by Nancy Muigei, a Kenyan journalist and researcher of social justice movements, deals with the legacies of social justice in relation to demands for historical justice and the framing of memory around the Mau Mau uprising in Kenya. By reflecting on the legacies for a group known in today's Kenya as *Mungiki*, and claiming descendance from the Mau Mau veterans, she considers the wider implications of the historic Mau Mau legal case against the UK government, which began in 2013. Linked with this are the different notions of justice, including legal, restorative and victim-centred, reviewed in Chapter 3 by Jackson Odong. His study is on 'Facing Justice', a radio programme produced in northern Uganda, with a focus on reconciliation, and supported by international NGO the Institute for War and Peace Reporting.

The third part of the study, on Land Rights in East Africa starts with a chapter by Tanzanian judge, Thomas Munzerere, who reflects on dilemmas for achieving land justice in the urban setting of Mbeya. He identifies the key constraints to be language barriers, dispersal of data sources, and lack of dispute resolution capacity among local professionals. Gender and land justice issues are addressed in Clare Cheremoi's case study of women's land rights in Eastern Uganda, in Chapter 5. This chapter is based on detailed fieldwork in a rural area close to the Kenyan border, and interestingly Cheremoi concludes that women's legal awareness of their land rights is not the main obstacle; instead she shows how women's capacity to claim land justice, is tightly constrained by the informal cultural institutions and gender relations which control local land use and allocation practices. In Chapter 6, Grace Chelimo explores the concept of legal pluralism as a useful way of theorising the connections between different, hybrid land-use and land ownership systems, following displacement and return of the population. Taking the case of Amuru District in northern Uganda, her chapter gives examples of how formal and informal legal institutions seek to resolve the multiple types of land conflicts arising from displacement, return and resettlement.

The third part of this volume goes on to examine more closely struggles for social justice from the margins, struggles that straddle the formal-informal division. Chapters 7 and 8 and 9 focus on such 'struggles for social justice' at the complex intersection of formal rules and informal sets of practices. In Chapter 7, Florence Nyakaisiki suggests that reforming, rather than abolishing, TBAs (traditional birth attendants) might be a better way to ensure safe delivery for poor, rural women, than banning TBAs, as had been proposed by the Ugandan government. TBAs are at the intersection of the formal and informal sectors. In Chapter 8, Jimmy Maguru shows that differential treatment may sometimes be needed to ensure equal outcomes for everyone, regardless of ability. Social justice for disabled refugees depends on access to participation. As one of Maguru's informants suggests: 'Disabled people should be separated because we have different needs and we are different people'. This is not an argument for permanent segregation; however, deliberate support may be needed if inclusion of disabled refugees is to be the outcome.

A key sector in this study is the Justice, Law and Order Sector, and the fourth and final part of the study focuses on how legal justice and social justice inter-connect, and how they may diverge. Chapter 9 is about 'street-level bureaucrats' who deal with the public in the Rwandan justice system. The researcher, Gervais Twahirwa, shows how officials directly in contact with the public manage to provide services under very demanding conditions. His main concern is to improve the efficacy of the criminal justice system, without sacrificing principles of social justice. Twahirwa's chapter is based on interviews with these 'street-level' officials and with citizens about the court system's workings in Rwanda. Whilst in Rwanda, formal legal systems appear quite strongly entrenched, in Uganda it is the informal that predominates, including with the use of violence. In the case of mob justice, the focus of Chapter 10 by Joshua Mugambwa and Helen Hintjens, the causes are a matter of debate. Comparing two local markets in Kampala, the study tries to explain why incidents of mob killings varied in intensity between the two locations, in spite of similar conditions. Possible wider explanations for mob violence are also discussed. Finally, Chapter 11 ends the whole study, and is a reflective chapter that reviews the JLOS sector reviewed from a social justice perspective. In this chapter, human rights lawyer, Freda Apio, who has worked with the ICC Coaliation of Uganda and with several other human rights-related organisations in East Africa, reviews the state of play in the EAC member states. What her discussion shows is how: 'a state structure that... would not tolerate any opposition and would rather lose its citizens than harbour people with different views' might be overcome throughout the region (Arendt, 1951: 278). Several sensitive issues have arisen in Uganda and elsewhere in the EAC in recent years, and this concluding chapter discusses many of them. Starting from the premise that sexual and minority rights need to be taken seriously if social justice is to mean anything at all, this volume builds on that understanding (Klugman, 2011). Issues of exclusion can affect women and men, young and old and are not to be ignored in any area of policy making, including in relation to justice, law and order, health and land rights, for example (Miller and Vance, 2004).

Each group of chapters contains cross-cutting debates, including how to define social justice, the benefits and costs of a multi-sectoral approach to social justice, and the significance of available evidence. These are discussed in all of the chapters. In most chapters, original fieldwork data is presented and analysed using key concepts from across professional specialisation, including education, health, land law, the judiciary and other JLOS institutions among others. This introductory chapter and the overall concluding chapter are intended to review questions that cut across chapters in all four parts of this volume. These questions include: How can respect for social justice be improved among policy makers and policy implementers? How can theoretical reflections help us appreciate the significance of specific and local case studies, in arriving at ways to tackle problems of social injustice, especially from the perspective of the worm's eye or grassroots perspective of the most vulnerable sections of the population? These are some of the key questions the chapters in this study will now address.

References

Arendt, H. (1994, orig. 1951) *The Origins of Totalitarianism*. Harcourt Books: New York.

Baines, E. (2010) 'Spirits and social reconstruction after mass violence: Rethinking transitional justice', *African Affairs*, 109 (436):409-430.

Brinkerhoff, D. (2004) 'Accountability and health systems: toward conceptual clarity and policy relevance', *Health Policy and Planning*, 19(6): 371–379.

Croke, K. (2011) *Politics, Child Mortality, and Health System Development in Tanzania and Uganda, 1995-2009*, draft paper. Available at: http://ihi.eprints.org/1163/1/Kevin_Croke(2).pdf (Accessed 24 March 2014).

European Commission (2013) *Study on Corruption in the Healthcare Sector*, Reference: HOME/2011/ISEC/PR/047-A2, Brussels, EU Commission, October. Available at: http://www.stt.lt/documents/soc_tyrimai/20131219_study_on_corruption_in_the_healthcare_sector_en.pdf (Accessed 24 March 2014).

Fraser, N. (1998) *Social Justice in the Age of Identity Politics: Redistribution, Recognition, Participation*, Discussion Paper FS/98-108, Berlin: Wissenschaftszentrum Berlin für Sozialforschung.

Harvey, D. (2009) *Social Justice and the City*. Revised Edition, Athens GA: University of Georgia Press (original 1973).

ICTJ & HRC (2005) *Forgotten Voices: A Population-Based Survey of Attitudes About Peace and Justice in Northern Uganda*, International Centre for Transitional Justice and Human Rights Centre, University of California, Berkeley. Available at: http://escholarship.org/uc/item/4qr346xh#page-1 (Accessed 2 September 2013).

Klugman, B. (2011) 'Effective social justice advocacy: a theory-of-change framework for assessing Progress', *Reproductive Health Matters*: 19(38):146–162.

Luckham, R., and Kirk, T. (2013) The Two Faces of Security in Hybrid Political Orders: A Framework for Analysis and Research, *Stability: International Journal of Security & Development*, 2(2): 44: 1-30.

Miller, A. M. & Carole, S. V. (2004) 'Sexuality, Human Rights and Health', *Health and Human Rights*, 7 (2): 5-15.

Nagy, R. (2013) 'Centralising legal pluralism? Traditional justice in transitional contexts', in Sriram, C. L., García-Godos, J. Herman, J., Martin-Ortega, O., (eds.) *Transitional Justice and Peacebuilding on the Ground: Victims and Ex-Combatants.* Routledge: Abingdon-New York: 81-99.

Nyamu-Musembi, C. (2007) 'Addressing Formal and Substantive Citizenship: Gender Justice in Sub-Saharan Africa', in Mukhopadhyay, M., and Singh, N. (eds.) *Gender Justice, Citizenship and Development*, Ottowa-Cairo-Dakar: Zubaan-Kali-IDRC: 171-232.

Nyamu-Musembi, C. (2005) 'Towards an actor-oriented perspective on human rights', in Kabeer, N. (ed.) *Inclusive Citizenship: meanings and expressions*, London-New York: Zed Books: 31-49.

Nyamu-Musembi, C. (2003) 'Review of Experience in Engaging with 'Non-state' Justice Systems in East Africa', report commissioned by the Governance Division, DfID, UK, February. Available at:

http://www.gsdrc.org/docs/open/DS37.pdf (Accessed 13 January 2014).

Phuong, N.P., Vinck, P., Wierda, M., and Stover, E. (2005) *Forgotten Voices: A Population-Based Survey of Attitudes About Peace and Justice in Northern Uganda,* International Centre for Transitional Justice, Human Rights Centre, Berkeley. http://escholarship.org/uc/item/4qr346xh

Pogge, T. (2005) 'Real world Justice', *The Journal of Ethics*, 9: 29–53.

Sjorgen, A. (2013) *Between Militarism and Technocratic Governance: State Formation in Contemporary Uganda*. Fountain Publishers-The Nordic Africa Institute, Kampala-Uppsala.

Uganda Human Rights Commission (2012) *15th Annual Report,* full report available at: http://www.uhrc.ug/?p=1873 (accessed 24.3.2014).

UN (2006) Department of Economic and Social Affairs, *Social Justice in an Open World: the Role of the United Nations*, UN, New York, Ref: ST/ESA/305, available at: http://www.un.org/esa/socdev/documents/ifsd/SocialJustice.pdf [Accessed 5 March 2014]

US Department of State (2012) *Uganda 2012 Human Rights Report,* Country Report on Human Rights Practices: available at: http://photos.state.gov/libraries/uganda/231771/PDFs/2012_Human_Rights_Report.pdf (Accessed 24 March 2014).

Part One

Historical and Restorative Justice in East Africa

Chapter 2

Social Justice: Recognition and Reparation: Connecting Kenyan *Mungiki* 'gangs' with the Mau Mau Legal Case

Nancy Muigei

Introduction

The aim of this chapter is to link inter-generational Kikuyu struggles for recognition to the question of criminal justice and social justice. *Mungiki* youth have been criminalised, just as the Mau Mau was during the struggle for Kenyan independence. The older generation of Mau Mau veterans and suspects have now opted for legally-framed claims on the former colonial government, whilst the younger generations again appears to be struggling for some form of liberation, through resort to arms. Both generations seek some form of justice and reparations for dispossession. But are the *Mungiki* really, as they claim, direct inheritors of the legacy of the Mau Mau? During the Emergency in the 1950s and early 1960s, the

Mau Mau experienced under colonial government repression, arbitrary killings and torture that were even worse than what today's younger generation, the *Mungiki,* experienced some years ago under the Kenyan government. Like their Mau Mau ancestors, the *Mungiki* were also martyred, and continue to be blamed for crimes during post-election violence in 2008.

So who are the *Mungiki*? In a discussion with Gachoka, one of the two *Mungiki* members I interviewed, I first sought to understand the meaning of the name *Mungiki*. His response in Kiswahili was that this was a name given by others, and that they did not call themselves by this name. He called this: '*Si Sisi Tulijiita Tuliitwa*' (Gachoka 2012, Personal Interview), an expression he used to explain that just like the Mau Mau, who first found out in the forest that they had been named Mau Mau, so too the *Mungiki* did not really understand the name they had been given, and which was now synonymous with their movement. *Mungiki* continue to contest their labelling although they do not contest that the group has its own cultural, religious and political aspirations, and is indeed a group.

In an interview with Muite, a young *Mungiki* himself, he explained the origin of the term *Mungiki* in this way: 'It was Ngonya wa Gakonya of the Tent of the Living God that coined the name *Mungiki*.' He told me that Maina Njenga and his fellow friends who travelled from Laikipia to Nairobi to sell vegetables, joined him in his tent and Ngonya wa Gakonya felt overwhelmed and told them that 'leadership is not for the *Mungiki*-Multitudes'. In Gikuyu, therefore, the term *mungiki* simply means 'a multitude of people'. There is no allusion here to violence, let alone the criminal forms of economic and political violence that have come to be associated with the *Mungiki* today. Arguably, such images of the group criminal, terrorists and highly dangerous, echo the heavily cultivated negative images of Mau Mau from the colonial past. The criminalisation of the movement has led it underground, just as with the Mau Mau. Depending on one's ideological perspective, the *Mungiki* today can be viewed as a gang, a cult, a sect, a social support network, or all of these (Rasmussen 2010:437).

In the early 2000s, on the occasion of a visit by Ngugi wa Thiong'o to the University of Warwick, it was announced that the newly elected democratic government of Kenya was giving serious thought to rehabilitation of the Mau Mau. They planned to begin by: '...erecting statues in memory of Mau Mau fighters ... and [there were] initiatives to found a museum to honour Dedan Kimathi in Nyeri' (Manji, 2003). In addition, already at this time it emerged that a legal battle would be fought in the UK courts by Mau Mau veterans, who were: '...planning to use [sic – this should read sue] the British government for human rights abuses suffered during the uprising' (Manji, 2003). A decade on, and the UK High Court has accepted that the Mau Mau case can proceed. Up to 8,000 families will be likely to sue the UK government for damages for torture, suffering and deaths inflicted on their relatives. Emergency powers were in force in colonial Kenya during the 1950s and early 1960s, and most of the evidence of systematic killings, torture and atrocities were deliberately destroyed, including reportedly by being dumped at sea (Cobain in *The Guardian*, 2013). The case, and the position of the *Mungiki* as outlawed Mau Mau 'descendants', claiming to carry the mantle of demands for social and historical justice, both in relation to identity claims and demands for restoration of their land.

Designing Fieldwork for a sensitive context

This study draws on a Masters thesis which focused uniquely on the *Mungiki*, and 12 respondents were interviewed during the summer of 2012. They included one victim of the *Mungiki*, two journalists, two members of the *Mungiki* themselves, one policy maker who is also a legal representative of the *Mungiki*, three human rights activists, one government official from the Truth, Justice and Reconciliation body, one official from Kenya's National Commission on Human Rights and one academic researcher.

The Mau Mau experience and the ongoing legal case against the UK government have now both been quite well researched, and much relevant information can found on the BBC and Guardian websites.[3] These two reasonably reliable media sources also carry links to the official statements by the UK and Kenyan governments about the case. Data was analysed to understand better how the *Mungiki* were constructed in the media, and the lack of recognition of the legitimacy of their claims for 'revolution' and social justice. Framed in the context of 'post-violence' Kenya, where the ICC

---

3 There are several scholarly studies, including Huw Bennett (2013) *Fighting the Mau Mau: The British Army and Counter-Insurgency in the Kenya Emergency*, Cambridge University Press (Cambridge-New York) and Daniel Branch (2009) *Defeating Mau Mau, creating Kenya: counterinsurgency, civil war, and decolonization*, Cambridge: Cambridge University Press: Cambridge-New York. The Guardian's special website on Mau Mau is located here: http://www.theguardian.com/world/mau-mau. The BBC website has a search function: http://www.bbc.co.uk/search/news/?q=mau+mau [both accessed on 2 May 2014].

is intervening to prosecute the head of state among others, the fieldwork was complex and access to *Mungiki* in particular was not easy, given their illegality and secretive, underground nature (Nyabola 2009:92; Henningsen and Jones 2011:4).

I was able to navigate this complex reality by working with gatekeepers who I had known before the research began, and who helped me contact *Mungiki*, and explain to them the purpose of my study so as to build trust. When the research was being conducted, in 2012-2013, the situation was tumultuous, since the International Criminal Court in The Hague heightened concerns for security more than usual in Kenya, including among local *Mungiki* in my own area of the city. I had to persuade them I had no links with the ICC, despite being a student in The Hague. When I introduced myself to *Mungiki* informants, they accepted me even though they knew I was from the Kalenjin community. One *Mungiki* man stated: '*Kama ungekuwa mlami, ingekuwa rahisi*', which translated means: 'If you would have been a white girl it would have been easier'.

Eventually, when meeting with *Mungiki* members, I was as much interviewed by them as the other way around. They first sought to establish my identity, and made phone calls to my gatekeeper, to check with him and to reassure themselves. I had my own security concerns when doing fieldwork, since I had chosen to work with members of an illegal organisation, whose members were known to have acted violently in the past. I had to overcome my own fear of the *Mungiki*, especially given the gruesome stories about them which I had so often read in the Kenyan media. Some topics we discussed, especially extrajudicial killings of *Mungiki*, evoked deep emotions among my respondents, and even a sense of (re)traumatisation. Researchers on conflict issues know all too well that sometimes we must listen, non-judgementally, to accounts of horror, where lives have been lost and where although the trauma may not be obvious, it can be deep-rooted (Smyth and Robinson 2001:3).

Mungiki justice claims

Mungiki claims are about jobs, income, resources; in other words, about distributive and redistributive justice. Their claims are also about dignity, cultural respect and the symbolic as well as practical value of lost land (Rasmussen, 2010a). Above all, *Mungiki* appear to demand what can be termed 'recognitional justice', which was also a concern in the Mau Mau court case, in which establishing the truth of historical memory, in the absence of colonial records, is a prime motivation alongside the quest for financial compensation. For *Mungiki*, as for Mau Mau, recognition is central to meaningful social justice (Fraser, 1998).

It is suggested that the *Mungiki* organisation has its origins in religious, cultural and traditional values, and its members claim historical and land justice and link these with historical land-related struggles in the past, especially among the Kikuyu community, which was the most heavily affected by colonial land appropriation. Using strategies similar to those the Mau Mau once used, the *Mungiki* cannot always combat their own repression (Gecaga 2007:85). From around 1992, the violence which took place in the rural areas of the Rift Valley, especially around election times, started to be framed as 'ethnic', even though much of it was criminal violence, involving robbery and political intimidation of voters (Turner and Brownhill 2011:1043, Gecaga 2007:85; Snow, 2009). Yet as for the Mau Mau, the targeted membership of *Mungiki* are the dispossessed and disenfranchised: hawkers, bus touts and internally displaced people. All have insecure livelihoods and low status in the labour market.

Perhaps the *Mungiki* are not all that new, in this case? However, the movement's leadership has made some significant shifts, moving first from traditional beliefs to Islam, and then from Islam to Christianity. *Mungiki* thus combine elements of continuity with elements that are new; their parallels with Mau Mau seem to merit further inquiry. Gecaga's suggestion that nothing much has changed is not adequate, given the unintended effects of internal displacement in the post-2007 era, and the redefinition of justice claims as 'ethnic'. The dominant view is now that violence results from ethnic identity struggles, and not from struggles between indigenous Kenyans and settlers from Europe, as during the Mau Mau period. This means that the task of reallocating resources has started to be accompanied by demands for recognition for identity, demands which are now perhaps the single dominant framing of injustice in Kenya among the *Mungiki* (Snow, 2009:116).

There is broad agreement among scholars and other researchers that the *Mungiki* emerged in Kenya around the 1980s, starting out as a mainly religious movement, and later becoming more overtly political, and finally being associated with criminal activities, violence and extortion (Rasmussen, 2010:306). The *Mungiki* have thus come to be understood mainly through a 'criminal' lens as a 'securitised other', widely reviled as a civil and political militia, using vigilantism to mobilise for violence, especially during election periods (Nyabola 2008, Anderson 2002, and Katumanga 2005). Banned since 2002, suspected *Mungiki* members have been subjected to brutal arrests and killings, especially in 2007, in a prelude to the terrible electoral violence that occured thereafter.

Already in 2002, in a prescient article about the politics of history and law in Kenya, Ambreena Manji noted that amidst the democratic reforms taking place at that time, there were signs that the historical injustices visited on the Kikuyu in particular, and on Kenyans in general, could become more overtly politicised. This, he already noted, opened up the possibility for recognition of some of the Kikuyus' historical justice claims in the form of cases under criminal law, and other claims for restorative and retributive justice (Manji, 2003).

Initially, most academic research on the *Mungiki* analysed their movement from the religious perspective; and the movement is still commonly viewed as a sect or cult (see Nyabola 2009:92, Ruteere 2009:8 for examples). However, it was the media that brought the movement to light in the 1990s, by reporting on their role in the re-introduction of multiparty politics in Kenya (Rasmussen 2010:302, Ruteere 2009:6, Servant 2007:521). At the same time, other state-sponsored militia groups emerged around this time, becoming central to how political power was maintained and how the electorate was controlled. Such groups were mainly activated around election periods, and to some it seemed they functioned to derail democracy rather than to defend it (see also Kagwanja 2005:56).

The *Mungiki* movement had begun in the mid-1980s as a youth movement focused on job creation and social advancement. During the 1990s, with the advent of multi-party politics, the use of violence, extortion and issuing of threats to businessmen became a tactic of some (not all) *Mungiki,* leading to their having a reputation as a network of criminal gangs, mainly operating within slums and some rural areas of Kenya. It was reported in interviews[4] that people believed President Daniel Arap Moi had invited these Kikuyu youth to control the transport system so as to help his party get more votes (see Githongo 2010, Gecaga 2007:68). Their emergence was thus linked to weakening state authority, ethnic polarisation and the widespread culture of impunity and corruption during the late Moi years of the early 1990s.

The founders of *Mungiki* were Ndura Waruinge and Maina Njenga, the latter now in the clergy. Both claimed explicitly to be heirs of the Mau Mau movement, following in their footsteps. They insisted that historical justice claims were behind the setting up of *Mungiki.* Kikuyu grievances following displacement from their land by white colonial settlers were aggravated by post-independence policies, which did not restore land to those previously dispossessed. Atrocities committed against the Mau Mau still remained unpunished, decades later, and were officially unacknowledged. The *Mungiki* leadership thus claimed to be struggling for land

4 One respondent highlighted how Moi had played part in allowing *Mungiki* to extort money in exchange for a youth constituency within Central Province. Moi learnt through intelligence of some disenfranchised young Kikuyu youth, and asked Hon. Njenga Karume to summon their leadership. It is said Moi granted him 400,000 Ksh approximately (EUR 4000), as money to be used for bail in case anyone of them was arrested (Muite 2012: Personal Interview, Moi did not want to be associated with the group, but offered them protection. Fairview Nairobi)

and freedom, just like their forefathers, and although they now embrace Christianity, they also subscribe to the Kikuyu philosophy that there should be major periodic shifts in inter-generational political authority, to bring 'outsiders' back into the mainstream, and shift power relations periodically (Kilonzo 2008:2).

When the KANU regime, started by first President Jomo Kenyatta, finally crumbled, official accounts of colonial history started to be reconsidered, especially in light of the neglected role of Mau Mau fighters. Historical injustices, through negative propaganda and disinformation, were countered by a campaign to secure recognition for the former Mau Mau leader, Dedan Kimathi. Unfortunately, the legacy of the past negative colonial images of Mau Mau influences reporting also on the *Mungiki*, who are still most often represented as savage 'others'. Like many post-colonial governments, KANU (under both Kenyatta and Moi): 'tried to suppress the narratives of the radical Mau Mau as an embodiment of the struggle for Kenyan nationhood', by recognising only '...a small portion of the multifaceted organisation...as the representative of those who fought for freedom' and social justice, on behalf of all Kenyans (Mwangi, 2010:92).

The current context: insecurity, youth and identity politics

Increasingly, semi-private militia groups are said to be taking over from government security forces in responding to civil disturbances and protests, and this has led to an increasing incidence of civil violence by non-government actors (Duffield 2007:67). The legitimating justice claims of the *Mungiki* are counteracted by their delegitimised resort to political violence. Yet their striving for recognition of their identity, and for distributive justice all serve to make them appear a legitimate social movement as well (Kamungi 2011). Interestingly, whether viewed as a social movement, a religious cult, a set of entrepreneurial and violent neighbourhood gangs, *Mungiki*, like Mau Mau before them, can be represented as both victims and perpetrators. This is indeed one of the connections between *Mungiki* today and the historical justice claims of the Mau Mau before them. A blurring of boundaries between *Mungiki* identity and other Kikuyu civilians remains a problem, and means that when *Mungiki* are targeted, their own use of violence is sometimes not questioned. Their propensity – like the Mau Mau before them – to sometimes target civilians, remains in need of acknowledgement, therefore (see Wegner and Mason, 2008:842 on this issue).

Interpreting *Mungiki* as privileged youth is one analytical lens that may help explain how the movement arose and how it uses cross-generational justice discourses to espouse its social justice objectives for youth in general, and Kikuyu youth in particular. Kagwanja's work has been central in sponsoring this view and he claims that youth within the movement use inter-generational discourses in a bid to capture power. His analysis is situated within the context of transitional politics and patrimonial leadership of the Moi successional debates of 2002 (Kagwanja 2005:51). Another proponent of cross-generational justice is Rasmussen (2010:315) who agrees with Kagwanja. Both claim that *Mungiki* have been key in bringing core issues to do with the priorities of youth onto Kenya's public political agenda. In 2002 and 2007, these youth were co-opted into serving the patrimonial interests of the elite in power (Kagwanja 2005:53). Using youth as an analytical lens has its pros and cons, especially when looking at issues such as vigilantism as well as criminality, as has been argued (Veit et al 2011:26). Youth as an analytical lens may fail to capture the complexity of the lived experiences of *Mungiki* as perpetrators. The analysis of historical and social justice claims by *Mungiki* youth needs to factor in how issues of gender, class and place intersect with one another. The point of departure of Rasmussen's work lies in the focus on the gendered dynamics of the youth movement, something on which Kagwanja's work does not shed light (Rasmussen 2010:315).

For some, the movement is not a serious force to be reckoned with due to the lack of principles demonstrated by its leadership (Murunga, 2006:30). Murungu claims the movement is weak and only functions as a means of survival and to negotiate with those in power on behalf of its members. Criticising Kagwanja, he opposes the idea that *Mungiki* is a mass movement. He instead states that 'straddling the urban and rural domains remains *Mungiki*'s central objective...for security concerns [and it is]...doubtful [that *Mungiki*]...is seeking state power' (Murungu, 2006: 30). As this study shows, *Mungiki* narratives point to deep-seated grievances related to living conditions, and also to a strong belief in historical justice (Henningsen and Jones 2011:14).

Kagwanja's work characterises the *Mungiki* as advocating for the return of Kikuyu traditional values, such as generational leadership transfer and views this as part of their ploy to 're-traditionalise the Kenyan society within the modern space' (Kagwanja, 2005:53). This thinking is criticised by Murunga

(2006:28) who claims it reflects Eurocentric views, and borrows from understandings of the failed African state, such as those of Stephen Ellis among others, which link anarchy, violence and warfare to all that is traditional. Instead, Murunga claims that those youth who are in the *Mungiki* are engaged in a struggle for power and that they use cultural symbols to project the forces operating behind the movement (Murunga, 2006:30). He also calls for an assessment of those who support the group from behind the scenes. Murungu points out that these forces have multiple interests, which sometimes do not converge with those of *Mungiki* youth; it is useful to thus distinguish the means and the goals of *Mungiki* and those of their supporters 'in high places'.

Recent scholarly work has also conceptualised the *Mungiki* as subaltern (for one example see Ruteere 2008:4, also Frederiksen 2010). From this perspective, the position occupied by *Mungiki* within the society is as the other, being both a Kikuyu underclass and unable to fit into the usual (neo-liberal) definition of 'civil society'. It was from this juncture that the group broke out from the Tent of the Living God and began their own religion (Muite August 2012, Personal Interview). From their origins, the *Mungiki* were mostly unemployed youth from Central Kenya who came together to plant vegetables in Laikipia. They would then ferry the vegetables and sell them in Nairobi. Their movement in and out of the city facilitated contacts with other underground movements, most at that time fighting the repressive regime of former Moi.

Frederiksen (2010:1068) frames the *Mungiki* as a 'political society', and views this as part of being subaltern as they are unconventional and viewed as outside the mainstream civil society. She argues for an extended understanding of civil society, so that such political groups can become part of a process of deepening democracy.

As noted earlier, relatively few researchers have concerned themselves with analysing the aspirations of ordinary members of *Mungiki* and with how they construct their own social reality. Henningsen and Jones (2011:6) use social movement theory to challenge understandings of *Mungiki* as subaltern and victims of deprivation and political exclusion. They instead propose an understanding of 'ordinary members' of *Mungiki* as actors within a social movement. They are concerned with how *Mungiki* manages to enroll young people despite its illegality and the risks involved for members.

Although *Mungiki* has been represented dominantly as male (Kilonzo 2008:1), recent studies indicate that the role of women within the organisation is also significant, if quite limited in terms of proportions. The study undertaken by Rasmussen (2008) identified *Mungiki* women – mothers, wives, daughters and sisters – as helping transform the media discourse around *Mungiki* claims and identity politics. They have done this by testifying and thus highlighting problems of extrajudicial killings, disappearances and the use of excessive force by police in 'search and destroy' operations against *Mungiki* suspects (Rasmussen 2010a:316; Wamue, 2001:454). There are women within the movement, but we do not have much information about their roles or distinctive outlooks. Another source, research by Brownhill and Turner (2004:98) enriches the discussion on the role of women within the movement, claiming that they view *Mungiki* as espousing the ideals of 'a New Mau Mau', and as advocating vehemently from below against globalisation and the land-grabbing that started during the colonial era, continuing today.

In 2002, after political reform and the installation of the Kibaki regime represented by the NARC party, the engagement of *Mungiki* in violence was taken as evidence of a strategy of collaboration by KANU, which was accused of using the *Mungiki* youth movement to try and undermine the newly elected government (Kagwanja 2005:66). The NARC administration responded with equal force towards the group, and the Internal Security Minister, Chris Murungaru, is cited by Kagwanja to have issued an order to shoot members of *Mungiki* on sight. At the same time, Murungaru also offered leeway for those who would surrender in 30 days to be granted amnesty (2005:67)

Primarily, therefore, the *Mungiki* are framed as a problem within the intra-Kikuyu community, and this is traced to narratives of how historical injustices around Mau Mau remain unresolved. The internal displacements of (1992, 1997 and 2002) framed as ethnic clashes, provided *Mungiki* with a base to recruit its members. During the violence in 2002, around 2000 people were killed and 400,000 displaced (HRW 2002:1), in 1992 and 1997 around 3,000 people were killed and an approximate 300,000 displaced (Stewart 2010:134) Subsequently, the ethnicisation of land was central to how conflicts around *Mungiki* were constructed. The original founders of the movement were squatters in the Rift Valley, and heirs of the former Mau Mau who were displaced and never resettled. The grievances advanced by the *Mungiki* stemmed from issues of how land and the Mau Mau had been subjected as well as structural issues to do with the political economy of Kenya (see also Anderson 2002: 532&553; Kagwanja 2009:325)

In terms of identity and their claims for recognition, the *Mungiki*'s claims are for a form of social justice rooted in religious and spiritual beliefs. Members of the movement claim that revolution is coming, and that the old corrupt order will be renewed, as it is swept away, in line with prophesies from both Gikuyu beliefs and the Old Testament. *Mungiki* used to have classically Mau Mau style dreadlocked hair. However, after police arrests and raids in the late 1990s and in 2002, Rasmussen notes how: '...most members have cut their hair and try to blend in with the general public' (Rasmussen, 2010a:309). Contrary to widespread belief, the *Mungiki* movement does not officially condone the use of violence. On the contrary, when one leader, Muigai, asked about why members sometimes seemed to resort to violence, another leader replied that youth 'impatience' and despair were perhaps to blame (Rasmussen, 2010a:310). Equally important may be the longer-lasting legacy of denial of recognition, and hence a feeling of resentment and even the temptation to use violence to achieve media attention, policy attention and hence, perversely, recognition. As Mwangi puts it, the *Mungiki*'s self-perceptions are linked with the way in which for some time: 'The Mau Mau discourse has had to become oppositional because the ruling elites have suppressed the memory of Mau Mau from the Kenyan nationalist imaginary' (Mwangi, 2010:92).

From Mungiki to Mau Mau and back again

Just like the *Mungiki*, the Mau Mau was a proscribed organisation over many years. When I interviewed Paul Muite, lawyer of leading members of *Mungiki*, he traced the origins of this organisation to social injustices and to historical grievances around the flagrant mistreatment and mass killings of suspected Mau Mau prior to independence. Muite observed that the socio-economic and political policies put in place after independence reinforced disillusionment among younger generation Kikuyu, since no real social transformation followed independence. In his words: 'The sons of chiefs and loyalists were co-opted into the minority elite, the use of ethnic mobilisation to cling to power was initiated, some people became extremely wealthy and the great majority shifted to poverty. The Nationalists that fought for the land never got the land, and were given no priority in access to the former white highlands (Sabar-Friedman, 1995:105). The socio-economic disparities, authoritarianism and land grabbing gave rise to the *Mungiki*'. (Muite 2012, personal interview).[5]

Another respondent likened the *Mungiki* struggle to the Mau Mau movement, suggesting that the *Mungiki*, like the Mau Mau, claim to be fighting for Land and Freedom '*Winyatti na Ithaka*'. Their goal, similarly, is to have the opportunity to decide for themselves how they live, and to have land in order to be able to fend for their own livelihoods. More ambitiously, he suggests: 'they want to reclaim their lost glory and are ready to go back to the forest' (Kamanda 2012, personal interview). In

5 Personal interview with Hon. Paul Muite (Former Member of Parliament Kabete and legal representative to Maina Njenga, the former *Mungiki* Leader), Nairobi, August 2012.

his view, *Mungiki* reinforce their bonds by adopting techniques similar to the Mau Mau's, including through oaths that bind the social group together.[6]

Whilst the root causes of both groups can be seen as claims for redistributive justice in terms of wealth, and good governance, as well as redress for previous human rights violations, both the Mau Mau and the Mungiki are seen as groups that organise under ethnicity and religion in particular. Their collective identity is itself forged through collective organising around an ethnic identity constructed as historically 'authentic' (Wegner & Mason 2008:836).

Not all *Mungiki* trace their heritage to the Mau Mau; some were first displaced by the direct electoral violence of 1988, of 1992 and of 1997. Violence at election times saw many Kenyans become internally displaced (IDPs) at this time, and many could not be resettled. Others within the movement are former robbers whom the *Mungiki* transformed. In a conversation with one member of the *Mungiki* movement, he informed me that the loyalists are still leading the country and took up much of the formerly dispossessed land after independence. This made it almost impossible for the Mau Mau to reclaim their lost land without criticising others, especially political elites, for injustices. The poor do not have the means to buy land, he claims '*tunataka usawa wa bindamu na mashamba*' – meaning 'we want all humans to be treated equally and [we all want] land' (Gachoka 2012, personal interview).[7] This statement

6 Personal interview with Kamanda (Human Rights Officer) in Nairobi, August 2012.

7 Personal interview with Gachara (Member of the *Mungiki*) in Nairobi, August 2012.

sums up the search for historical and land justice that lies at the heart of the continued mobilisation of the *Mungiki* today.

Media perceptions of *Mungiki*: shades of the past

In this section, we sum up briefly the findings of an earlier study by the author, which looked at media attitudes towards *Mungiki* in much more detail. The media analysis was conducted to show how images of *Mungiki* in the Kenyan media suggest their marginalisation and even stigmatisation as a social grouping. The data analysed came from two Kenyan newspapers, *The Daily Nation* and *The Standard*, from articles published in March 2009 about *Mungiki*-related topics. The articles were found in the electronic archives of both dailies, and retrieved and headlines relating to *Mungiki* used to code the data. Of six articles selected from each of the two dailies, frame analysis was used, as proposed by Entman (1993) and a matrix table designed for comparative analysis. The question posed was: 'How are narratives about *Mungiki* constructed within the Kenyan print media'? The findings were relevant to the extent that there are echoes of earlier research about how Mau Mau was constructed at the time of the Emergency in Kenya. The *Mungiki* are defined by frames, labels and metaphors, found in our analysis of media coverage during March 2009 in the two selected newspapers. Once headlines that made reference to *Mungiki* were analysed, the researcher read stories produced in both papers, and then analysed them in terms of the sources of information provided. Then the labels used for *Mungiki* were analysed, their actions identified and metaphors analysed in each of the 12 selected articles. Figure 1 shows the labels used in *Daily Nation* and *The Standard* articles. These were analysed from headlines making reference to *Mungiki*.[8]

Figure 1: *Mungiki* labels in headlines of *The Daily Nation and Standard* newspapers

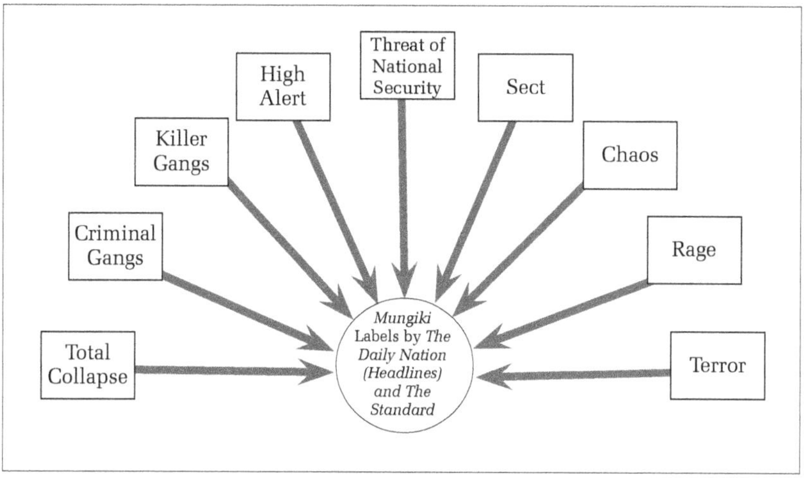

Looking more closely, *The Standard*, unlike the *Daily Nation*, avoided explicit mention of tribe, but referred to *Mungiki* as a problem in 'central region'. Since colonial administrative boundaries established by the British divided the country into Provinces, so that in each province some tribes were dominant, the reference to central region implies that the *Mungiki* are Kikuyu. The history of how Kenya was divided up and tribes distributed across the space, suggests that the *Mungiki* are being framed as a Kikuyu problem, in a way very similar to the tribal framing of the Mau Mau by the British colonial regime (Sabar-

8 Other terms like 'thorn in the flesh' and 'outlawed gangs' were also used. There was also reference to 'climate of fear' and *Mungiki* were described as 'Lords of illegal government'.

Friedman, 1995:103). A deeper analysis points to alienation and mistreatment of Mau Mau families within the same region in the past, and this makes clearer the linkages with how Mau Mau were constructed in the past. The common features are the insistence on a specific tribal identity, and a preference for a psychological treatment of the groups, as if they did not have any meaningful grievances, but were simply manipulated by their leaders to express anger through violence, and act in criminal ways in order to terrorise others. Sabar-Friedman refers to the 'savage, psychotic and religious cult image of the Mau Mau', fostered by the colonial British through their counter-insurgency operations (Sabar-Friedman, 1995: 103).

Redistributive Social Justice claims: *Mungiki* and Mau Mau

Interestingly, when interviewed, and in the rare media report where they can speak, *Mungiki* members themselves often claim their movement 'saved' them from a previous life of despair, crime and poverty. By joining *Mungiki*, they claim to have gained self-respect and to have rediscovered hope for a better future (Rasmussen, 2010a: 312). As Diouf puts it: 'Taking for granted their despair with regard to the disjunction between their dreams and aspirations, on one hand, and the opportunities offered them, on the other, the religious discourse calls for a complete and deliberate rupture with the past and lays out a different future'; to this extent the religious framing of the group as a cult may not be entirely mistaken (Diouf, 2003:7). *Mungiki,* however, according to some researchers, also represent landless Kikuyu lineages, directly traceable to those clans with the strongest support for the Mau Mau during the colonial era (Kamungi 2009:360). Colonial dispossessions affected some areas more than others, and Mau Mau were recruited from among those most adversely affected. Later on, after independence, this was why the *Mungiki* came to be constructed as part of an 'intra-Kikuyu set of conflicts between the 'old guard' and 'new guard', the 'haves' and 'have-nots' (Sabar-Friedman, 1995:104-106). Whilst this construction reflects some elements of the historically differentiated impacts of land dispossession on Kikuyu people, it does not take on board resulting ideological and class differences that underpinned the Mau Mau movement, and may underpin recruitment into *Mungiki* today.

In a final discussion with both Ngare and Gachoka, I sought to more fully understand how the *Mungiki* movement, like the Mau Mau before it, had come to be associated with mindless and criminal violence. They responded as follows: '*Vita yetu ni kati yetu na matajiri wa Kikuyu, hawa wengine ni kuskia wa husskia, Mungiki wako Mombasa, Kisumu, na Kenya mzima, kwanini mambo haitendeki huko? Hatauwezi nyanyasa wananchi, Vita haijaisha mpaka nchi ibadilike*', which translates as follows: 'The war is between us and the Kikuyu rich upper class, *Mungiki* exists countrywide, why haven't you heard that *Mungiki* has attacked people in those places but only in central Kenya? The war is not over until the country changes' (Gachoka 2012, personal interview). They also explained that their motivation centred on the desire for greater equality and respect between the rich and poor, '*Kaa na watu kama bindamu nikiwa tajiri wewe maskini tuheshimiane*', 'You should stay with people like human beings. If I am poor and you are rich, let us respect one another' (Gachoka 2012, personal interview).

Although *Mungiki* has been defined as a Kikuyu problem, a conversation with the members revealed that an important issue for the *Mungiki* is a class conflict between dispossessed Kikuyu and members of the Kikuyu elite. The two *Mungiki* interviewees explicitly invoked narratives of the Mau Mau and the past issue of land, and how elite within the community were able to take over land previously occupied by white farmers. That the Kenyatta regime failed to resettle the Mau Mau, and that their previously seized lands were then sold to the highest bidders, was seen as the root cause of their grievances, a source of class conflict and a profound sense of injustice. Since the Mau Mau, of whom many were still in the forest, could not buy land, their descendants claim that Mau Mau were never acknowledged as those who freed Kenya from colonial rule. Now, those who claim to have inherited the injustices first inflicted on Mau Mau, offer up an alternative leadership model, through which they hope that the future of Kenya can become more promising than under the liberal policies pursued more or less since independence under the Jomo Kenyatta 'sellout' regime (Kinyatti 2008:xxi)

A Justice, Law and Order Perspective

There is a need to deeply interrogate the interests and goals of the Mau Mau and *Mungiki*'s use of violence, and this research goes further and asks what this violence has been aimed at achieving. Asking this question breaks with an interpretation of *Mungiki* and Mau Mau as criminal to the extent that they have employed violence. Violence can, however, be political, criminal, economic and social; not all forms of violence are viewed in the same way by society (Viet et al 2011:26). Thus after 2002, with the Kibaki regime in power, *Mungiki* violence was viewed in political terms, as evidence of collaboration with KANU, and was given a specific meaning, interpreted as a way to undermine the newly elected democratic government (Kagwanja, 2005:66). The NARC administration responded with a show of police force towards the group. Internal Security Minister Chris Murungaru then issued an order that police should shoot members of *Mungiki* on sight. At the same time, Murungara offered some leeway for those *Mungiki* who surrendered in 30 days, offering them amnesty (Kagwanja, 2005:67).

Subsequently, another interpretation of violence by *Mungiki* has been proposed, a more materialist one. This suggests that members of the movement use violence to protect and promote their own economic interests, rather than for any political reasons (Anderson 2002:542). Government has even been accused of strategically protecting the movement, opposing them only when *Mungiki* interests clash with those of the ruling elite (Nyabola 2010:93). Occasionally, in times of crisis, *Mungiki* violence has even been perceived in positive terms by some Kenyans, especially in 2007, when the *Mungiki* were said to have come to the defense of civilians being targeted for attack within their local communities during post-election violence, and to have taken the brunt of the violence themselves (Frederiksen 2010:1066). Rather than being criminal or self-interested, from a broader perspective, *Mungiki* use of violence can be related to the weakening of the 'monopoly of legitimate force' on the part of the Kenyan state. The failure of internal security systems to manage the electoral reform process, for example, placed many *Mungiki* in the position of a civil guard, defending the citizens from their own state security forces and hired thugs. The growing *Mungiki* movement can be viewed, from this perspective, as symptomatic of the breakdown of law and order in Kenya (Kagwanja 2005:73).

For the most part, government-proposed solutions to the '*Mungiki* problem', have involved excessive use of force. Kenyan police have been blamed by several human rights groups for extrajudicial killings of suspected members of the movement, and for torture and mistreatment (KNCHR 2008, OHCHR 2009). However, the use of force by police has been justified on the grounds of 'terrorism' of the group, and the need to respond to public panic and pressure to act tough. All this is very reminiscent of the arguments of the late colonial regime in Kenya that 'extreme' measures were needed to reassure white farmers and 'moderate' Kenyans that the state was still in control, when patently the state was no longer in control at all. To curtail the *Mungiki*'s activities in a more sustainable manner, without adding to their recruits, will require different tactics in future, if the past is anything to go by. What must be acknowledged is that even if the Kenyan public tends to approve of violent direct action by police against *Mungiki*, and even if police are constructed as heroes, and *Mungiki* as villains, a sustainable solution cannot come from violence-based policies (Ruteere, 2008). Human rights movements and social justice advocates may not have a wide audience, but in the end their argument that negotiation needs to focus on grievances and restoring a sense of justice for the members of

Mungiki appears more realistic and hopeful than the policy of eliminating this movement physically (Ruteere 2008:2).

Growing concern over how police deal with *Mungiki* has brought attention from Amnesty International, which reported that in a single operation to recover what were said to be stolen weapons, almost 30 innocent lives were lost in the swoop, through random police shootings. Michuki, who was then Minister for Internal Security, said on camera:

> We will straighten them and wipe them out. I cannot tell you today where those who have been arrested in connection with recent killings are. What you will be hearing is that there will be a burial tomorrow. If you use a gun to kill you are also required to be executed. (Amnesty International 2007, cited in Atieno 2007: 527).

Concluding Thoughts

This research has focused on questions of historical and criminal justice in relation to the *Mungiki* today, in light of the precedent of the Mau Mau during the late colonial era. The reasons for connecting these concerns in this way is the belief that potential lessons that are there to be learned may not yet have been taken on board by policy makers. In particular, the belief in social justice can be a powerful recruiting tool among disenfranchised youth, for a movement like the *Mungiki* or the Mau Mau. Civilians caught in crossfire between such groups and the police remain vulnerable so long as violence is a principal means of resolving power disputes. The Achilles heel of any violent policing solution is that the dividing line between *Mungiki* and ordinary civilians is very blurred indeed. Unless less physical, and more social justice-oriented, approaches are adopted in future, police operations risk engendering forms of localised ethnic cleansing and a form of contemporary counter-insurgency that resonates with past colonial counter-insurgency in disturbing ways, as Michuki's statements about funerals suggest. For those who are civilians and who may have been multiply displaced, lost land, been tortured and suffered the deaths and disappearances of family members in the past, more violence from police may not discourage recruitment into *Mungiki*, but rather hasten this process (Kaldor 2007:169).

Overall, the *Mungiki* revolt can be linked to a failure to realise an inter-generational and inter-class handover of leadership and positions of authority, especially within the Kikuyu community (Fredriksen 2010:1081). Discourses around youth are often used to explain *Mungiki* use of violence (Rasmussen 2010:315). More widely, since the *Mungiki* also appear to be renegotiating within the wider society who they are in relation to other classes, the older generation, and the state, questions of historical justice remain an active part of their agenda. Whilst youth within *Mungiki* do use violence to define their own political spaces, the prospect of their disarmament depends on making other spaces open to them, and respecting due process, including through putting them on trial for their crimes, instead of shooting them in shoot-to-kill police operations (Rasmussen 2010: 315, Kagwanja 2005: 52).

If marginalised and disadvantaged youth are attracted to movements that inspire messianic hopes of future redemption, for example through being 'born again' or returning to 'fundamental' cultural roots of resistance to both elders and foreigners, then the Mau Mau and *Mungiki* both start out as youth movements of this kind. Yet, as is becoming apparent, 60 years later, the main hope for historical justice still lies in recourse to formal legal institutions in the colonial heartland – the courts of the UK. The hope that long-denied historical justice can be achieved, if not through the Kenyan government, or through land reallocation, then through the revealing of truths long hidden by the colonial power itself, then the connections between Mau Mau veterans and the *Mungiki* today have become more tangible. As surviving Mau Mau veterans become old and are dying, their legal battle is being handed over to their children, grandchildren and great-grandchildren. In 2013, over 8,000 Kenyan families of those tortured and killed as Mau Mau during the colonial era, were granted permission to proceed with their court case through the UK courts. They are now suing the UK government for the first time in post-colonial history, for damages for past injuries, suffering and loss. A key witness in this case was a British colonial official, responsible for overseeing part of the Emergency anti-terrorist operations in Kenya at the time, who gave evidence, testimony that helped to expose the secrecy of the colonial records, their destruction and their burial in archives not opened up to the public until 2013, decades after they ought to have been released.

References

Anderson, D.M. (2002) 'Vigilantes, Violence and the Politics of Public Order in Kenya', *African Affairs,* 101(405): 531-555.

Atieno, A. (2007) '*Mungiki,*'Neo-Mau Mau'& the Prospects for Democracy in Kenya', *Review of African Political Economy,* 34(113): 526-531.

Cobain, I. (2013) 'Revealed: the bonfire of papers at the end of Empire', *The Guardian,* 29 November.

Diouf, M. (2003) 'Engaging Postcolonial Cultures: African Youth and Public Space', *African Studies Review,* 46: 1-12.

Duffield, M. (1998) 'Post-modern Conflict: Warlords, post-adjustment States and Private Protection', *Civil Wars* 1(1): 65-102.

Fraser, N. (1998) *Social Justice in the Age of Identity Politics: Redistribution, Recognition, Participation,* Discussion Paper FS/98-108, Berlin: Wissenschaftszentrum Berlin für Sozialforschung.

Henningsen, E. and Peris, J. (2011) 'Crisis and the Regeneration of the Self:The *Mungiki* Movement's Power of Mobilisation' Kagwanja, P. (2009) 'Courting Genocide: Populism, Ethno-Nationalism and the Informalisation of Violence in Kenya's 2008 Post-Election Crisis', *Journal of Contemporary African Studies,* 27(3): 365-387.

Kamungi, P. M. (2009) 'The Politics of Displacement in Multiparty Kenya', *Journal of Contemporary African Studies,* 27(3): 345-364.

Manji, A. (2003) 'Law, Literature and the Politics of Culture in Kenya', *Law, Social Justice and Global Development,* 2: no pages (electronic journal). Available at: http://www2.warwick.ac.uk/fac/soc/law/elj/lgd/2003_2/manji/#a4 (Accessed 13 January 2014).

Mwangi, E. (2010) 'The Incomplete Rebellion: Mau Mau Movement in Twenty-First-Century Kenyan Popular Culture', *Africa Today*, 57 (2): 87-113.

Nanjala Nyabola, H. (2009) 'The legal challenge of civil militia groups in Kenya', *African Security Review*, 18 (3) 89-102.

Rasmussen, J. (2010a) '*Mungiki* as youth movement: Revolution, gender and generational politics in Nairobi, Kenya', *Young: Nordic Journal of Youth Research*, 18(3): 301–319.

Rasmussen, J. (2010b) 'Outwitting the Professor of Politics? *Mungiki* Narratives of Political Deception and their Role in Kenyan Politics', *Journal of Eastern African Studies*, 4(3): 435-449.

Ruteere, M. (2009) 'Dilemmas of Crime, Human Rights and the Politics of *Mungiki* Violence in Kenya', *Human Rights and the Politics of Mungiki Violence in Kenya (August 27, 2009)*.

Sabar-Friedman, G. (1995) 'The Mau Mau Myth: Kenyan political discourse in search of Democracy', *Cahiers d'Etudes Africaines*, 35 (137): 101-131.

Snow, S. (2009) 'Unhindered by the rule of law: ethnic terrorism and the 2007 Kenyan presidential election', *South African Journal of International Affairs*, 16 (1): 115-127.

Smyth, M., and Robinson, G. (2001), 'Researching Violently Divided Societies: Ethical and Methodological Issues'. United Nations University.

Wenger, A., and Mason S. J. A (2008), 'The Civilianization of Armed Conflict: Trends and Implications', *International Review of the Red Cross* 90(872): 835.

Chapter 3

Justice on the Radio? An Assessment of Justice Frames in 'Facing Justice', an NGO-supported Radio Programme

Jackson Odong

> *"Our main task as media is just to set the agenda and let people discuss. We started with the issue of peace – people said yes, we think that is a brilliant idea, we did it, and now the peace is there. Now we said our second agenda is post-war recovery and post-war recovery cannot be comprehensively achieved without discussing the issue of Justice" (interview with a radio presenter in Gulu, Uganda, August 2014).*

Introduction

This study arises from the starting point that radio can be an active and vital tool and participant in post-war justice and development. The belief that radio can offer more up-to-date and accurate information, coupled with well-packaged and interesting features and music, can make radio an attractive form of media, especially since it is free at the point of delivery, and relatively cheap to produce. Radio can become an alternative platform for discussing development issues, and this applies especially to peace, and to justice, including social justice.

Through an analysis of the *Facing Justice* radio programme, this chapter reveals that there is no single meaning of justice; instead, there are multiple meanings of justice. Justice in people's minds is not necessarily this or that but a combination of meanings which can include: justice as a tradition, justice as forgiveness and reconciliation, rehabilitation and reintegration, justice as fairness, and justice as truth-telling. All of these include elements of legal justice, social justice and restorative justice. Material compensation, ICC style justice, and peace as justice are three main strands that were found to be dominant in the *Facing Justice* radio programme, and were each associated with three further broader categories of justice, namely: legal justice, distributive justice and rectificatory justice. Social justice, in any meaningful sense, and also positive peace, would require all three of these components.

As will be shown, the meanings of justice produced by the *Facing Justice* programme relate to different levels, which can be described as international, national, regional and local, representing various intra-perspectives on justice. Local justice initiatives at community and sub-community level tend to be rectificatory or distributive; national level justice tends to be legal and criminal justice, and international justice initiatives tend to be both legal and rectificatory, and from a donor-led perspective.

Overall, as the chapter shows, what is meant by justice varies widely among different stakeholders and is sometimes much closer to 'social justice' as it is usually defined, and to peace, than in other cases. Realising justice can prove challenging and risky for all those involved, including for victims, prosecutors and the media. Understanding and achieving justice that includes, but is also broader than legal justice, becomes harder when it comes to war crimes, where neither prosecuting crimes under cumbersome international justice system mechanisms nor pardoning perpetrators through traditional restorative justice mechanisms, appears able to reintegrate the perpetrators and reconcile them not only with the victims, but also their crimes with the need for justice as a prelude to lasting peace.

The role of media in achieving peace and justice

Since 2004, popular debates over justice in northern Uganda have been reduced to merely international criminal justice versus traditional justice. Controversy has raged since then among various stakeholders and justice experts, including trading of accusations regarding "tolerance of impunity and imposing of Western ideas of justice" as noted by Branch (2014:10). How do the views of different actors about the meaning of justice differ (Armstrong 2014:3)? And if war and humanitarianism have been replaced with the perspectives of peace and justice in northern Uganda, to what extent has radio played a part in this process (Branch 2014:1)? How have Western ideas entered into local and national debates on justice? Debates around justice have occurred, and as Kimberley (2014:3) has argued: "the news media was particularly important in framing the debate... media focused on the apparent dilemma between peace and justice". Whereas many debates in the 1990s considered peace and justice to be mutually exclusive, more recently it could be argued that they are more often viewed as mutually reinforcing goals. In part this is the outcome of how justice has been defined and framed in several different ways, creating a wide array of meanings of justice and ending the notion that only one dominant definition of peace or justice exists.

By exploring the *Facing Justice* radio programme, this chapter examines how the co-producers, the Institute for War and Peace Reporting (IWPR), based in The Hague, and the northern Uganda Media Club (NUMEC) collaborated to produce the programme and to frame justice in particular ways. The study addressed key questions, including:

(i) What are the meanings of justice represented in the radio programme *Facing Justice*?

(ii) How are meanings of justice framed, produced and whose perspectives are expressed?

(iii) Who are the *Facing Justice* target audiences for whom justice issues are framed and broadcast?

The analysis begins by describing the *Facing Justice* radio programme, and methodology. It then reviews existing literature (both print and electronic) on media and justice in the context of post-war situations in which different discourses on broadcast journalism and transitional justice are reflected upon. Parallel with this, I analysed organisational documents of the IWPR and NUMEC about the content of the *Facing Justice* radio programme, where I applied framing and focalisation analysis as my main analytical research tools.

Research Context

From April until October 2014, I conducted a study on the *Facing Justice* radio programme. I set out to triangulate three sources of information, namely: secondary data (such as literature, published organisational documents, reports, manuals and other studies on the subject), 46 episodes of the *Facing Justice* programme, and semi-structured interviews with individual staff of the IWPR, NUMEC, and 102 Mega FM which broadcast the programme. First, I would like to give a brief description of what *Facing Justice* radio programme is and who the different actors involved are.

Facing Justice, a specialised justice reporting radio programme, was organised by IWPR in partnership with NUMEC between 2011 and 2013. It was a 25 minute radio feature that focused on issues of justice, peace, conflict, and human rights, particularly in relation to northern Uganda. In addition, the *Facing Justice* episodes aired on 10 radio stations in Acholi, Teso, and West Nile sub-regions and was posted on IWRP website.

The IWPR describes itself as an international media development charity set up in 1991 during the conflicts in the Balkans, and was purposely set up to contribute to peace and human rights through balanced and accurate reporting. IWPR has since emerged as a global media NGO that works on international justice issues, and The Hague office specialises in work that relates to the ICC. A flagship programme, and one of IWPR's longest-running initiatives has been the International

Justice programme, through which IWPR has closely followed developments at the ICC as well as other accountability mechanisms at the local level such as in northern Uganda. This programme provided extensive multimedia coverage of experiences of victims of atrocities during the violent conflict between the Lord's Resistance Army (LRA) and the government of Uganda (1986-2006). IWPR assumes that access to accurate, and balanced information helps empower local populations and also international justice-related decision-makers, as well as linking them in such a way that local populations will be better able to drive and shape global justice processes for social change.

NUMEC is an association of journalists and media professionals organised in the form of a regional media organisation working in conflict-affected northern Uganda. To date, NUMEC claims to have over 80 members spread across the region, but its coordination office is located in Gulu, northern Uganda. Furthermore, its primary goal was to revitalise the media terrain within the region and to help catalyse the reconciliation, resettlement, and recovery efforts in northern Uganda. NUMEC attempts to provide information on development initiatives, enhancing peace, justice, accountability, and good governance. When IWPR supports NUMEC as an organisation, as in other partnerships, it does so through encouraging NUMEC journalists to report on international and post-conflict justice issues.

With funding from IWPR and various other donors, NUMEC runs a well-equipped media resource centre that comprises a radio production studio, audio recorders, audio editing software, computers and Internet through which they have been able to produce a number of radio programmes. *Facing Justice* was one of these, and was developed alongside other development-oriented media reporting. NUMEC radio programming thus extends well beyond the traditional role of radio – as – entertainment.

To understand the potential role of radio in realising justice, as well as the meanings of justice produced through radio programming, is the main motivation of this study. To find out more, I considered the case of the *Facing Justice* radio programme which was a joint collaboration of NUMEC and IWPR. I chose this programme because of its uniqueness within programming, wholly devoted to peace and justice in northern Uganda. Secondly, I chose this case study because several notions of justice appear to be holistically embedded within this single case study. With a focus mainly on framing and the wider politics of representation, I focused on *Facing Justice* even though it is no longer broadcast. This choice was made because there has, until now, been no detailed or systematic analysis at all of media's representational practices in relation to the post-war situation in northern Uganda. By considering how the framing of justice takes place in one programme, this study attempts to bridge some gaps in the available media research.

Framing concerns the selection and emphasis on central ideas, themes, and an understanding of the wider context through which meanings of justice are produced. How a radio programme deals with differences between themes, participants and their positions vis-à-vis various justice issues, is referred to as categorisation, which is a minor concern. Finally, although framing was central, my approach to focalisation is to try and establish what hegemonic impositions of meanings of justice can be found in the radio programmes. Thus the aim is to answer the question: whose perspective and position is privileged by the *Facing Justice* programme? This combination of techniques aided this study, helping to identify what topics, people and voices were included and excluded from the programme, and how these relate to the various dominant definitions and meanings of justice as reflected in the contested space of the radio programme *Facing Justice*.

Facing Justice, a Uganda radio programme, despite being a new initiative in media practice particularly in relation to influencing justice outcomes in northern Uganda, ended in June 2013 barely four years after its initial launch in September 2009. The reason for the closure of the programme also intrigued me, I wondered why, despite the perceived achievements of the programme, there was no further funding. Perhaps, however, this was not that surprising given that many development agencies choose to sponsor radio programmes but usually only for fixed periods of time, and with specific goals. Finding follow-on or sustainable financing is often much harder than getting initial start-up money for a good media idea, for two, three or in this case four years.

Northern Uganda Conflict and Post-War Situation

Uganda, in East Africa, is sometimes described as a country with promising development prospects and a historically violent past. Since attaining independence in 1962 from Britain, Uganda has experienced over 20 armed conflicts (Rogers et al. 2008:134) with the longest and most gruesome being the LRA war in northern Uganda. This erupted in 1986, taking the form of a violent armed conflict between the Government of Uganda (GoU) and the LRA.

However, since there are several contested definitions and meanings of war, "it is never easy to know when a war truly began" (Azar as cited in Dolan 2013:39). The analysis of the northern Uganda civil war never escaped the complexities concerning the mainstream discourse of today's wars. To tell precisely when war starts remains a point of contention. For instance, one may ask; is it the day the first shot is fired? Or when death per year reaches a certain level? Or even when the conditions of structural violence (Galtung 1969) are created that eventually lead to physical violence? Raising these questions is vital to understanding different meanings of justice in post-war northern Uganda.

The conflict in northern Uganda, popularly known as the 'LRA war', has often been framed and described in multiple narratives, sometimes using actors, concepts or the region in which it occurred. The most prominent narrative is that it was "exceptionally protracted and brutal in its impact on the civilian population" (Dolan 2013:4-10). The result of this conflict was the displacement of about 1.8 million people representing 80 percent of northern Uganda's population at that time, into Internally Displaced Persons' (IDPs) camps in search of protection (Murungu and Biegon 2011:202). This displacement created a catastrophic situation of fragile communities and a total dependence on donor aid.

On August 26, 2006, the signing of a Cessation of Hostilities Agreement between the GoU and the LRA in Juba reduced direct hostilities. The subsequent signing of protocols on comprehensive solutions as well as accountability and reconciliation provided hope for peace and perhaps justice; argued Dolan (2009:57). However, "Joseph Kony's[9] failure to sign the final agreement in April 2008 inevitably created doubts about whether any of the potential of the protocols would be realised" (Dolan 2009:57). The LRA has since moved out of northern Uganda but continues to commit atrocities in the DR Congo and Central Africa Republic (Darehshori and Evenson 2010:5).

Currently, northern Uganda is relatively calm but the consequences of armed conflict and prolonged displacement continue to manifest in the region. Frustrations related to inadequate justice processes are gradually translating into community violence and organised crimes, notably: widespread land conflicts and gender-based violence. According to the northern Uganda Conflict Analysis Report[10], 'perceptions of neglect cannot be resolved in the absence of post-conflict truth, reconciliation, and transitional justice processes'. This implies the need for a neutral platform where accurate information about the past and grievances can be debated. One such a platform in post-conflict societies is a 'Truth Commission' (Dancy et al. 2010, Hayner 2010, Mazzei 2011).

However, in the absence of a Truth Commission, radio has become an alternative platform for reflecting on the past, expressing grievances, and discussing possible options for redress. The *Te-yat* programme sponsored by Refugee Law Project, *Voices of Peace*, supported by USAID, and formerly

9 Leader of the Lord's Resistance Army fighters.

10 http://www.saferworld.org.uk/resources/view-resource/762-northern-uganda-conflict-analysis

Facing Justice programme supported by IWPR are a few of the many radio initiatives dedicated to debating the issues of reconstruction, truth and justice in post-war northern Uganda.

The Meanings of Justice in *Facing Justice*

Our analysis of programme content and discussion will show that justice, as represented in the *Facing Justice* radio programme, has multiple meanings, which are however interlinked, and which intersect and overlap with each other. The intersection and interlinkages are embedded in four main thematic frames: service delivery, access to justice, war crime trials, and gender-based violence as discussed below.

Justice as a Tradition:

Proponents of traditional justice suggest that justice is part of the Acholi tradition. Perspectives from traditional, cultural, religious and opinion leaders, including native Ugandans, whose voices are projected in the FJ radio programme, argue that justice is a common principle or value based on collective community responsibility. They suggest, for instance, that Kony can be pardoned using cultural and traditional mechanisms such as *Mato Oput* so that justice can result.

Justice as Forgiveness and Reconciliation

The rhetoric of forgiveness and reconciliation strongly featured in some episodes of *Facing Justice,* particularly those episodes where the main framing of justice was in relation to war crimes trials and access to justice. Linked to the perspective of justice as a tradition, there is a claim that some of the ethnic groups or tribal groups in northern Uganda, such as the Acholi, are merciful and easily forgive, provided there is some sort of cleansing. Perspectives from locals tend to point to how forgiveness and reconciliation can also bring about justice, and have the advantage over criminal justice of being able also to restore broken social relations.

Rehabilitation and Reintegration

Justice is not only about arresting and jailing perpetrators, of course, and the *Facing Justice* programme reflects this; it is also about healing and offering psychosocial forms of support. On the one hand, justice should be victim-centred; on the other hand, even the rights of prison inmates should be protected, and their reintegration after serving their prison sentence, should be assumed.

Justice as Fairness

Scholars and civil society professionals who were interviewed in the FJ programme as experts particularly on the thematic frame of service delivery generally held this perspective of justice as fairness. Justice in this sense implies effective service delivery in health, education, water, and road networks. It also implies a relatively equitable distribution of resources, for example through the actions of local government officials. Furthermore, justice would mean no corruption as was vividly discussed in an episode focused on the aspect of paying for justice, where police were accused of taking bribes before assisting locals in the search for justice. In addition, justice means gender equality and that property ownership is a right for all including women. This can be associated to all, the identified forms of justice mostly, legal, distributive and gender justice.

Justice as Truth-telling

This arises from the fact that "individuals have a right to know the truth or information about the past abuses as affirmed by treaty bodies, regional courts and international and domestic tribunals" (E/CN.4/2004/88). Reconstructing narratives/accounts of war is seen as justice. In an episode published on 21 December 2010, a cultural leader observed that: "truth should come out, I should be allowed to ask Kony why he did so many bad things to me". This can be linked to the rectificatory form of justice more specifically, restorative justice. Expert opinions seemed to suggest that the idea of truth telling is a necessary process, but it is difficult to get it started let alone achieved. Diverse perspectives were presented ranging from victims, former LRA fighters, opinion leaders, politicians, CSOs, academics, and government officials on this aspect.

Material compensation

Justice here means paying victims for damages caused or inflicted on them. There seemed to be a consensus among all stakeholders who were interviewed over the issue of compensation as a form of justice. The discussion focused not on whether it was right or wrong to compensate victims of war but instead on the modalities through which the compensation package would be provided. The perspectives appear to suggest that once compensation is paid, then justice would have been achieved.

ICC-Style Justice

ICC-style justice relates to war crime trials and all the punitive or retributive aspects. Justice in this context means bringing perpetrators to account especially with the use of international legal instruments. According to several episodes on war crimes trials, the discussion hinged on possibilities of prosecuting Kony and his top commanders at the ICC in the Hague or any special court that would later be established. This is linked to Legal justice with aspects of rectificatory justice.

Peace as justice

About two or three episodes discussed the issues of peace as justice. The argument advanced was that arresting Kony or putting an end to the LRA war and its cruelty would bring about sustainable peace and eventually justice. This means that justice was seen as the flourishing of peace. The episode published on 7 November 2011 as well as that of 15 February 2015 discussing the military options to addressing war crimes, give the impression that war and peace are the alternate means to realising justice.

War, Peace, and Justice

The meanings of war, peace, and justice are constantly changing and complex as it is about their practice and realisation. Today, it is evident that states are not so much engaged in violent and brutal war with each other, but appear to cooperate and engage as partner states under the premise of globalisation. This trend is attributed to mainly economic interdependence (liberal peace thesis) and ideational factors (democratic peace thesis), with the argument that democracies do not go to war with each other (Wenger and Mason 2008:838). Since the end of the Cold War of 1945, wars between states have significantly reduced with a corresponding shift to intra-state armed conflicts, civil wars, protests and political uprisings arguably in the global south and the Middle East (World Bank 2011), particularly in fragile states.

While global relations are largely driven by neoliberal interests in natural resources and prospective geostrategic interests, the approach to peace, justice and development in fragile states is influenced by viewpoints on bad governance and ethnicity rather than contextual analysis of social realities. Wenger and Mason (2008:842) argue that most contemporary conflicts relate to "disagreements over wealth and power-sharing, bad governance, human rights violations and poor human security conditions". Conflict analysis studies on intra-state conflicts and civil wars in the global south highlight colonialism, continued greed, and unresolved grievances as key causes and drivers of violent conflicts.[11] For instance, colonialists amalgamated an estimated 10,000 African ethnic nations to about 54 modern-day nation states like Uganda. "Thus while wars between states are still conceivable, they occur primarily in the form of territorial conflicts among regional opponents, or as interventions by great powers or loose coalitions that seek to change the status quo in badly governed states" (Wenger and Mason 2008:838). This implies that, just as the resolution of such wars may require a combination of national, regional, and global approaches, realising peace, and justice after war may necessitate a similar combination of approaches or even more.

Kaldor (1999) states that, the majority of new wars are financed by the government, Diaspora, and neighbouring states

11 http://www.saferworld.org.uk/resources/view-resource/762-northern-uganda-conflict-analysis

in the name of fighting for freedom and justice. According to Jabri (2006), war seems to be a policy option in which peace is equated to war. Nonetheless, grievance and economic greed, and not necessarily ethnicity, appear to be behind many of the civil wars and conflicts in Africa. Yet, in today's society that is so conscious of realising rights, we need to question whether wars can be ethically justified under any circumstances. For example, the LRA struggle and opposition to the ruling NRM government may be founded on legitimate grounds but its catastrophic effects on civilians nullifies its legitimacy, besides violating the rules of war.

Genocide, war crimes and crimes against humanity constitute the worst acts of war and violence. The dominant notion of justice in the case of genocide and war crimes tends to be legal and punitive, and justice is understood to be something delivered through criminal prosecution of perpetrators (Opotow, 2001). Various legal instruments and institutions including the International Humanitarian Law and the Statute of ICC support the prosecution of war crimes (Cassese et al. 2002). The ICC specifically came into force in 2002 to prosecute international crimes so as to bring about justice and to end impunity. In essence, a potential case can be referred to the ICC in one of three ways: (i) first by the Chief Prosecutor as in the case of Libya, (ii) second by the UN Security Council, as in the case of Darfur, and (iii) third by a member state as in Uganda's case (Adebajo et al. 2012, Cassese et al. 2002). Drawing on the latter, Uganda became the first country in the world to refer a case to the ICC in December 2003. This led to the indictment of LRA leader Joseph Kony and his top commanders (namely; Raska Lukwiya, Okot

Odhiambo, Dominic Ongwen, and Vincent Otti), in July 2005 (Eichstaedt 2009:8-10). The five were all indicted in the same case with a list of 33 crimes: 21 counts of war crimes and 12 counts of crimes against humanity.[12] Until now, the LRA leadership continues to elude capture and as a result, many victims still await justice (Armstrong 2014, Branch 2014).

While the ICC is yet to prosecute Kony and his associates, the potential of this international court to deliver justice in northern Uganda depends on a clear understanding of what justice really means. Often, "when victims of a transgression say they want justice done, this is commonly understood as meaning that they want to see the offender punished" (Okimoto et al. 2009:156). Sarah Nouwen, in her analysis of ICC as an instrument of peace and justice, asked, "What is justice?" Thus, mentioning three common categories of justice namely legal justice, distributive justice and rectificatory justice (Adebajo et al. 2012:171-172). Furthermore, Nouwen describes the ICC-style justice as "individual rather than communal, criminal rather than distributive, and punitive rather than restorative" (Adebajo et al. 2012:172). This understanding and meaning of justice pursued by the ICC and its proponents seem disconnected from the local aspirations and expectations of justice right from the start of ICC's operations in Uganda as the findings in this study later reveal.

With the aim of delivering justice, regulating the conduct of war, and ending impunity, the ICC has come under enormous scrutiny relating to its capacity to prosecute crimes, including a tendency to polarise society as in the case of Kenya

---

12 http://www.beyondintractability.org/casestudy/sikenyi-great-lakes

and Uganda (Adebajo et al. 2012). Additionally, the future of this global crimes court remains uncertain, especially with the fluid political landscape in most African countries in which the criminal justice system continues to be politicised. This is made worse with a perception that national and international justice systems do not bring about appropriate redress for war crimes or deliver timely justice as critics of the ICC suggest.

Equally, transitional justice scholarship by contrast tends to support more of restorative approaches as opposed to prosecutions per se. The victims and survivors of armed conflict tend to search for truth and justice as well as decent livelihoods that transcend both prosecutions and mere survival. Justice in this context would mean a "process of re-humanisation and empowerment to live a life of dignity" (Kagoro 2012:15). In the case of northern Uganda, the meaning of justice seems to be widely dispersed and loosely categorised into international, regional, national, and local perspectives. While analysing traditional justice in northern Uganda, Branch noted that:

> Justice is 'yet to come', in Hountondji's phrase, in the sense that it is open to new voices, new opinions, new formulations and ideas into the indefinite future. There is no single true justice, for justice is a domain of ultimate uncertainty, a fact that ethnojustice rejects. (Branch 2014:21).

This, however, points to the plurality of meaning of justice on one hand and the complexity of achieving justice on the other hand. For instance, it is assumed that retributive and restorative justice results in resolution and transformation of conflict respectively, but northern Uganda still needs a platform that brings out and accommodates the various 'truths' on justice as an ideal step towards establishing which justice mechanism would be more feasible. As such, I now turn to analyse how radio has come to be an alternative platform for discussing development issues, including debating justice.

Radio development and broadcast culture

Technological advances have made communication, transmission of information faster, reliable, and far-reaching. Development and perfection of computer technology, has made the Internet the most revolutionary technology, allowing for mass broadcasting and mass production of media while combining all other forms of media (newspapers, radio, cinema, and television) for a wider broadcast. Since 1919, radio has been one of the most popular mediums of mass communication globally. This is simply because radio is "relatively cheap, efficient, immediate, and undemanding as a technology" (Fardon and Furniss 2000:16). Historically, the 1920s are considered the boom of radio, particularly in the US during that period people rushed to buy radios, whilst business and social structures adapted to the use of radio. According to Anderson (2005:26), "universities began to offer radio-based courses; churches began broadcasting their services; newspapers created tie-ins with radio broadcasts". Subsequently, "entertainment came to rule the radio waves much more than governmental or educational content" (Anderson 2005:26). This suggests that, radio has three cardinal functions, namely: entertain, inform, and educate.

According to Fardon and Furniss (2000:4), the "primary function of radio is to provide entertainment and pleasure". They further suggest that, "in situations of crisis, radio comes to the fore as an informational medium" (Fardon and Furniss 2000:2). During the World War II for example, Anderson writes that, "radio was a key lifeline of information for the masses. Listeners around the world sat transfixed before their radio sets as vivid reports of battles, victories, and defeats were broadcast by reporters" (2005:26). Since then, radio has variously been used as a powerful medium for propagating war as much as influencing public opinion through various representational strategies. In the case of 1994 Rwandan genocide, radio Télévision Libre des Mille Collines (RTLM) is accused of generating genocidal violence. The popular argument is that RTLM, in its broadcasts and representation of the ethnic and political tensions, reinforced stigma, social divisions, and stereotypes that eventually propagated violence between Hutus and Tutsi (Rothbart and Bartlett 2008, McCordic 2012). Straus (2007:610), however, disputes such a claim, arguing that; "despite the central role regularly attributed to radio, there has been little sustained social scientific analysis of radio media effects in the Rwandan genocide". Nevertheless, one cannot simply dismiss RTLM's involvement and influence in genocidal violence while it was playing its cardinal role of informing the Rwandan public about the political events of the time, especially through regularly repeated practice of framing. Simply because, "radio, long established as the voice of government in Rwanda, defined the enemy as the Tutsis, and inspired an obligation by Hutus to protect themselves and their families" (Kellow and Steeves 1998:123).

Though the role of radio in reinforcing genocidal violence may not be conclusive in this study, the Rwandan case brings to the fore the fact that radio can be an influential representational tool that touches on people's emotions. As such, "if radio can be used so effectively to promote hate, can it not then also be used at least as effectively to promote peace?" (Betz 2004:43-44). Betz's perspective seems to have inspired the spread of donor-supported peace radios, mostly in fragile and post-war communities. Radio Okapi and Mega FM in the DRC and northern Uganda respectively are some of the many radio stations that have been set up in Africa by the United Nations, donor agencies, churches, and NGOs to help communities overcome the challenge of rebuilding after war. One such challenge is realising justice in a more objective approach.

Radio development in Uganda can be described as progressive. Since 1986, there has been liberalisation of the radio airwaves, with more commercial and community broadcasting stations entering the market to compete with the state-funded radio broadcasters (AMDI-Report-Uganda, 2013). By 2006, Uganda had about 92 radio stations and currently there are over 122, with about nine radio stations which broadcast daily to an estimated five to six million listeners in Gulu alone. Most radio stations in northern Uganda focus on 'infotainment' with a recent adaptation to an 'edutainment' broadcasting approach. They broadcast information about conflict, development, health, and education, all of which are geared towards conflict transformation, justice, peacebuilding, and reconciliation.

The first radio station in northern Uganda was Freedom FM, set up in 1989, which operated on 88.8 MHz (Ibrahim 2007:9). Radio Freedom was largely managed by the military with the primary objective of bringing about peace and communicating with the people affected by civil war in northern Uganda. In 1999, the "British government through its agency, Department for International Development (DfID) started building Mega FM to replace Radio Freedom and 102 Mega FM went on-air in August 2002" (Otim 2009:1). Today, 102 Mega FM stands at the freedom square, a place where the British put up their first flag in Gulu in 1907.

Politics of Representation in Media

Representation, as argued by Hall (1997:15), refers to the use of language to convey meanings. In the context of this chapter, representation is defined as the use of selected words, themes, topics, and language by media to construct and convey meanings to their audience.

According to Hall, representation takes on three forms: reflective; intentional and constructionist approaches (Hall 1997:15). Reflective representation is grounded on the notion that a meaning already exists and can be located in the real world. Language here then becomes like a mirror, to reflect the true meaning as found in the real world. Hall, however, subscribes to the constructionist approach, in which the material world is mediated through language systems embedded in social relations of power that convey meanings. This implies that, meanings depend on discourse as a system of representation that combines language and practice (Hall 1997:44).

One of the roles of media in reconstruction and post-war development is agenda setting. Media agenda, very much correlate with public agenda as well as policy agenda (Tan and Weaver 2009:454-456). This means for instance that daily politics and webs of cultural practices influence the media and vice versa. Power relations shape the media's representational practices and meanings of war, peace, and justice it produces. According to Žarkov, "competing and conflicting meanings are produced through dominance, subordination, exclusion and marginalisation; the shifts and ambiguities in meanings reflect changing domains of power" (Žarkov 2007:8). Žarkov's reasoning is particularly important in understanding why some perspectives dominate while others are excluded in media reporting during and after war. This is also related to issues of framing, categorisation and focalisation of justice.

The media coverage of the LRA war and cycles of violence including killings, rape, torture, and abductions as the conflict unfolded into a large-scale war helped popularise this conflict. However, media's representation of the LRA war was full of less analysed facts and ambiguities, including some misrepresentations and disinformation. Dolan noted that daily media created ambiguities of the extent of the war rather than drawing a careful analysis of the conflict (Dolan 2013:103).

The misrepresentation and disinformation meant that Government, NGOs, LRA fighters and the media framed the conflict on their own terms. At local and national level media, the LRA war for example was represented as an 'ethnic conflict' targeting the Acholi people. The interpretation of this representation nationally and regionally was that the LRA war was only a northern Uganda problem and not a Uganda in general problem. In relation to international media, the LRA war was equally framed and represented as a regional problem in Uganda. The implication of such representation was inaction from the global community since it was not a global issue then. The world continued to watch, listen, and read about this conflict, hoping that it would burn out on its own. Later, the perceived ethnic slaughter of Acholi people began to spread to the neighbouring Lango, Teso, West Nile, and partly Karamoja sub-regions.

As the conflict gained prominence in the news media both nationally and internationally, as well as in public and policy agenda, it started to be seen as a bigger threat. First, a threat to the Great Lakes region, which would imply the need for regional measures to combat its impact. Second, a global threat, perceived as acts of terrorism, in which interventions, especially military options, were designed within the framework of 'war on terror'. One journalist I interviewed suggested that during war, radio reporting agenda is framed around peace that those affected purportedly need, and after war, the reporting is more justice oriented. He observed that "in a post-war situation, it is more about realising justice and sustainable development in which people reckon with critical questions such as; whether to leave perpetrators go free, reconcile them with their communities, or hold them to account". (Interview in Gulu, Uganda, August 2014). This then brings me to the discussion of meanings of justice represented in the radio programme *Facing Justice* including: how such meanings are framed, produced and the perspectives focalised.

Perspectives and meanings of justice

The *Facing Justice* programme offers various perspectives and a wider context of meanings of justice in post-war northern Uganda. The programme often began with a background, an introduction of the topic and mention of the main question or focus of the episode. Issues raised ranged from service delivery in the education, health, and water sectors for the former Internally Displaced People (IDPs), returning to their homes following decades of displacement, to gender equality, trials of rebel leaders accused of war crimes, land rights, livelihoods and reconciliation. These issues were produced within four main thematic frames namely: a) Service delivery, b) access to justice, c) war crime trials, and d) gender-based violence. Although seemingly different, these themes are not mutually exclusive. Rather, they are overlapping and were purposely created for at least two reasons. First, the concept of justice as earlier stressed is complex and needed to be broken down in order for the target audience to understand it. The second reason was that of reporting, follow-ups' and tracking of any new developments.

The *Facing Justice* programme focalised largely 'local stakeholder's perspectives' but often ensured that a wide range of perspectives were represented in each episode; thus, making it difficult to identify the most dominant perspectives even within the local stakeholders. Each podcast presented a combination of different perspectives representing various stakeholders such as victims, government officials, civil society, traditional/cultural and religious leaders relevant to the theme of justice under discussion.

The meanings of justice produced from the *Facing Justice* radio programme can be associated with three broader categories of justice; (1) Legal justice, (2) Distributive justice and (3) Rectificatory justice as mentioned by Nouwen (in Adebajo et al. 2012:171-172). Understanding what justice really means in relation to each of these forms of justice may vary but this study describes them as follows:

First, legal justice also seen as the enforcement of the rule of law involves the aspect of proper administration of the law within the system of law. This means that justice can be found in the application of the law in which there is fair and equitable treatment of conflicting claims. Justice then tends to be measured through processes involved such as arrests, detentions, and trials of suspects by police, courts, and other judicial institutions. Thus, it is procedural and does not prejudge any outcome at all, for example, whether there will be compensation or any punishment. The assumption here is that once the process is just then the outcome is also just, which may not necessarily be the case.

Second, distributive justice refers to the elimination of structural and systematic injustices such as political and economic discrimination and inequalities of distribution. Therefore, justice is achieved through proper distribution of wealth and power for example. Distributive justice focuses more on outcomes. The assumption for instance is that, a solution to war, violence, and impunity would be to redistribute wealth or power, prevent further violence and then justice would be realised. This suggests that the process does not matter but rather what matters is the means. Interestingly, both legal and distributive justice, have the element of the 'proper' as a yardstick for measuring a just outcome. However, what proper distribution actually means is equally relative and surprisingly not justice for some. For example, you cannot justify dictatorship because it redistributes wealth or even power and neither can one justify a court proceeding because it has a fair process.

Third, justice is considered as a process of addressing direct consequences inflicted on individuals. This is known as rectificatory justice. This is further divided into two forms: restorative justice and punitive justice. 'Restorative justice' implies the restoration of the position of the victim and of the affected relationships. Punitive justice, by contrast, refers to inflicting a penalty on the perpetrator.

One other form of justice that seems to originate from restorative justice is victim-centred justice. This very specific type of justice sharply contrasts legal and distributive justice, simply because it targets only the victim who is assumed to have unfairly suffered atrocious harm, more so against their will.

Another form of justice that has risen to prominence in recent years is gender justice. It aims at realising gender equality and therefore targets anyone who is disadvantaged or suffers unfair treatment based on his or her gender. However, gender justice, as any other form of justice described in this chapter, does not follow a straitjacket approach but may be realised through other forms of justice such as legal justice, distributive justice or even victim-centred justice. In relation to gender justice for example, media has reportedly argued that there are high levels of sexual and gender-based violence (SGBV) in northern Uganda. However, more accurate data about sexual violence during the war in northern Uganda is yet to be established as revelations of its systematic and deliberate nature continue to emerge as people now start to speak out and report cases to the concerned authorities and civil society actors working on post-conflict development, such as Refugee Law Project.

Conclusion

As this chapter has suggested, the potential role of the media and perhaps especially of radio, in aiding post-war recovery in northern Uganda, depends in part on its approach to justice.

As Betz (2004:38) has stressed, radio is often the most readily available form of media when it comes to promoting social justice and social development. In northern Uganda we have seen how one radio programme, *Facing Justice,* has been engaged in debating sustainable peacebuilding and the different views on how justice can help achieve lasting peace in the wider region. Preliminary findings suggest that the *Facing Justice* radio programme used thematic frames to produce meanings of justice, which can be associated to legal, distributive and rectificatory categories of justice. Victim-centred justice and gender justice appear to be the most marginalised perspectives on social justice, and yet arguably are among the most important for sustainable peace and a sense of overall justice being done. What this case study suggests is that though justice after war may be vital, and is an obvious part of the desire for sustainable peace and development, there will be no single meaning of justice, and rather, there are likely to be multiple meanings that are intertwined and complex. In a nutshell, the chapter has shown how the debates around the meanings of justice in northern Uganda reflect the competing sovereignties of different actors. The main actors and positions on justice identified were those of victims, the view of the state, and the views of international institutions and actors.

References

Adebajo, A., Curtis D., and Dzinesa, G.A. (2012) *Peacebuilding, Power, and Politics in Africa*. Ohio University Press.

AMDI-Report-Uganda(2013) http://africanmediainitiative.org/content/2013/07/22/AMDI-Report-Uganda.pdf

Anderson, J.Q. (2005) Imagining the Internet: Personalities, Predictions, Perspectives. Rowman & Littlefield.

Armstrong, K. (2014) 'Justice without Peace? International Justice and Conflict Resolution in Northern Uganda', Development and Change, 45 (3): 589–607.

Betz, M. (2004) 'Radio as Peacebuilder: A Case Study of Radio Okapi in the Democratic Republic of Congo', *The Great Lakes Research Journal,* 1: 38-50.

Branch, A. (2014) 'The Violence of Peace: Ethnojustice in Northern Uganda', Development and Change, 45 (3): 608–630.

Cassese, A.,Gaeta, P., Jones, J.R., and Eser, A. (2002) *The Rome Statute of the International Criminal Court: A Commentary:* 1. Oxford: Oxford University Press.

Dancy, G., Kim. H., and Wiebelhaus-Brahm, E. (2010) 'The Turn to Truth: Trends in Truth Commission Experimentation', *Journal of Human Rights,* 9(1): 45-64.

Darehshori, S., and Evenson, E. (2010) 'Peace, Justice and the International Criminal Court', *The Foundation for Law, Justice and Society, (ed.) Oxford Transitional Justice Research: Debating International Justice in Africa*. Oxford: The Foundation for Law, Justice and Society & The Centre for Socio-Legal Studies, University of Oxford.

Dolan, C. (2013) *Social Torture: The Case of Northern Uganda, 1986-2006:* 4. New York: Berghahn Books.

Eichstaedt, P. (2009) *First Kill Your Family: Child Soldiers of Uganda and the Lord's Resistance Army.* Chicago: Chicago Review Press.

Fardon, R. and Furniss, G. (2000) *African Broadcast Cultures: Radio in Transition.* Oxford: J. Currey; Westport, Conn.: Praeger; Cape Town: David Philip; Harare: Baobab.

Hayner, P.B. (2010) *Unspeakable Truths: Transitional Justice and the Challenge of Truth Commissions.* London: Routledge.

Jabri, V. (2006) 'War, Security and the Liberal State', *Security Dialogue,* 37(1): 47-64.

Kagoro, B. (2012) 'The Paradox of Alien Knowledge, Narrative and Praxis: Transitional Justice and the Politics of Agenda Setting in Africa', *Where Law Meets Reality: Forging African Transitional Justice*: 4-52.

Kellow, C.L., and Steeves, H. L. (1998) 'The Role of Radio in the Rwandan Genocide', *Journal of Communication,* 48(3): 107-128.

Mazzei, J.M. (2011) 'Finding Shame in Truth: The Importance of Public Engagement in Truth Commissions', *Human Rights Quarterly,* 33(2): 431-452.

McCordic, C.R. (2012) , The Use of Stigma as a Marker of Otherness by RTLM during the Rwandan Genocide, PhD Thesis, University of Guelph, Ontario, Canada.

Murungu, C., and Biegon, J. (2011) *Prosecuting International Crimes in Africa.* Pretoria: PULP.

Okimoto, T.G., Wenzel, M., and Feather, N. (2009) 'Beyond Retribution: Conceptualizing Restorative Justice and Exploring its Determinants', *Social Justice Research,* 22(1): 156-180.

Opotow, S. (2001) 'Reconciliation in Times of Impunity: Challenges for Social Justice', *Social Justice Research,* 14(2): 149-170.

Rothbart, D., and Bartlett, T. (2008) 'Rwandan Radio Broadcasts and Hutu/Tutsi Positioning', *Global Conflict Resolution through Positioning Analysis:* 227-246. Springer.

Straus, S. (2007) 'What is the Relationship between Hate Radio and Violence? Rethinking Rwanda's "Radio Machete"', *Politics & Society*, 35(4): 609-637.

Tan, Y. and D.H. Weaver (2009) 'Local Media, Public Opinion, and State Legislative Policies: Agenda Setting at the State Level', The International Journal of Press/Politics, 14 (4): 454-476.

Wenger, A. and S.J. Mason (2008) 'The Civilianization of Armed Conflict: Trends and Implications', *International Review of the Red Cross (2005)* 90(872): 835.

World Bank (2011) *World Development Report 2011: Conflict, Security, and Development*. World Bank.

Žarkov, D. (2007) *The Body of War: Media, Ethnicity, and Gender in the Break-Up of Yugoslavia*. Durham: Duke University press.

Part Two

Land Justice in East Africa

Chapter 4

Law and Land Justice in Urban Tanzania: The Case of Mbeya

Thomas Munzerere

Introduction

This chapter will give meaning to the view that good governance is essential to effective land administration, and that together they can help to ensure that land justice can be achieved. By referring to the Tanzania National Land policy, the Land Act 1999 and the Village Land Act 1999, it is shown that there are several signs of weak land governance and administration, which make injustices in land allocation more likely. Taking the example of urban Mbeya, the study considers the high rates of land disputes, the prevalence of illegal land developments, and the problem of land grabbing. All imply difficulties with realising land rights and land justice for the poorest inhabitants. Since this chapter explores the urban area of Mbeya, we will outline some key factors that influence land justice through the modalities of land governance, focusing on the situation within this urban setting.

In summary, the chapter suggests that three main issues will influence the extent to which land justice can be attained in urban Mbeya under the existing laws, policies and institutions. These three issues are: (i) Land law; (ii) Land information (iii) Leadership in the land sector. To understand how these three factors shape outcomes and processes related to land justice, an FAO good governance framework is adapted for the purposes of this study.

In relation to the first factor, although land laws should be available for public consultation, and their status and accessibility matters for land justice, in Mbeya, although good laws are available, the documents themselves are not accessible to most ordinary members of the public. This is first of all because such laws are in English only, whilst Mbeya's inhabitants mostly are educated and speak and read Kiswahili. Later we discuss some contradictions within the land laws, but it can be noted that the problem lies in accessibility rather than in the letter of the extant laws. Secondly, an unclear, largely unaccountable and inefficient land court administration system is a problem in Mbeya, as will be shown, and means that the pursuit of land justice can be frustrated by the lack of detailed and available information. This means that a detailed analysis of the situation with respect to land disputes may not always be possible, or manageable within the provision of the local land administration offices. The weaknesses in the present land information systems can also jeopardise the quality of land justice outcomes. Not only is language a barrier – in addition, the information needed and laws themselves are not always available in one place, in a secured and translated form. Most land data is recorded in English only, contrary to the provisions of the Land Act, Section 3, which, following the Food and Agricultural Organisation (FAO) guidelines, requires that land records should both be computerised and translated into the locally spoken language, in this case Kiswahili. The kinds of information available and the extent to which such information is accessible and reliable, is a second major problem. Thirdly, leadership is a crucial obstacle to achieving land justice in terms both of procedures and outcomes. Weaknesses of leadership include corruption, unethical behaviour and weak decision-making among local officials in Mbeya, as noted in Presidential land commission reports. Surveying and allocation of land plots in urban Mbeya has fallen far short of demand, due to both inefficiency and misallocation and corruption. Leadership can thus be seen as both inefficient and weak, and an obstacle to land justice being achieved.

To gain deeper insights into these three issues, or obstacles, I will first consider land justice in the light of theories of good governance, especially in relation to the challenges of the 'elasticity' of good governance theories as applied to the governance of urban land. Good land governance like land justice, is an elastic concept that borrows the general term – governance or justice – to the context of one specific resource, land. Criteria like rule of law, human rights, fairness, accountability and responsiveness compete with criteria related to efficiency, value for money and cost to taxpayers, in the operationalisation of terms like governance and justice. There are many different definitions of good governance, with both differences and similarities. Useful definitions vary depending on which institution or individual is involved. Understanding and applying governance theories to land governance thus becomes a question of contextualising. Similarly, justice as a concept when applied to land can be simply too broad and all-inclusive to be operationally useful. After considering a range of different approaches to good governance and to justice, the three aspects mentioned above will be focused on, all three being drawn from a set of FAO guidelines for good governance.

The Land Administration System in Tanzania

Mbeya urban area is located in the southern part of The United Republic of Tanzania, and occupies around 6.4 per cent of the total land area of mainland Tanzania, as well as forming the border between Tanzania, Malawi and Zambia. Most parts of Mbeya region are arid and semi-arid, and the total area is estimated at 61,868 square kilometres, of which 57,000 square kilometres are arable land (Planning Commission, 1997:1-5). There is some degree of competition over land for agriculture and settlement purposes, with demand for land for construction around the urban area far outstripping allocation of building permits.

Land in Tanzania is legally defined as 'the surface of the earth and the earth below the surface and all substances other than minerals and petroleum...' (Tanzania 1999:3). All land is deemed to be public property, and is held by the President in trust for all citizens of the United Republic of Tanzania for present and future generations (Tanzania 1999:5). Day-to-day land administration activities, however, are delegated by the President to the Commissioner for Lands, responsible for providing and disseminating information about land ownership, value and use across Tanzania as a whole. Land administration tasks fall under two separate ministries, however: The Ministry of Lands, Housing and Settlement Development (MLHSD) and the Prime Minister's Office for Regional Administration and Local Government (PMO-RALG). This dual system of governance is further complicated by the division between central government and local government. Village land councils and City or District land committees fall under local government control, under the Prime Minister's Office, while the Commissioner for Lands is accountable to the Ministry of Lands at central government level. The Ministry of Lands also provides technical expertise, is responsible for the policy and regulatory framework, while the local government ministry deals more with implementation of such laws and policies. All seven land departments of the Ministry of Lands, Housing and Settlement are located in Dar es Salaam, except for land tribunals, land registration offices and land commissioner services. These are dispersed in the regions with six zone offices, including one in Mbeya town.

The local government ministry, on the other hand, has a much stronger local presence, with 21 administrative regions and 161 local government authorities in place in mainland Tanzania (Tanzania 2013:1-5). Each district has a land office providing a limited range of land services. Since land allocation depends on the type of land, only village land allocation is dealt with at the level of village land councils. For general or reserved land, land surveys and allocations are the responsibility of District Land Offices. In Tanzania, land allocation is just one way in which a person may access and use land. There are other ways including inheritance, clearance of virgin land, land purchase and gift (Rwegasira 2012:93-118). However, land registration is not compulsory in the country, reflecting that ultimately all land belongs to the state.

The Problem of Just Land Governance in Tanzania

In recent years, governance issues and injustices in the land sector have come to attract more attention from scholars and practitioners alike. There are growing calls for proper land governance, partly as a result of increased demand for land from investors, mining companies and other commercial interests. This growing demand makes it harder to ensure that vulnerable groups such as poor women, small farmers and other marginalised citizens benefit from protective measures and governmental accountability (Deininger et al. 2010:250-251). The National Land Policy of 1995 and The Land Act of 1999 were intended to place good governance principles into practice (Tanzania 1999:5-7, MLHSD 1997:6, 42). Unfortunately however, land disputes, illegal land developments and land grabbing have all continued today to pose a challenge to aspirations for land justice in both urban and rural Tanzania.

Land disputes often relate to social justice concerns regarding land access, use and ownership, and to disputes between generations, classes and gendered conflicts over access and use. Unfortunately, land disputes in Tanzania have increased steadily from year to year (Askew et al. 2013:120-121). Discussing land tribunals, Massay indicates that 12,643 land cases were filed in 2009, compared with 9,216 cases in 2010. By December 2011 land tribunals in Tanzania admitted 10,428 land cases while by 2012 the number of land cases increased to 12,074 (Massay 2013:6). The trend in land disputes appears to be upwards, and the land tribunals in Mbeya region are among several in the country, overwhelmed by such disputes.

A rise in illegal land developments and unplanned settlements is a commonly cited example of the injustices and weaknesses of Tanzania's current land governance system. Studies suggest that around 75 per cent of the general urban population in Tanzania live in unplanned housing, some in potentially hazardous areas (Lugoe 2010:4-5, Kyessi and Tumpale. 2013:1- 4). In the areas of urban Mbeya, the figure is even higher, since close to 80 per cent of the total population live in unplanned areas (Kyessi and Tumpale. 2013:1-4). Lugoe argues that while the national population is growing at half a million people per year, legally only 6,000 new land plots are provided annually (Lugoe 2010:4-5). That means most people who need land plots for settlement and other economic activities cannot find them, even assuming that they could afford the land. Consequently, most people simply opt to build in unplanned or hazardous areas where services like water, electricity, schools and roads are likely to be very poor or non-existent. This has huge implications for the wellbeing and quality of life of people living in such unplanned communities. Large land acquisitions, some of them through means of bribery and malpractice, are another emerging phenomenon that is linked to land injustices and can be seen as an outcome of poor land governance. According to Teeffelen (2013:33) land grabbing by foreign and local companies and business people has increased by 36 per cent annually in sub-Saharan

Africa in the past few years. He found that in Tanzania, of 4 million hectares of land requested by investors, 640,000 hectares had been allocated by 2009 (Teeffelen 2013:39). This left many local communities landless or with insufficient land for planned farming and settlement in future, making their lives even harder.

Despite documented evidence that suggests unjust and weak land governance, the problems of land disputes are too often disconnected from wider struggles for social justice. One of the aims of this chapter is to reconnect the common understanding of land conflicts to theories and approaches to social justice more generally, and land justice in particular. Land governance issues can offer relevant insights into how social justice issues can be approached in relation to the weaknesses of law, the problem of useful information and the poor quality of leadership when it comes to implementation and adjudicating.

Good Land Governance Theory and Frameworks

Good governance in land administration cannot be strictly differentiated from good governance overall. Many institutions and scholars promote good land governance in their research. There are thus three distinct frameworks for good governance in land administration, developed by UN-Habitat, the World Bank and the FAO. The first, the UN-Habitat framework was first developed in 1999 and finalised by 2004. Based on Amartya Sen's concept of development as freedom, the UN-Habitat developed five good governance principles for land administration. With the addition of security, the principles were similar to those that underpin policies of good governance more generally: effectiveness, equity, accountability, participation and security (UN-Habitat 2004:14). UN-Habitat also proposed an Urban Governance Index (UGI), to lay down key principles for promoting good urban governance around the world.[13] Yet, whilst the UGI could be useful in understanding urban planning issues, it does not explicitly refer to land, and thus lacks the conceptual clarity needed for resolving land disputes in an urban context like that or Mbeya town. Additionally, since the UN-Habitat approach rests on Sen's notion of development as freedom,[14] it was viewed as not that relevant to a context where market principles do not exclusively guide allocation decisions around land, as in Tanzania's case.

A second important framework worth mentioning is the World Bank's approach, developed by Burns and Dalrymple, whose Conceptual Framework for good land governance rests on eight principles (Burns and Dalrymple 2008:7). The principles include fairness and equity, market justified land management control, transparency, good land information, clear procedure in land disposition, recognition of social land rights, and market-based valuation of land, with a good land disputes settlement system. The World Bank approach is an important contribution to expanding knowledge about good land governance and how to improve land justice. However, the framework is again biased towards a Washington consensus view that makes market-oriented approaches

13 http://www.undp.mn/publications/Urban_Governance_Index_Guidelines.pdf

14 While Amartya Sen advocated for freedom in the market (in this case total liberalisation of land) his ideas were questionable given the historical point of view where for example Karl Polanyi in the Great Transformation argued that market economy was not free in its origin and could therefore not be left free to operate without the control by the state.

central to allocation decisions. This ignores the customary and less marketised land models that remain so significant in the Tanzanian context, and that also inform the context of land governance and land disputes in urban Mbeya.

As opposed to these two frameworks, an FAO framework devised in 2007 appeared to fit much better with the requirements of this study to find an approach to land governance that aimed to achieve land justice as one of its key outcomes. The FAO model establishes 12 good governance principles, which include the usual ones of efficiency, responsiveness, competence, transparency, accountability and security. However, in addition, and unlike the World Bank or UN-Habitat models, the FAO list of principles also includes: equality, sustainability, participation, integrity of land officials, and locally-responsive land administration systems (FAO 2007:9). It is noteworthy that marketisation is explicitly not part of the FAO framework, and this makes it more appropriate for the specific Tanzanian context, where, as explained earlier, the freehold on all land is held in trust by the President.

Adapting the FAO-Good Governance Principles for Research on Urban Mbeya

For the purposes of clarity and manageability, the twelve FAO good land governance principles have been condensed into three broader requirements of any land governance system at local level, namely:

(1) good land laws,

(2) accessible and transparent information and

(3) honest and accountable leadership.

The first of these, the land laws, should be consistent, just, ensure security of tenure and provide for impartial land disputes to be settled (FAO 2007:9). Land laws and policies, to be helpful to decision makers, need these qualities of consistency and predictability, so that smooth decision-making is possible by both judiciary and land officers. Good land laws can also promote public security by reducing the incidence of land disputes, and ensuring that impartial, efficient and amicable dispute resolution are the norm.

It is important that land legislation adheres to non-discrimination principles, since different groups in society, the poor and the rich, men and women and young and old, must be able to access land services on the basis of rules seen as equally applied to all. In that respect, the FAO model requires that land laws be locally responsive, and that land services be located closer to the end-users, both geographically and technologically through making land information accessible, for example through computerisation and keeping the text of the law and accompanying regulations available for the public at little or no cost, and in the local language(s) (FAO 2007:9).

This relates to the second aspect of a good land governance system – the importance of accessible information. Land information should be made available, accessible and should be reliable. Unless this is the case, the public's participation is based on partial information, and there is no real transparency of policy-making. Land information includes all the records on land. Generally, land information refers to physical, legal, economic or environment data that provides details about land registration, transfer, ownership, mortgage, land disputes and others. Good land information is important to good land governance because it helps the government and the public in day-to-day planning, decision-making and evaluation. That being the case, the absence or weakness in the land information system will cripple the performance of the land governance system. Making such information transparent should also mitigate the cost to government of providing land services to the public (FAO 2007:9-12). A good land information system should be locally sensitive in terms of languages, and the costs of making information available to the public, of translation, and making copies, should be offset against the costs of unnecessary travel and informal charges associated with poorly managed land information systems.

Thirdly, with respect to good leadership, this entails that cases of corruption should be the exception rather than the rule among land officials, so that efficient and competent land officers are promoted, and those who are corrupt can be retrained or removed from service (FAO 2007:9-10). Leadership of good quality is of great importance in urban land governance since decision-making by those entrusted with power to provide land services will influence outcomes. And zooming in on leaders, within the prism of good governance theory provides a more nuanced understanding of obstacles to achieving land justice in practice within the local setting, than the more neutral-sounding term, 'governance'. Using general concepts can tend to disguise what may simply be questions of poor quality leadership. This may need to be tackled directly, rather than through systemic changes of governance or public management arrangements.

The three principles outlined here are of course closely interrelated. Providing transparent land information is one of the functions of accountable and efficient leadership, and this requirement is important to effectiveness of the law, since laws alone cannot ensure that good land governance is possible and that outcomes of laws imply greater land justice. A working system of land governance depends on an active interplay between good laws, good information systems, and good leadership. Together, these three aspects if combined may help improve land governance and promote greater land justice in the eyes of the public. Even if one of these three basic principles is absent or weak, this does not imply that the whole system of land governance will be crippled; on the contrary, each can also act as a counterweight to deficiencies in the other two.

Rather than being absolute, land governance can be represented as a continuum, from good practice to poor governance practices, and combinations of these in different respects. The point is that the more the land governance system fulfils the three principles the more it is likely that land governance will be improved, and that more just outcomes will be possible, irrespective of the class of citizens involved. We cannot, however, claim to know what the broader effects of land governance will be on the overall patterns of land justice, as it affects different groups of people in Tanzanian society.

Figure 2: The FAO Good Governance Model for Land Governance and Administration

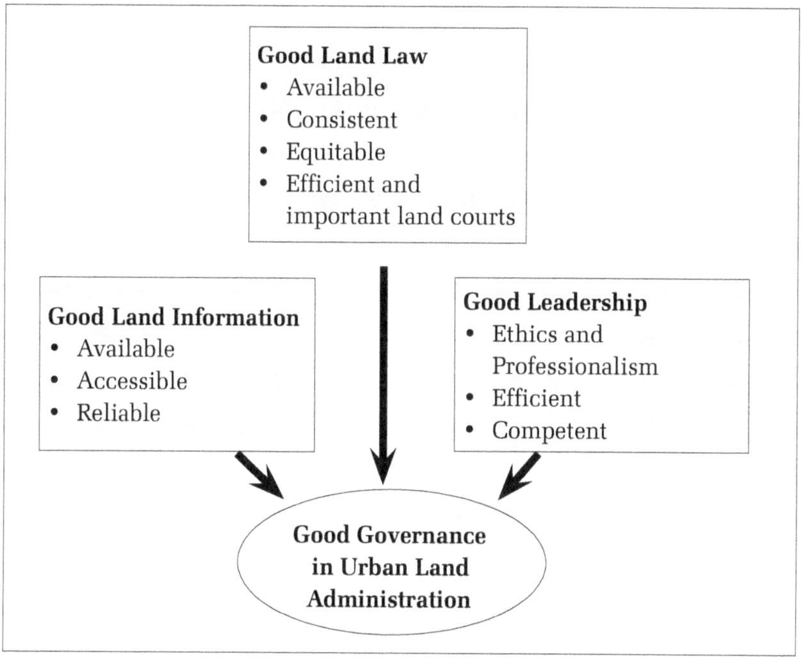

Source: FAO 2007:9

Good land law, information and leadership are key and central aspects in order to establish good governance in land administration. Land laws define what constitutes land, accessibility and use both by the government and public in urban areas. The laws and regulations provide land authorities and elaborate on their core functions. Therefore, weakness in the land legislation can be an obstacle to good governance while strength of the law is likely to improve land administration and possibilities of addressing land justice concerns.

Land Law, Information and Leadership

The relative strength or weakness of land laws can be influenced by various factors, including the clarity and consistency of the law itself. Where there is considerable ambiguity and inconsistency in land law, this can reinforce tendencies for misinterpretation both by land officers and in the courts (Burns et al. 2007:15-20, Deininger et al. 2010:75-77). Stringent legal procedures and the use of unfamiliar language, can mean that those involved in land disputes can find their way to accessing land services barred by incomprehensible laws (Kironde 2009:23). In my view, unless laws are clear and consistent, justice delivery in the land sector will be compromised. One factor that makes law less coherent and comprehensible is the multiplicity of land authorities and laws that are sometimes in place. There are divergent views on this, with some studies suggesting that such complex situations can create a breeding ground for patronage, corruption and informal fees (Burns et al. 2007:15-20, Deininger et al. 2010:75-77). Along similar lines, Cotula explains that pluralism 'creates confusion and tenure insecurity, which in turn foster conflict, discourage investment and enables elites to grab common lands' (Cotula 2005:3). The contrary view is expressed by other authors, however, who suggest that: 'tenure dualism needs to be recognised as a resource not an obstacle' for good land governance; this suggests that legal recognition of complexity is preferable to streamlining legislative provisions (Adams and Turner 2005:6-7).

The first set of literature discourages legal multiplicity, whereas the latter shows that recognising complex hybridity in the law is preferable and that acknowledging pluralism can be helpful to good land governance, and thus needs to be encouraged. In a more cautious way, Ben Cousins argues that multiplicity in land laws needs to be dealt with in terms of the legitimacy of different land law systems, including customary land practices and the role they play for local communities in land allocation, use and access (Cousins et al. 2005:12-18).

Despite this range of differing views about the pros and cons of multiple land regimes and laws, and the undoubted complexities in land governance at local level, including in Mbeya, it remains my considered opinion that multiple land tenure regimes and legislation can create the danger of duplication, reduce security of tenure and significantly increase costs associated with providing transparent information, for example. When there is weak local leadership, among whom there is minimal coordination and lack of necessary skills and technology, the problem of complexity is compounded. Although I recognise that this may be a minority view among scholars of land governance and land justice, I feel that the present plural land governance system in Tanzania, poses distinct challenges for improvements in law, in information provision and in the quality of local land leadership.

Some scholars have shown that when land laws are violated this can lead to a breakdown in land governance systems, resulting in social instability and sometimes even in the low-level violence that can be associated with the onset of civil disturbance and, eventually, civil wars (Byamugisha 2013:97, Elhawary and Pantuliano 2013:25-69). Examining land governance in Ghana, Roth et al see weaknesses in land legislation as being to blame for property rights uncertainty, land conflicts that sometimes became violent, and very high litigation costs (Roth et al. 2012:83). In my view, however, such fractures in land legislation could most effectively be mitigated by regular amendments in the law to close down loopholes and ensure that violations in the law can have consequences.

Subjectivity is embedded in notions like 'good land governance', as when it is argued that good land laws must adhere to basic constitutional principles such as justice, gender equality and even protection of private property (McAuslan 2006:2). Experience indicates that law alone is never enough, since there are definite limits to the extent to which land disputes are amenable to purely legal solutions, and there are usually a number of strategies for bypassing or avoiding legal solutions to such disputes (Woodiwiss 2006:34, Askew et al. 2013:120-122). There is no rule that fits all scenarios, and whether a law is judged as good or not is to a large extent, therefore, a matter of experience with the law following its implementation.

This is why land information is such a vital ingredient of good urban land governance, since it can help ensure that public participation is based on sound understandings of the law, and of how decisions related to land matters should be taken, and by whom. With land being public property in Tanzania, cheaply accessible land information is especially vital and clearly the responsibility of government to provide. In recognition of this, sound land information was one of the core principles of the 1999 Land Act (Tanzania 1999:15). Good land information is determined by its availability; accessibility and reliability (see Koroso et al. 2013:423). Here, too, however, the indices used to judge these normative labels, vary from one source and one scholar or study, to another. Thus Derby argues that a functional land information system should be complete, accurate and consistent (Derby 2002:6). Ciparisse expands the list by explaining that good land information should be secure, simple, complete, accurate, cheap and suitable for the local context (Ciparisse 2003:96).

In contrast, Enemark suggests good land information is not necessarily about accuracy but about completeness, adequate identification and credibility of data (Enemark 2013:10). He suggests land information should be flexible enough to fit the purpose of one particular area, rather than simply being copied in identical form from one location to another. Both Hespanha et al and Zevenbergen et al agree with Enemark that accuracy is less important than contextual relevance for land information to be termed 'good' (Zevenbergen et al. 2013:597, Hespanha et al. 2013:1-19). For Zevenbergen, there are eight principles for good recording of land information: affordability for citizens and the state, preventive justice to avoid disputes, systematic recording, recognition of existing land rights, transparency of data, inclusive and equitable data, flexible data that is co-managed (Zevenbergen et al. 2013:597).

It is suggested that simply organising a proper filing system and modernising and computerising land information systems can improve the reliability of land data (Margulis et al. 2013:4-5). More specifically, Haldrup and Stubkjær clarify that maps and land registers must be freely available for public scrutiny (Haldrup and Stubkjær 2013: 1663). Nevertheless, based on experience, the idea of total transparency is not attractive to most local leaders in Mbeya involved with land, since they would usually suggest that a balance should be struck between total accessibility of land information and the need for some aspects of land data to remain confidential, for example to prevent potential escalations of disputes.

However, confidentiality comes with a price, since absences in land information can imply that land governance may not be functioning properly, or according to the law. Research conducted in China found that publicly available and fully accessible land information was vital for creating a well-functioning land market there, after decades of state ownership of land (Koroso et al. 2013:423). There may be lessons in this experience for Tanzania in future. In contrast, costly and unreliable land records are found to cause uncertainty in the market and generate disputes; corruption and nepotism are all more likely when land transactions are less transparent (Deininger and Feder 2009:236-237). Clearly, what this suggests is that well-documented land information can not only improve land rights and land justice, but can also reduce the tendency towards fraud by cutting land transactions costs, and reducing incentives for local leaders to claim rent on land services and administration in their dealings with the public. For this reason, such transparency may precisely be resisted, since it can erode the privileges and spoils available to those involved in land administration.

Human resource data was collected from all three land offices visited during fieldwork, and this data suggests that there was an acute shortage of professional land officers in all three offices. Indeed, there were only six graduates employed in total across the three separate land offices visited during field research in 2012. This meant that most land administration was being handled by officers with relatively little formal training. Leadership weaknesses could be the result of lack of trained staff, rather than lack of will of those employed to do a decent job. Lack of trained staff can work against wider efforts to make land administration systems more accountable, effective and just for the public. Finally the mix of formal and informal processes of decision-making, combined with technical difficulties of coordination, given that computerisation has not even begun, make urban Mbeya's land administration system likely to suffer from overlap, partial documentation and ineffective leadership. This will be considered in more detail after the next section, which explores the issue of gender justice, as it relates to administration of land laws, through setting one specific case in its wider context.

Striving for Land Justice: Gender Relations and Case Analysis

According to Kironde, 'Laws can be passed or inappropriate laws upheld by those who control land policy to help them benefit from this policy rather than meet the perceived ends of society' (Kironde 1994:1-2). This implies that laws need to be assessed in terms of how appropriate they are for different sectors within society, and citizens overall. In this part of the chapter, we consider the gender implications of some of the local land administration systems in urban Mbeya, and report on findings from fieldwork in the summer of 2012.

An important indicator of land justice is the degree to which gender equality in land access and use is achieved. In the context of Tanzania, gender equality refers to equal opportunity between men and women irrespective of other differences of class and status, with respect to access and use of land. Land laws in Tanzania are in principle in line with principles of gender equality. This aim of respecting and promoting gender equality in land rights is reflected in four main aspects of Tanzania's land laws. The principles are: equal access to land for men and women; spousal consent in cases of disposition of land; co-ownership provisions and equal representation of men and women before land decision-making bodies. By contrast, neither males nor females have the right to own land at Mbeya or elsewhere in the country since the land remains public.

The National Land Policy categorically states that: 'in order to guarantee women's rights to land and security of tenure women will be entitled to acquire land in their own right' (MLHSD 1997:12). That is cemented in both the Land Act 1999 and The Village Land Act 1999, where it was provided that 'the right of any adult woman to acquire, hold, use and deal with land shall be equal [to the]... right of any man' (Tanzania 1999:14, Tanzania 1999:8). Similarly the land laws were carefully crafted to accommodate both men and women in land-related decision-making bodies such as land committees, village land council, ward tribunals, and the District Land and Housing Tribunals.[15] Although gender equality goes beyond men and women, recognition of various genders and their inclusion in decision-making bodies are certainly among the more commendable aspects of Tanzania's land laws.

Despite these declaratory provisions on gender equality, realising equal land rights is not easy in practice. This emerges with especial clarity in the differential and unequal treatment of men and women in relation to land inheritance,

15 See section 11, 5 (1) 26, (1) of the Land Act 1999 and sections 3, 53 (3) and 20 of the Village Land Act 1999

land allocation, co-occupancy and purchase rights, the principal means in Tanzania of accessing land. In Mbeya and in Tanzania in general, land can be accessed in six different ways: allocation by the state; inheritance; purchase; clearance of virgin land; gift and co-occupancy (Rwegasira 2012:93-118). Most land is held under customary land rights, which are transferred from one individual to another through inheritance, gift or sale. Recognition of customary property rights is provided for under the Land Act 1999, the Village Land Act 1999 and the National Land Policy of 1995. In the 1995 Land Policy, for instance, it is stated that 'inheritance of clan land or family land will continue to be governed by customs and traditions' (MLHSD 1997:12) that were already in place. Given this provision, laws of inheritance need to be understood to cast light on how they affect outcomes in terms of gender dimensions of land allocation. Land inheritance can be guided by statutory, customary or Islamic law, or a combination of these (Kudo 2012:6-7, Rwegasira 2012:220-225). In urban Mbeya, application of these legal systems depends on the ethnicity and religious affiliation of the deceased.

Broadly speaking, statutory law applies to all people of non-African descent and those of African descent who have abandoned their historical customs and tradition. The law allows for both the widow and children of the deceased to inherit land equally, but excludes illegitimate children (Rwegasira 2012:221). Since Tanzania has more than 120 tribes, and each has its own customs and traditions, it is quite unlikely that most people will abandon their customary land provisions. Statutory law is thus rarely applied in inheritance cases, and is hard to apply to such cases in court.[16] Thus statutory law applies mainly to those who are of either European or Asian descent, and this leaves the majority African population mainly subject to customary or Islamic law for land inheritance and allocation. Even statutory law is gender biased, however, since it precludes illegitimate children from inheriting their deceased parents' land.

Customary laws of inheritance apply to all citizens and residents of African origin who wish to be guided in local customs and traditions and who are not Muslims. In the absence of any will, the law identifies customary heirs as first, second and third degree heirs (Rwegasira 2012:224). The first degree heir is the first-born male from the deceased's household, and he obtains a larger share than any other males or females. The second degree heirs are all other male heirs and they get a smaller share than the first degree heir but larger than third degree heirs. The third degree heirs are all daughters and they in turn receive a smaller share than first and second degree (i.e. male) heirs.

The law does not allow the eldest female child to claim the clan land as a first degree heir, or even as a second degree heir. It allows a woman to inherit her father's land only as provided for by custom, and with no rights to sell the land. Similarly to statutory law, customary law does not allow for any land (or anything else) to be inherited by illegitimate children, whether male or female. Widows are only allowed to stay in the deceased husband's home and live with their children until remarriage or death, and cannot inherit land however

16 At least I know only of one case where it was successfully proved to be applicable to a native person of African origin since 1977 to date.

long they have been in the marriage and irrespective of how much they may have contributed towards the acquisition of land in the past. Altogether, customary laws of inheritance around Mbeya are clearly and explicitly gender biased, since they apportion inheritance in three categories and all females are confined to the category that obtains the smallest shares of land. Widows and illegitimate children are discriminated against, and yet it is customary law that is most often applied in land inheritance procedures in Tanzania today.

The Islamic law of inheritance applies only to Muslims, wherever they are located, and under Islamic rules, as under customary rules, a son is entitled to a greater proportion of land – his share being the equal to that of two daughters (Rwegasira 2012:233). When there is only one son and one daughter, therefore, the son inherits two thirds of the whole estate. Like customary inheritance law, Islamic inheritance law reinforces gender inequality in land access, undermining the formal provision of the law which explicitly favours gender equality in land allocation and distribution.

Apart from customary and Islamic inheritance provisions, in Tanzania land may also be accessed through allocation by the state, co-occupancy and purchase. According to Section 3 of the Land Acts (Tanzania 1999:14, Tanzania 1999:8), it was expected that state land allocation, co-occupancy and purchase, could all serve to improve gender equality, by allowing women equal opportunities with men in acquiring access to land. Registered land, allocated by the state, however, was investigated in urban Mbeya, and it was found that only 16 per cent of those who had registered land in urban Mbeya were women.[17] This finding was corroborated by an earlier study conducted in Dar es Salaam, which found that there the proportion of women who held registered (state-allocated) land was only 13 per cent (Ali et al. 2013:3).

Similarly, co-ownership may not deliver on promises of gender equality either. This study found that of 30 land disputes reviewed at the DLHT-Mbeya, all but seven were matrimonial land disputes, in which the women complainants were asking for men who unlawfully disposed of land, to be sanctioned by the Tribunal. This finding is confirmed by a recent study that indicates that less than half of all the men surveyed had obtained their female partner's consent before renting, selling or mortgaging the land. The same study found that 70-75 per cent of all matrimonial land registration was done in the name of the male only, not following the formal co-occupancy rule which requires that both spouses' names should appear on the land title (Ali et al. 2013:3, 5). This suggests some of the reasons why women are still largely under-represented in land ownership and access, compared to men. To illustrate this point, one case study will be explored in more depth. This concerned Esta Mwambene, a complainant whose case shows how women's land rights can be jeopardised under co-occupancy arrangements.

Case Analysis: Land Application Number 24 (2012)

The case of Esta Mwambene versus 1), Musama Auction Mart. 2), NMB Bank 3), Kikondya Mwakilasa centred on

17 Personal analysis on land register showed that land plots registered since 1984 to June 2013 were 7,463, of which only 1,194 were allocated to women.

Mwambene, wife of Kikondya Mwakilasa, who was suing the other three respondents, including her husband, for selling the matrimonial home. Esta had married Kikondya Mwakilasa 14 years earlier, and was disputing the legality of the sale of their house at Plot Number 13 in the Majengo area of Mbeya. She claimed the house was sold unlawfully by her husband at Musama Auction Mart. However, the auction mart claimed that they had been given the house to sell not by her husband, but by NMB Bank. In the reply to the complainant, the bank's lawyer explained that the house in dispute was mortgaged by Kikondya Mwakilasa, and that he had defaulted on mortgage repayments, leading the NMB Bank to repossess the house and force its sale in order to recover their losses on the loan. While the bank maintains that both spouses including Esta Mwambene signed the mortgage contract, Esta disputed this in court. Her husband, on the other hand, sided with the bank and claimed that his wife had given her consent on the original mortgage form.

In this case, if she signed the form, Esta Mwambene was by implication a co-owner under the law, and yet her husband seemed to have colluded with the bank and the land officers, who facilitated the mortgage, and later the sale and transfer of the land. This indicates that even though the law explicitly provides for protection of women in relation to matrimonial land, it can be hard in practice to ensure that this right is respected, given the prevailing male dominance mentality, which in my view remains pervasive (for a similar argument, see the chapter on women and land rights in Eastern Uganda by Clare Cheremoi).

Thus, co-occupancy based land allocation can be as discriminatory against women as customary law, making land laws not that useful a tool in promoting more equal gender relations, given the crushing weight of discriminatory customary laws in particular.

Whilst land laws formally promote respect for principles and practices that promote gender equality in land access and use, many women, and some poorer men, and illegitimate children, continue to be discriminated against in terms of land allocation in practice. The application of customary laws in land matters affects vulnerable people disproportionately, since as for married women, most customs and traditions do not allow for inheritance through marriage. The outcome is that women and men do not inherit land equally. Women are more likely to end up landless, excluded from customary land use, than men. The complex intersection of gender with class (poor/rich), marital status, and education and with existing power structures and social conditions (e.g. being a widow, or being illiterate) will tend to work in favour of men, other things being equal).

What this means is that good laws cannot promote more just outcomes on their own. Those land laws that apply in the setting of urban land governance in Tanzania are only a starting point; legislation can fall into underlying cracks that can jeopardise good land governance in practice, by discriminating against some citizens at the expense of others. What has been said here about gender, in the case of Esta Mwambene could also be said of poorer land holders being in a weaker position than wealthier ones.

Obstacles to land justice in urban Mbeya

Land laws as such may be rather weak instruments for achieving land justice, and this makes it doubly important that information about the law should be accessible and that there should be committed leadership. Clarity, consistency and responsiveness to local language are imperative features of any good land law, so that land legislation provisions can be understood by the wider public. This also helps to ensure that the law's strengths are appreciated, since it is more likely that a law that is accessible will be viewed as clear, as just, as equitable and as supported by impartial courts (FAO 2007:12). Public perceptions of the law will certainly influence the extent to which individual citizens are willing to settle their land disputes in court, or not. To gain more insight into this matter, five broad indicators can be used to assess the key laws that govern the land sector in urban areas of Tanzania. They are in turn: (i) availability of land laws for public scrutiny; (ii) consistency of the law; (iii) language of the law; (iv) gender equality provisions, and (v) perceived efficiency and impartiality of the land courts system.

To begin with, most land laws were indeed found to be physically available within the land offices particularly the District Land and Housing Tribunal (DLHT), the City Land Office (CLO) and the Land Registry Office (LRO). The relevant legislation identified includes: The Land Registration Act 1967, The Land Acquisition Act 1967, The Land Act 1999, The Village Land Act 1999, The Land Courts (Disputes Settlement) Act 2002, The Urban Planning and Development Act 2007, and The Unit Titles Act 2008. Most of this identified land legislation can be found in the large collection of legal instruments known as JUTA. The JUTA collection was available at the time of fieldwork both at the City Land Office and at the Land Registration Office. While the DLHT had no JUTA collection, the individual pieces of legislation were available at that office for public access.[18]

Nevertheless, I established that in none of the offices were the identified pieces of legislation available in soft copy. All the laws were only available in hard copies, and this suggested that unless an individual personally travelled to the office and knew that they could request to make a copy of the law(s) or to read them personally, they would not be able to access the legislation or share it with others, despite the formal availability of the laws within the various institutions, the DHLT, the CLO and the LRO. In addition to availability, the language used in the laws should be responsive to local conditions, and the official language used in education should be applied in land legislations, in policy and in regulations. Despite this internationally recognised provision, the land laws and policies of Tanzania are written and are only are available in the English language, which can be considered a foreign language for most Tanzanians.[19] The Land Act 1999, Section 3 and 181 for instance, clearly stipulates that this law should also be translated into Kiswahili, thus making it more readily accessible to all Tanzanian citizens (Tanzania 1999:5,

18 Personal review of the National Land Policy 1995 and legislations.

19 Personal review of the Land Act 1999, The village Land Act 1999, Land registration Act, Land Acquisition Act 1967, Urban Planning and Development Act 2007 and the Land Disputes Courts Act 2002 done on 24 July 2013

151). Despite such provisions, a Swahili version of this Act and other land laws was found to be unavailable in most of the relevant offices in urban Mbeya.

Since at least 95 per cent of the Tanzanian population does not speak or understand English [20], most urban and rural people are denied the opportunity of knowing the contents of land laws without recourse to legal and interpretation skills. Hiring a translator, and seeking legal counsel in order to pursue the settlement of a land dispute is a costly business. And without knowing the basic information about land laws and regulations, it is unlikely that an individual will be able to access the land services needed to effectively settle their case. This makes land justice more unattainable, and removes the possibility of dispute settlement from all but the better off citizens; justice in matters of land administration remains unaffordable for the poor.

Another important indicator, the consistency of land laws should also be considered; this refers to the uniformity and clarity of legal provisions. Scholarly evidence suggests that 'legal clarity contributes to compliance, reduces the possibility of arbitrary interpretation of the law by government officials and facilitates the task of the judiciary' (FAO 2005:25). Yet some of the land laws in place in Tanzania contain inconsistent and ambiguous provisions, as will now be explained. One example is Section 3 of The Land Act and Village Land Act 1999 which defines 'general land' and 'village land'. The Land Act 1999 defined 'general land' as all 'public land' which is not

---

20 Personal experiences as a lawyer, public officer and citizen of the United Republic of Tanzania.

'reserved' or 'village land' including 'unoccupied' or 'unused'[21] parts of village land. In contrast with this, The Village Land Act 1999 describes 'general land' as all public land which is not 'reserved land' or 'village land'. What this means is that The Land Act 1999 includes village land as general land while the Village Land Act 1999 does not, and indeed explicitly excludes village land from the category of general land.

This inconsistency can lead to maladministration in the case of land disputes, with the more favourable interpretation being referred to, and the less favourable being ignored, depending on the biases of the official administering the law's enforcement. This is an example of an inconsistency that can create confusing interpretations by land officers and the judiciary. This can reinforce other forms of injustice, by producing delays in land services and encouraging illegal land use in the absence of legal clarity that can guide a definitive decision. For obvious reasons, this can even set back the cause of achieving longer-term land justice for weaker groups in the population.

To see how such a legal inconsistency can influence practices of land administration, the researcher interviewed the city land officer in Mbeya, and this interview revealed two possible consequences. The first was that confusing and conflicting interpretations of the general land law by urban land authorities could cause land authorities to survey and allocate unused or unoccupied parts of village land for urban use. The second consequence was that inconsistencies in how land was defined could trigger land disputes between

21 Personal review of section 2 of the Village Land Act 1999 and the Land Act 1999.

the urban and rural (City and Village) land authorities over boundaries[22] and similar disputes could arise between urban and rural populations.

Moreover, another provision, which allows for presidential powers to acquire and transfer this land for other uses, was pointed out as an additional grey area in the law. The Land Acquisition Act 1967, The Land Act 1999 and The Village Land Act 1999 all empower the President to acquire and transfer any land from anybody, anytime and anywhere within the country, provided this is in the public interest (Tanzania 1999:8-9). To quote, the President may 'transfer any area of village land to general or reserved land' as long as this is in the 'public interest' (Tanzania 1999:8-9). This provision implies that the power conferred on the President in the land laws is so wide as to result in a permanent and pervasive insecurity of tenure, a clear source of injustice in relation to land. Examining these powers of the President over land more closely, Issa Shivji concluded that enormous power placed on one individual, had become a source of uncertainly and all kinds of related problems of corruption, nepotism and informalised, patronage-based forms of land allocation (Shivji 1999:4). In the case of village land, such provisions could even work against the more general purposes of the Village Land Act 1999 (Mousseau and Sosnoff 2011:10) and could end up with villages being denied autonomy over their own land.

The structure of land courts in Tanzania poses an additional challenge for improving land governance, since under the

22 Personal Interview with Kastor, the City land officer who cited misunderstanding between Mbeya city council and Iwambi and Itende villages as some examples, on 22 July 2013.

law there are five kinds of land courts, whose competences overlap and can conflict. These are village land councils, ward tribunals, the DLHT, the High Court and the Court of Appeal of Tanzania (Tanzania 1999:137, Tanzania 2002:5). The aim of having five levels was to facilitate administration of land justice by resolving disputes where possible locally, more cheaply and in a timely fashion. However, this multi-layered court structure means that decision-making falls under three different ministries. Village councils and ward tribunals are answerable to the Prime Minister's Office for Regional Administration and Local Government (PMO-RALG). The DLHT on the other hand falls under the authority of the Ministry of Land, Housing and Settlement Development (MLHSD). The final two levels, the High Court and the Court of Appeal, however, come under the Ministry of Justice and Constitutional Affairs (and the Judiciary).

This means that the High Court has no direct administrative control over the DLHT, or over lower level land courts, nor does the DLHT have powers over the ward tribunals and village land councils. Neither is the DLHT accountable to the High Court. In such a situation, there is likely to be little or no accountability between different levels of the judicial system, a situation that also reduces the accountability of court officers, and can potentially cause inefficiency on the part of courts at all levels regarding land-related cases, thus defeating the purposes of justice in general and land justice in particular. Thus, it seems that chairpersons of the DLHT and of ward tribunals are rarely called to account for decisions they make in the name of justice.[23]

A related difficulty is that DLHT chairpersons are paid per session as well as a monthly salary. Since they are employed on three-year renewable contracts, in the absence of resources, the DLHT can be incapacitated, since members only sit if they are paid a daily fee. Unfortunately, even when money is available, members tend to adjourn cases more often than necessary, so as to prolong the payment of daily fees.[24] These kinds of considerations mean one can conclude that the system in place may in some instances create more land conflicts, chaos and ultimately more land injustice, through delays and self-interest.

An indicator of whether a land administration system is working properly is that land courts work impartially and efficiently. By this criteria, officials working in land courts should be free to perform their duties with due regard to law and evidence alone. Secondly, they should be able to settle land disputes in a timely manner, fairly and inexpensively. However, the fieldwork revealed that the efficiency and impartiality of land courts was being undermined by at least two significant factors. First, the complex administrative structure of land courts as observed earlier, with land courts falling under three separate ministries, did not facilitate

---

23 Personal analysis on High Court Inspection Report on DLHT 2010, where delayed decisions, corruption and unfair treatment of clients were among the noted issues against DLHT chairpersons. Sometimes the ward tribunal chairperson/secretary refuses to bring cases files when ordered to do so by DLHT.

24 Personal analysis on Land Disputes Register, land cases and the Land Disputes Courts Act 2002.

speedy decisions. Since arrangements fell under three separate ministries, this could cause overlapping powers, complicate practical tasks of administration, and reduce accountability, as suggested in the literature (Palmer 1999:4, Maoulidi 2004:29). Secondly, there was a problem with poor security of tenure for chairpersons and tribunal assessors, appointed for three years (Massay 2013:3-5). As temporary employees, they had insecurity of tenure and this meant their decisions were more likely to be influenced by political pressures, than would have been the case for permanent appointments. Coupled with the poor leadership already noted earlier, this could serve to reduce the efficiency of the land courts, and could even encourage corrupt tendencies among land administration officials.

Several studies have shown that corrupt practices and forms of misgovernance by officials involved in land administration result in double allocation of land, or misallocation, increasing a tendency for land disputes to emerge and even resulting in mass forced evictions or land invasions in some cases (McAuslan 2002:36, Report, 2012:34). Whilst such studies imply that corruption is a challenge for land governance worldwide, in Tanzania this does not mean that land administration systems are dominated by scoundrels. On the contrary, problems may arise in spite of good intentions, because of inefficiency and incompetency rather than corruption as such. Poor leadership in most African countries can be attributed at least in part to the lack of technical capacity and the low level of human resource development because of the deficiencies in the educational systems of those countries (Burns et al. 2007:19-20). However, lack of technical and human capacity may not be the only problem, where the extremely meagre incomes of some public servants may be at fault. Thus, if salaries are too low in relation to the costs of living, this will also thwart wider efforts to secure good land services through training in ethical norms of good governance.

Conclusion: Key Findings

In summary, in urban Mbeya the main problem was that land laws and land regulations and land administration procedures were not translated into Kiswahili, and that this prevented accessibility for the general public. It also increased the cost of information for the majority of local people. Not only were they compelled to translate the documents, but for this reason, they were often obliged to seek legal counsel simply in order to be able to decide what the meaning of the data and the law implied for their situation. Since the laws themselves were available only in English, the vast majority of the population of urban Mbeya was effectively excluded from understanding it.

Equally, the land information that was available was located in three separate locations – for example being divided between the District Land and Housing Tribunal (DLHT), the Land Registration Office (LRO), the City Land Office (CLO) and various other local government offices and courts. None of this information was found to have been computerised, and some of the data was in poor, and incomplete, condition. Making the information safe from natural disaster damage was a priority and would imply computerising it, as well as making it more centralised and thus easier to locate and access for the public.

In line with this, there was found to be no single consolidated land information system within urban Mbeya. Instead, land information was scattered in multiple, independent and uncoordinated land offices, with no established system of communication among them. Deciding how such bodies of data should be maintained, updated, stored and shared, was found to be something that nobody had given serious attention to at local level. And not surprisingly, this meant that for the public (as for the researcher, despite his familiarity with the local land administration system) the costs of obtaining full and contextualised information about land law and land services, are prohibitively high for the public. Given the generally poor economic conditions of most of the population, obtaining data on land becomes a priority, so that land diputes can be resolved without requiring access to the courts, to lawyers and to intermediaries of all kinds.

Finally, leadership was found to play a vital part in influencing how land governance systems operated within urban Mbeya. Leadership can be defined as the ability to influence other people and to achieve wider goals (Hughes et al. 1996:1029). This implies that a good leader should not only avoid corruption, but also strive for efficiency, ethical professionalism and impartial service to the wider public (Hughes et al. 1996:1029). Corruption among land officers has been found to pose a major challenge to good land governance generally (Møller-Jensen 2010:5, Tuladhar 2007:1-5). Examples from The Netherlands, Tanzania, Pakistan, India, Sri-Lanka, Bangladesh, Kenya, Vietnam, Lithuania and other countries confirm that corruption among land officers is widespread and a global problem (Tuladhar 2007:4-5). In some instances, public servants ignore land laws in their own interests or in their family's interests – in other cases they manipulate such laws against those they take as enemies, and in favour of their political or personal friends (McAuslan 2002:36).

In this context, defining good land governance and how this can contribute to wider social justice in relation to land allocation, use and access is not an easy task. Regardless of disagreements over what constitutes good governance, however, the three identified components of good land law, and committed and able land officers, all seem vital for improved future performance.

In conclusion, I propose that through regular amendments of land legislation, particularly the Land Act, Urban Planning and Development Act and The Village Land Act, weaknesses in the law could be reduced and the outcomes tailored towards better attainment of land justice for the local population. Similarly, translating land laws into Swahili and allowing for the proceedings and record of land court cases to also be in Kiswahili would enable the general public in Mbeya and Tanzania to access far more relevant land information and to obtain land services more easily and cheaply, which would tend to promote greater land justice. Consolidating land records that are held in different land offices into one central location could also help improve accessibility, as could computerisation, and reducing the costs of maintaining and duplicating records in each separate office.

Finally, the operationalisation and monitoring of the ethical standards and professional integrity of land officers is essential if a more robust local leadership is to emerge that is capable of delivering more socially just outcomes through the land governance systems in place. It may be necessary to reward the most efficient land officers and to take some corrective measures against officials who have been found to be involved in malpractice in the past. Ensuring that the officals, as well as the public, have a clear understanding of the land administration system, the land laws and the overarching land disputes settlement system in Tanzania, will be key to addressing the remaining challenges for improving land justice more generally.

References

Adams, M., and Turner, S. (2005) 'Legal Dualism and Land Policy in Eastern and Southern Africa', *Land Rights for African Development*: 6.

Ali, D.A., Collin M., Deininger, K., Dercon, S., Sandefur, J., and Zeitlin, A. (2013) 'The Price of Empowerment: Experimental Evidence on the Demand for Land Titles and Female Co-Titling in Urban Tanzania': 2-26. Accessed at www.american.edu

Askew, K., Maganga, F., and Odgaard, R. (2013) 'Of Land and Legitimacy: A Tale of Two Lawsuits', *Africa: The Journal of the International African Institute,* 83(1): 120-141.

Burns, T., and Dalrymple, K. (2008) 'Conceptual Framework for Governance in Land Administration', Australia Article of the Month August.

Burns, T.B. (2007) Land Administration Reform: Indicators of Success and Future Challenges, Agriculture and Rural Development Discussion Paper 37, IBRD/World Bank, Washington.

Byamugisha, F. (2013) Improving Land Governance in Sub-Saharan Africa: A Ten Point Programme to Scaling Up Land Policy Reforms and Investments. World Bank Publications.

Ciparisse, G. (2003) Multilingual Thesaurus on Land Tenure: English Version. FAO.

Cotula, L. (2005) 'Making Law Work for the Poor', London, IIED, Sustainable Development Opinion Paper.

Cousins, B., Cousins, T., Hornby, D., Kingwill, R., Royston L., and Smit, W. (2005) 'Will Formalizing Property Rights Reduce Poverty in South Africa's 'second Economy', questioning the mythologies of Hernando de Soto.Plaas Policy Brief (18).

Deininger, K. W., Augustinus, C., and Enemark, S. (2010) Innovations in Land Rights Recognition, Administration, and Governance. World Bank Publications.

Deininger, K., and Feder, G. (2009) 'Land Registration, Governance, and Development: Evidence and Implications for Policy', *The World Bank Research Observer,* 24(2): 233-266.

Derby, W. (2002) 'Improving and Facilitating Land Title Registration Processes in Tanzania', Proceedings FIG XXII International Congress, April, 19-26.

Elhawary, S. and S. Pantuliano (2013) 'Land Issues in Post-Conflict Return and Recovery', *Land and Post-Conflict Peace Building*: 115.

Enemark, S. (2013) 'Fit-for Purpose Land Administration', *GIM International*, 27(7): 26-29.

FAO (2007) Good Governance in Land Tenure and Administration, 9. Food & Agriculture Organization of the UN (FAO).

Haldrup, K., and Stubkjær, E. (2013), 'Indicator Scarcity on Cadastre and Land Registration in Cross-Country Information Sources', *Land Use Policy*, 30(1): 652- 664.

Hespanha, J.P., Ghawana, T. C., Lemmen, H.J., and Zevenbergen, J.A. (2013) 'Can LADM contribute to a more fair large scale land acquisition?' in: Proceedings of FIG working week 2013, Abuja, Nigeria, 6-10 May.

Hughes, R. L., Ginnett, R. C., and Curphy, G. J. (1996) *Leadership*. Cambridge University Press.

Kironde, J.M.L. (1994) 'The Evolution of the Land use Structure of Dar Es Salaam 1890-1990: A Study in the Effects of Land Policy', PhD Thesis, University of Nairobi.

Kironde, J.M.L. (2009) Improving Land Sector Governance in Africa: The Case of Tanzania Paper prepared for the "Workshop on "Land Governance in support of the MDGs: Responding to New Challenges" Washington DC, March 9-10.

Koroso, N. H., van der Molen P., Tuladhar, A. M., and Zevenbergen, J. A. (2013) 'Does the Chinese Market for Urban Land use Rights Meet Good Governance Principles?', *Land Use Policy,* 30(1): 417-426.

Kudo, Y. (2012) 'Marriage as Women's Old Age Insurance: Evidence from Migration and Land Inheritance Practices in Rural Tanzania', IDE Discussion Paper 368, Institute for Developing Economies, Chiba, Japan.

Kyessi, A., and Tumpale, S. (2013) Formalizing Property Rights in Informal Settlements and its Implications on Poverty Reduction: The Case of Dar es Salaam, Tanzania.

Lugoe, F. (2010) The World Bank. 'Prioritizing urban land access in the economy of Tanzania'. Tanzania: The World Bank.

Maoulidi, S. (2004) 'Critical Analysis of the Land Laws in Tanzania', a study prepared for Hakiardhi, Dar es Salaam, September.

Massay, G. E. (2013) 'Adjudication of land cases in Tanzania: a bird eye overview of the district land and housing tribunal'. Dar es salaam: Haki Ardhi. Accessed 14 October, 2013 http://www.

hakiardhi.org/index.php?searchword=ADJUDICATION+OF+L AND &ordering=&searchphrase=all&Itemid=1&option=com_search.

McAuslan, P. (2002) 'Tenure and the Law', in G. Payne (ed.) *Land, Rights and Innovation: Improving Tenure Security for the Urban Poor*, (2nd edition, 1:36). London: ITDG Publishing.

McAuslan, P. (2006) 'Legal Pluralism as a Policy Option: Is it Desirable? Is it Doable', Land Rights for African Development, Washington, DC: Consultative Group on International Agricultural Research.

MLHSD (1997) 'National Land Policy 1995'. Tanzania. Accessed on 15 July 2013 at www.ardhi.go.tz/

Møller-Jensen, L. (2010) 'Land Management System, Urban Governance and Leadership: The Future of Urban Tanzania'.

Mousseau, F., and Sosnoff, G. (2011) 'Understanding Land Investment Deals in Africa', Country Report: Tanzania. The Oakland Institute, Oakland.

Palmer, R. H. (1999) The Tanzanian Land Acts, 1999: An Analysis of the Analyses. Oxfam.

Planning Commission (1997) 'Mbeya Socio-Economic Profile', 1: 1-191. Dar es Salaam: The Planning Commission, Dar es Salaam and Regional Commissioner's Office, Mbeya.

Roth, M. J., Cochrane, J. A., and Kasanga, R. K. (2012) 'Land Markets and Legal Contradictions in the Peri-Urban Area of Accra Ghana: Informant Interviews and Secondary Data Investigations'.

Rwegasira, A. (2012) *Land as a Human Right: A History of Land Law and Practice in Tanzania*. Mkuki Na Nyoka Pub.

Shivji, I. G. (1999) *The Land Acts 1999: A Cause for Celebration Or a Celebration of a Cause*? Oxfam.

Tanzania (2013) '2012 Population and House Census: Population Distribution by Administrative Areas', :1-244. Dar es Salaam: Ministry of Finance.

Tanzania (2002) 'The Land Disputes Courts Acts 2002'. Law, Tanzania.

Tanzania (1999) 'The Land Act 1999'. Law. Tanzania.

Tanzania (1999) 'The Village Land Act 1999'. Law, Tanzania.

Teeffelen, J. van (2013) 'Fuelling Progress or Poverty? The EU and Bio-fuels in Tanzania: Policy Coherency for Development in Practice', Evert Vermeer Foundation, Amsterdam, available on-line at: http://www.fairpolitics.nl/doc/Impact%20Study%20DEF.pdf [accessed 7 August 2015].

Tripp, A. M. (2004) 'Women's Movements, Customary Law, and Land Rights in Africa: The Case of Uganda', *African Studies Quarterly,* 7 (4), available on-line: http://asq.africa.ufl.edu/files/Tripp-Vol-7-Issue-4.pdf [Accessed 10 May 2014].

Tuladhar, A. (2007) 'Corruption and Land Administration', *Surveying and Land Information Science,* 67(1): 5-13.

UNDP (1994) Good Governance and Sustainable Human Development. Geneva, Switzerland: UNDP.

UN-Habitat (2004) 'Urban Governance Index: Conceptual Foundation and Field Test Report, 4: 97. Nairobi: UN-Habitat.

UN-Habitat (2002) 'The Global Campaigning Urban Governance Concept Paper', No. 2nd ed. 3-25. Washington, DC: UN-Habitat. org/wbsite/ external/countries/menaext/extmnaregtop

WB (2013) 'Governance and Good Governance: Varying Definitions' (a webpage of World Bank).
http://web.worldbank. governance/0, contentmdk:
20513159~pagepk:34004173~pipk:
34003707~thesi tepk:497024,00.html [accessed 25 April 2014].

Woodiwiss, A. (2006) 'The Law Cannot be Enough', The Legalization of Human Rights: Multidisciplinary Perspectives on Human Rights and Human Rights Law: 32-48.

Zevenbergen, J., Augustinus, C., Antonio D., and Bennett, R. (2013) 'Pro-Poor Land Administration: Principles for Recording the Land Rights of the Underrepresented', *Land Use Policy* 31(0): 595-604.

Chapter 5

Beyond Rights Awareness: Women, Men and Land Rights: A Case Study from Eastern Uganda

Clare Cheremoi

Introduction

The need to improve access to land and strengthen women's land rights in East Africa generates a lot of discussions, with women's rights activists arguing for increased access to and control over land and other productive resources. This chapter examines inter-relations between women's land rights in the Ugandan context and customary law, placing this in the context of debates around women's land rights in East Africa more generally. What governs the allocation of land in practice, between women and men? This is the key question the chapter seeks to address through a range of evidence drawn from fieldwork conducted in a rural area near Busia, on the Ugandan-Kenyan border. The focus of the study was to assess women's awareness of their land rights, and the role of local council courts in promoting equal land rights for women and men. The findings highlighted how discriminatory customary practices of land allocation continued to work against women's best interests, in relation to accessing, controlling and owning land, compared with men. The main problem was found to be not women's lack of knowledge or awareness of their rights, as is sometimes thought, but the enforcement of customary norms and cultural practices that rest on prevailing patriarchal norms transmitted also through the local informal justice systems.

It is evident from the data available that for land access and ownership, the gender gap in sub-Saharan African is wide. Efforts have been made to redress this situation, through drafting gender-sensitive laws and constitutions. Several East African countries have explicitly provided equal access for women to both land and legal justice, in effort to redress gender inequalities in land rights. A new wave of land reforms in East Africa has also had gender equality as one of its main aims (Wily 2003b:4; Lipton 2009:258, cited in Pedersen, 2010). In East Africa, as in most Sub-Saharan countries, such reforms make economic sense since women play a dominant role in agricultural and especially in food production. Their equality can thus be seen as conducive to improved overall food security for these countries, as well as in itself as an indicator of socially just policies.

In Uganda, Kenya, Rwanda and Tanzania a large proportion of the population remains involved in farming, and most farmers are still engaged in subsistence agriculture, usually alongside commercial crop production. The economies of all East African countries depend heavily on women's labour, since they are the backbone of subsistence farming. Yet women continue to face disproportionate difficulties, compared with men, in securing land ownership and accessing land for use, in spite of some recent reforms. Most East African countries have favoured a decentralised system for achieving more gender equality in land management and in land dispute settlement. Yet it is not clear that decentralising decision-making to the local level, and to local-level legal institutions, will achieve the goal of greater gender equality; it may be that quite the reverse is the case. As referred to in the Introduction, the view that decentralisation can devolve oppression, rather than ensuring greater citizen participation and equality for all, has been forcefully expressed by Mamdani in his research on the late colonial state in Uganda (Mamdani, 1996).

The data used for this local-level study included data collected directly from respondents, through Focus Group Discussions (FGDs), in depth interviews, and a questionnaire which was completed in order to provide more information on what women knew about their land rights. Key informants were able to add local in-depth knowledge about how land disputes were administered in practice, when it came to women's rights. Data collection in June, July and August 2012, involved a total of 27 respondents, including two local council members, the District Land Officer, Assistant Commissioners from the Ministry of Gender, Labour and Social Development, and two FGDs with a total of 23 participants, in the two selected sub-counties of rural Busia. Most participants in the FGDs were women over 30; some men were also included in one of the FGDs. Women in attendance freely discussed issues arising in relation to their land rights. It became clear that whilst quite a few of the women did know some of their land rights, they had made little effort in practice to gain equal land rights with men, or enforce those rights they formally had under the law, and were aware of. I concluded that this reluctance was mainly due to the continuing hold of customary law and customary norms over the way in which land rights were understood at local level. The women suggested several times that assertively claiming their equal land rights with men, would tend to destabilise their marriages. Such demands for rights might even endanger the livelihood of the household, or make women more vulnerable to different kinds of violence, which they said; they were not ready to face in order to secure their legally defined land rights.

The in-depth interviews carried out showed that different actors with different ideologies and institutions were trying to scrutinise the question of women's land rights, in the hope that women would not remain indefinitely at the mercy of customary norms and value, unable or unwilling to take the risks of the socially unacceptable behaviour of claiming equal land rights. What emerged for the researcher was the delicacy and sensitivity of the question, which provided a bigger picture about why the attaining of equal rights and social justice in relation to women's land rights is such an intractable issue, including at local level. The questionnaires distributed to local leaders and to women in the two sub-counties suggested that a straightforward human rights approach to overcoming injustices faced by rural women in relation to land would be unlikely to achieve the desired result, given the level of resistance to equal rights for women. In the rest of this chapter, the research findings are placed into the context of legislation in Uganda to promote women's equal land rights, and provisions intended to deliver decentralised justice through Local Council Courts. Before that, the context of women's land rights in the wider East African region is briefly outlined, country by country.

East African Land laws and gender equality strategies

In Tanzania, the 1995 Land Policy recognises dual systems of land tenure, with both customary and statutory rights of occupancy. However an estimated 80 per cent of all land under cultivation in Tanzania is held under customary tenure, making this by far the most important tenure system in operation (Behrman et, al 2013:4). The Tanzania Land Policy makes provision for registration of customary and statutory titles to land, and the policy also explicitly entitles women to acquire title deeds in their own names through purchase or as a gift. The land policy finally allows for the application of customary practices of inheritance, but only insofar as these are not contrary to the constitution or to wider principles of justice, including equal rights for men and women. The Tanzanian Land Act of 1999 provided for co–occupancy between men and women of land, which was divided into three parts: village land, reserve land and general land. The Village Land Act 1999 at the same time declares null and void any customary law that denies women and other vulnerable groups equal access to, ownership of, occupation and use of land. The law thus prohibits gender-based discrimination in relation to customary rights of land occupancy and use. Despite all these provisions of the law, significant inequalities in land rights and ownership between men and women persist, with women representing only one fifth, or 19.7 per cent of all agricultural landholders in Tanzania in 2010 (FAO 2011).

To resolve disputes, the Village Land Act makes provision for establishment of Village Land Councils that are tasked with mediating and resolving disputes. These Village Land Councils are also required to set gender-based quotas, so that three of the seven members must be women. Whilst Toulmin and Quan (2000) suggest that women would typically have stronger rights under statutory law, very few land cases in Tanzania involving the African population, fall under statutory law, which is more or less reserved for non-nationals or those without a customary African identity group. The influence of statutory provisions is thus very limited, in this context.

In the case of Rwanda, a new constitution enacted in 2003 and approved by national referendum brought in a new era where gender equality and principles of gender justice have been placed at the centre of policy making. Like other East African countries, Rwandans rely heavily for their survival on agriculture, which still forms the backbone of the country's economy and trading sectors. Agricultural products remain the main exports, and women represent around 80 per cent of the rural agricultural workforce (Rurangwa, 2013:11). This means that women also suffer from the poor income levels, and from customary practices that limit their ownership and control of land. Typically, women's plots are small or very small, and it is this group of micro-farmers that has been most under pressure from a new land law introduced in 2005. At the same time, national legal frameworks in Rwanda safeguard the rights of women. Thus the 2003 Rwanda Constitution provides that all men and women have equal rights to land. Article 9 (4) provides for equality among Rwandans and ensures that women and men are represented by providing that at least 30 per cent of posts in all decision-making organs should be allocated to women. The National Land Policy and the Organic Land Law of 2005 were intended to provide for greater gender equality in terms of land rights.

As has been noted by researchers (Daley et al, 2010:1), land administration in Rwanda has been decentralised to five person committees at local level, of which at least two members should be women. These committees operate at grassroots level in each village within Rwanda. In addition, more than 50 per cent of parliamentarians in Rwanda are now women, well above the minimum 30 per cent level required by the constitution. This is a fascinating development that has undoubtedly fostered greater gender equality and respect for women's rights in Rwanda than in some other East African countries. Women representatives have spearheaded several issues related to land succession that this has led to the enactment of a Bill into law in 1999, which called for equal inheritance rights for sons and daughters and also for joint land ownership for husbands and wives (Daley et al 2010:3). According to one study, as a result of changes in the law of inheritance, many women have managed to claim their land rights, which makes it more likely that issues of gender equality cannot be ignored, whether in marriage or in the disposal of property and in sharing of land (ibid).

The Rwandan situation contrasts sharply with that in Kenya, where gender equality may even have been reversed in recent years. The 1999 Land Law in Kenya was based on a decentralisation process intended to make an important contribution to promoting gender justice in land allocation, through ensuring respect for gender equality in the workings of the legal justice system. The land laws passed in 1999 devolved significant responsibility for land administration to village councils. They became responsible for managing land under national principles of governance which were to include equity, social justice, inclusiveness, equality, human rights, non-discrimination and protection of marginalised people, as well as the establishing of agreed property boundaries through adjudication committees.

Despite the existence of gender-sensitive laws in Kenya, marked imbalances remain the norm in land ownership across different regions. Nyamu (1999:21) asserts that Kenyan women are largely excluded from the control of land and other key economic resources. Most registered land is held in men's names, and although gender-disaggregated statistics are difficult to obtain, estimates suggest that only around 4 per cent of all registered land is registered in women's names (Nyamu, 1999:21). This is in spite of Article 5 of the Kenyan constitution, which requires that land be held, used and managed in an equitable, efficient, productive and sustainable manner. Article 61 of the Kenya constitution clarifies that land belongs to the people of Kenya collectively as a nation, as communities and as individuals, and Article 10 (2) provides for gender equality in general.

Considering an example, in this wider context, from local-level land administration and land use in Uganda, close to the Kenya border, this chapter tries to move from national to local level to identify the kinds of practices that can strengthen women's land rights and those that can undermine their implementation in practice. Possible benchmarks and indicators that might track progress in strengthening women's land rights are examined, and the 1995 Ugandan Constitution, which provides for equality between men and women with respect to the acquisition and holding of land, is a starting point. However, in spite of such promising provisions, the study on which this chapter is based, found that while many women in this particular rural area were aware that laws and policies in place did protect their land rights, they were rarely aware of how such protection could mean anything for them personally. The gap was between law, the awareness of law, and their position in relation to local practices and customary law. It is suggested that this gap resulted in many of the injustices observed at local level, in land use, allocation and control. One woman advocate thus lamented that whilst: 'Ugandan land laws offer a lot of protection to women on paper… many women particularly those in rural areas, have not benefited from these policies in reality' (Esther Kodhek, Africa Programme Director for COHRE). In this regard the Uganda land laws may need to be reconsidered in terms of the difficulties in their implementation in the desired direction of great gender equality.

A recent study on 'Improving access to land and strengthening land rights of women' by the Commission of Land Policy Initiative was an important component of the implementation process of the African Union Declaration on land. In addition, a number of Regional Assessment Studies on Land Policy were conducted, including for Eastern Africa, by the Land Policy Initiative between 2007 and 2008. These reports highlighted the problem of women's access to secure land rights, seeing this as a key constraint on the socio-economic development of the region, and of the African continent more generally (Odeny, 2013:2). Customary and statutory laws on marriage and inheritance are especially crucial for women, and it may be that sector-specific legislation is required to give general statements in the law a firmer footing in practical realities on the ground (Wily 2003: 57; see also Manji 2006:106).

One reason that women's land rights are considered such a key priority for many women's groups in East African countries, is that achieving greater equality in this domain could help to underpin future efforts for women to attain equal rights in other domains and sectors as well (Goetz and Hassim 2003:20; Tsikata 2003). Throughout East Africa, including in Uganda, this has led many women's NGOs to focus on collective efforts to attain more equal land rights for women, given the fundamental importance of land in what remain predominantly agrarian societies. Indeed, for East African populations generally, 'land is absolutely essential to economic survival' (HSRC, 2006:8), and even more so for women who often bear the primary responsibility for feeding their families, and rely mainly on farming in order to do so. For these women, if laws on paper are not implemented, then they remain largely meaningless, and have little impact on their daily lives.

Land Tenure and Land Law in Uganda

Following independence in 1962, the Government of Uganda took control of Crown Land and managed its operation through a variety of government agencies (Schreck, 2012:3).[25] Land tenure systems in Uganda were complicated during the Idi Amin regime. In 1975, Amin nationalised all land and established a leasehold system (ibid). In practice, frequent overlapping land claims made fair compensation practices difficult to implement (Deininger & Ali, 2007).

Currently, land in Uganda is held under four tenure systems namely: customary, freehold, leasehold and mailo system. Each of these land systems has different characteristics. Land in Uganda is held differently in each of the regions, that is to say the Northern, Eastern, Western and Central regions. All these regions have different ways of land management and ownership. The majority of the land (80 per cent) is held under customary tenure, meaning that land use is governed by the clan and customary laws (Bomuhangi et. al, 2012).

As noted by Margare at. al 2007, most research has indicated that communities in Uganda do not recognise individual ownership of land. (Cited in Cheryl, et.al, 2013:6) The rising concern today, which has resulted in several debates amongst organisations that deal with land issues, is how to reorganise the system of land distribution and inheritance in order to make it more socially just, and to promote gender justice at the same time. Since 1998, when the Ugandan Land Act attempted to formalise all land tenure systems by recognising customary land ownership and providing a process by which customary landholders could obtain a certificate of customary ownership, there has been little evidence that respect of women's land rights has improved. On the contrary, Similar

25 For a description of the land ownership regime in Tanzania, see Chapter 3 above.

problems with customary land tenure have also been noted in other East African countries (Tripp, 2004; see discussion in Munzerere's chapter on Tanzania, in this volume). Limited institutional and implementation capacity has hampered the effectiveness of the Ugandan Land Act where gender justice is concerned, and the role of Local Council Courts, this chapter suggests, is critical (Hunt, 2004; the theme of Local Council Courts' role in land allocation and access is also discussed in the next chapter by Chelimo).

Yet the trend internationally is to stress that women's equal land rights are essential to progress in agriculture and in human development indicators. In East Africa too, most governments want to be seen to comply with international human rights standards and obligations; Uganda, Kenya, Tanzania and Rwanda have all ratified the Convention on the Elimination of all forms of Discrimination against Women (CEDAW). Some countries also explicitly provide for gender equality in their Constitutions. Thus Uganda, South Africa and Mozambique have Constitutional provisions that prohibit discrimination, including on the basis of customary law and practice (UN-Habitat, 2006). CEDAW states that women should have equal entitlement to property, protection and well-being including protection from all customs that stifle the progressive realisation of women's rights. These principles of equity are clearly stated in the Convention[26] which also requires state parties to actively intervene to ensure that women's position is equal to men's before the law, and that outcomes are also as equal as possible. Similar ideals inspired

---

26 Article 15(1)

the Protocol on the rights of women, of the African Charter on Human and People's Rights.[27] Uganda has ratified this Protocol, and together these ratifications set a clear standard for the treatment of women concerning land rights in local legislation and implementation. Domestic law is intended to give effect to the broad requirements of international law, by ensuring measures that will have the ultimate result of safeguarding women against injustices, including in relation to property, land and inheritance rights.

The 1995 Constitution of Uganda has played an important role in ensuring that gender issues cannot be ignored, and sought to remedy the historical discrimination faced by marginalised groups in general, including women, ensuring steps should be taken to redress social imbalances that already existed in Ugandan society.[28] Article 21 of the 1995 Constitution provides that all persons are equal before the law, in all spheres of political, economic, social and cultural life, and should enjoy equal protection of the law. Article 21 (3) further explains that discrimination means giving different treatment to different persons attributable only or mainly to their respective characteristics such as sex, race, colour, ethnic origin, tribe, disability, birth, religion or political opinion. This article sets the stage for equal treatment in all spheres including equality and fair treatment in land ownership and access between men and women. With specific reference to women, Article 33 provides that women shall have a right to dignity equal with men and that the state should prohibit and take action to protect women from laws, cultures, customs or

27 Article 15

28 Article 21, 32 and 33

traditions which undermine their dignity, welfare, interests or status. The right to affirmative action in order to redress imbalances created by history, tradition and custom is explicitly enshrined in the Ugandan Constitution. In relation to land rights, the Constitution gives the right to all Ugandans to own property regardless of sex.[29]

Principles of affirmative action for women have been affirmed through several laws and the creation of institutions like the Ministry of Gender and Social Development, which is empowered to tackle issues that hinder women's equal rights. Despite all these commitments and efforts, the question that remains is whether such provisions in the law for equal access, ownership and the constitutional guarantees to freedom from discriminatory practices that women won, have actually been implemented and enforced since 1995. It seems that, to a large extent, respect and observance of these constitutional principles has come into confrontation with the resilience of customary law in relation to women's ability to claim and realise their own land rights. Since rural women need access to land for survival and to feed their families, whilst questions of ownership and control are still largely decided by men, it is clear why women's bargaining power might not be great, given their dependence for food security on their husbands, on their husbands or fathers' families, and on Local Council Courts, still dominated by prominent local men.

Similarly, the Succession Act Cap. 162 deals with succession and the protection of the family of the deceased. It is relevant for the protection of women's rights to property

29 Article 26

acquired during the lifetime of their husband, and to women retaining such rights after the husband's death. The Succession Act is one of the most efficient laws governing inheritance of property, but leaves a lot to be desired from the perspective of gender equality. Indeed, Sections 2 (e), 27, 31 and 43 of the Act all acknowledge the patriarchal nature of Uganda.

Securing women's land rights through decentralised justice?

The Local Government Act Cap 243 was one of the decentralisation provisions introduced in Uganda in 1997. This was designed to give Ugandans improved access to services through recourse to duty bearers at local government level, including district chairpersons from district to village level. According to Article 176 of the 1995 Constitution, decentralisation should be the principle applicable to all levels of local government. This would ensure that functions, powers and responsibilities are devolved and transferred from government to the local population. Section 3 of The Local Government Act provides for the establishment and composition of the local councils who are a manifestation of decentralisation as per Section 2 (1) of the Local Government Act.

Uganda's strategy to decentralise power to locally-elected bodies reflected a paradigmatic shift in perspectives on the state and society (Nsibambi, 1998; Ottemoeller, 1996; Tideman, 1994; Villaden and Lubanga, 1996). As Khadiagala observes, since local government offices are embedded in the community, their staff should be well placed to find:

> ...sustainable solutions to the challenges faced by a community because they are in a better position to operate with strong networks...with greater efficiency, efficacy, fairness and also to craft local solutions to local problems. Decentralisation combined with democratisation ought to result in a more responsive, accountable, equitable, efficient, and transparent state (Khadiagala, 2000:57). In practice, is this the case?

It was partly in a search for socially just outcomes that the NRM government committed itself to decentralise power decentralising and providing for local access to justice, creating the powerful institutional structure of Local Council Courts, established to advance and administer justice locally. Table 5.1 shows the outlines of these complex locally-established justice systems.

The Local Council Courts Act, 2006 is another piece of legislation designed to bring access to justice to the grassroots population who include women. This legislation reflects the commitment of the government to devolve judicial power to the lower government authorities with the aim of serving and bringing justice to all Ugandans. Section 3 of the Act establishes a local council court at every village, parish, town, division and sub-county level. The court is mandated to sit as often as the business of the court requires for speedy discharge of cases. The quorum of the court at any sitting shall be represented by two women in case of village or parish and one woman in cases of town, division or sub-county. Section 3 (3) provides that at least two members of the town, division or sub-county Local Council shall be women. The Act requires all the deliberations in the local council courts to be determined by consensus or majority vote. In line with this, Section 6 (2) provides that the vice-chairperson shall be a woman if the chairperson is a man and vice versa.

Table 5.1: Structure of LCs and local justice systems

Local council level/area	**Political head**	**Procedure for selection of representatives**	**Status of LC level and Administrative Head**	**Technical staff**	**Percentage of locally generated revenue retained**
LC5/District	District Council Chairman	(a) Chairman elected by universal adult suffrage (UAS)	Local Government	Full team	35%
		(b) One councillor elected from each sub-county by UAS	Chief Administrative Officer (CAO)		
		(c) Women make up 1/3 of council			
		(d) Special councillor for youth and disabled			
LC4/County	LC4 Chairman	(a) Council made up of all LC3 executives, who then elect LC4 executive	Administrative Unit Assistant CAO	-	5% of 65%
LC3/Sub-county	Sub-county council Chairman	(a) Chairman elected by UAS	Local Government	Sub-county executives and other technical staff	
		(b) Councillors elected by UAS from each parish	Sucounty Chief		
		(c) Women make up 1/3 of council			
LC2/Parish	Parish council Chairman	(a) Selected by LC 1 executive members	Administrative Unit Parish Chief	-	5% of 65%
LC1/Village	LC 1 Chairman	(a) Direct election by universal adult suffrage (UAS)	Administrative Unit		25% of 65%

Source: Francis and James 2003:4.

With regards to jurisdiction, the local council courts have jurisdiction over matters of a civil nature, including issues related to land held under customary tenure. Since most land in Uganda is held customarily, and since Ugandan women reside mainly in rural areas where customary ownership is practiced, in principle local courts could be useful in ensuring that women's land rights can be realised through enforcement measures. However, the courts are not as accessible to local women as might be expected, and even in cases where women may be in dire need of protection from exclusion and denial of their land rights, for reasons of livelihood, the courts may not assist them in practice.

Local Council Courts are not generally as fair to women as had been hoped; and localisation thus cannot be equated with greater gender equality; on the contrary, since the Local Council Courts mainly apply customary law to land disputes, and most customs remain rooted in beliefs that men remain for their lifetime within their home areas (whatever the reality may be), women have often been disadvantaged in relation to decisions of the Local Council Courts. From this perspective, women are viewed as mobile persons, who get married and divorced and each time move away from 'home'. From this perspective, women are not able to control and therefore inherit land in their area of birth, as men do, since women are assumed to leave the parental home at some point, and live with their husband's family in another place, where they again do not 'belong' qua land rights and customary inheritance rights; women are perpetually viewed as from 'elsewhere', in this perspective.

In terms of active participation in the sittings, women's active involvement in Local Council Courts is supposed to improve delivery of justice, in terms of overall principles of equality and bringing government closer to the local level. The difficulty is that women's claims for land rights are hindered both by the historically dominant voice of men in society, and by women's marginal position in the Local Council Courts themselves. We now consider some of the main findings of research in the field.

Key Findings of the Case Study

This study found that although women to some extent knew about their land rights, they were surprisingly reluctant to speak out about these rights in public, or to take steps to claim these rights themselves vis a vis men in their community, by asserting their rights publicly. Their reluctance was found to be partly attributable to the high expected social and economic costs of challenging gender barriers discriminating against and sidelining women in decision-making around land. The risks involved may also be what discouraged women from directly accessing justice institutions, including notably Local Council Courts, to pursue their legitimate (i.e. legal and human rights-based) land claims formally. Customary practices, cultural norms, discriminatory traditional laws and socially endorsed practices of male dominion and oppression, especially from male heads of households, clans and justice institutions, thus all served to silence women's claims for equal land rights. Women feared losing their reputation as well-behaved women members of the local community. Such cultural and status barriers appeared to be an effective way for those with land – most of whom were men – to prevent those without land – most of whom were women – from even proposing more equal treatment in land-related justice systems. Women were dissuaded from advancing their own rights claims in relation to land; in effect they could be treated as if they did not belong fully to the local community. To paraphrase Hannah Arendt, it was as if they were not considered to have the 'right to have rights' in the first place, and perhaps even considered themselves as such.[30]

In order to understand and provide a clear picture of land rights issues pertaining to women's access to and use of land, the roles played by Local Council Courts can be considered important. Some implications of their role will be discussed in the context of Busia District in Eastern Uganda, focusing on two sub-counties: Dabani and Lumino. According to the Uganda 2002 National Housing and Population Census, Busia had a population of just under one quarter of a million (225,008, of whom 52 per cent were female). This population was growing at 2.7 per cent per annum and 83 per cent of the total population of Busia district lives in the rural areas and largely depends on subsistence farming. This suggests that land in this district is mainly used for agrarian production, and that its distribution can make the difference between having sufficient food and income, and not.

There are two predominant 'ethnic' groups in rural Busia District: the Samia and the Bugwe. However, mainly in urban areas, there are also other social and language groups, including

---

30 There is an echo of this in the debate around the Ugandan Marriage and Divorce Bill 2009 (115-116), where women's views were also not sufficiently taken into account, since women were hardly represented in Local Council Courts, which informed the Bill about local views. In this sense, if the Bill is passed into law, women's access to land rights will continue, and will even be further compromised by this legislation. Since those who participated in discussions around the Bill were mostly men, in reality male dominance and authority figures, including clan leaders and husbands of relatively better-off households, were in charge, and could hardly be expected, in most cases, to become advocates of women's land rights in relation to men's. Hannah Arendt's idea of the 'right to have rights', based on the idea of recognition, comes from her text *The Origins of Totalitarianism,* Meridien Books, Cleveland (OH) – New York, 1951.

Iteso, Basoga, Bagisu and Karimojong, most of whom live in Busia Town (FHRI and HIVOS Netherlands 2009:12). Being the eastern border point of Uganda, along the border with Kenya, Busia is transversed by many different individuals and businesses carrying out various trading activities adjacent to, and back and forth across the shared border. The relatively high level of economic activity due to cross-border trade has tended to push up the price of land through market transactions. At the same time, land disputes have been growing, including between men and women, as inequalities create pressures of poverty, ownership disputes, and conflicts over access and control rights.

Several studies have shown that there are numerous interlocked land conflicts, involving gender dimensions, including class formation, international land grabbing across the African continent, East Africa, and in Uganda itself, and long-term commercialisation of former customary land (Verma, 2014, 2007; Tripp, 2004; Peters, 2004). Busia seems to be no exception to this, and the problem centres on debates around whether customary land tenure is better for women or whether women tend to face even more difficulties accessing land justice when customary land use is the norm (Verman, 2014). In most cases, the battle for women's land rights is partially lost already at marriage, even when women are still young girls, living with their parents. Most customary law does not recognise women as heirs in the family set-up, and marital status can be a key determining factor. A woman's ability to protect her land rights in particular, or indeed access land at all can also depend on other people (Ravnborget, et al 2013:50). However, it should be noted that women's demands for land rights or the right to land use, arise for different reasons, including because of women's responsibility for food production for households, and in their capacity at other times as food harvesters and marketers.

Some more positive stories from the field, show how some exceptions suggest that there could be room for greater equality within the existing system, if patriarchal assumptions are challenged, on the side of men. The key point that was found from fieldwork was that land justice in Busia involves a great deal of political influences and political affiliations along party lines. Politics plays a key role in influencing the outcome of decisions on whether you have land rights or not, especially in regard to women. One example was when a respondent reported that:

> I had a problem of a land wrangle with my neighbour. He grabbed my piece of land and so I took the matter to the Local Council Court II. Days after, however, I was advised not to go far and was threatened to leave the issue. [They said] that I could not win the case because he is a well-known person and works for the political system that has the authority and power today (Interview conducted 20 July 2012).

It was found that political party affiliation more or less determined whether a woman's case would be treated seriously in the Local Council Courts or not. It was also revealed in the field, that women were victims of injustice and discrimination, on the basis not only of gender and patriarchal attitudes, but also because of which political party they supported. Abel (1982:6-7) asserts that when political parties are at loggerheads, with each demanding the diversion of the Local Council Courts in their service, then rural women in particular, like those I studied, fall victim to such situations. Local Council Courts would sideline their cases if they did not support the political party in power, and this happened. If they took their case to the Local Council Courts, women could find their cases delayed or they might simply not be handled at all. This arbitrariness really undermined the quest for justice of women whose land rights were denied. Rural Busia women continue to face challenges that they should not have to face. There were examples where Local Councillors demanded sexual relations with women before allowing the women to access Local Council Courts for justice in relation to a land case. As stated:

> One of the workers asked me for a sexual advance [i.e. favour], so as to help pass through my file for at least an early hearing in the court, and when I refused, my file got lost as well, in the file records (Inteview, 5 August 2012).

Women's awareness of the law and access to justice is one important step to the full realisation of women's rights. However, Busia women expressed that they have little information or limited understanding of the operations and jurisdiction of the local courts. Although some understood the Local Council Courts as duty bearers meant to provide local justice within communities, they did not appreciate their full mandate. Other women were sceptical about LCCs, and many women in Busia explained that they did not really know about their role. Some women reported that communities were not sensitised about issues of the law and procedures to be followed in order to access justice.

A feeling of exclusion from Local Council Courts, failure to receive fair treatment and attention from the local courts in the past, was often attributed to poverty. Some women expressed more concern about the local council courts because their demands to land rights are usually not respected. They lack resources to facilitate the court sittings or bribe the members of the court to influence outcome of decisions in their favour. This has made most women reluctant to seek remedies at the Council Courts because it appears that only a few rich, and usually influential people receive justice. Kigula (1992:5) asserts that influential members of the court by virtue of their social and economic status influence the decisions especially when they are interested parties in a dispute, where ultimately women's land rights are compromised. In this respect, one respondent stated that:

> After my husband passed away, my brother in law grabbed the land that my late husband and I owned. I then resorted to the council courts for help but they have been tossing me for a very long time yet at the moment I cannot even access the land or grow crops for production and even have some to sell (interview on 20 July, 2012).

In general, most respondents I interacted with in Busia, gave the Local Council Courts little credit for efficiency or effectiveness. Several women explained that although they had tried to seek justice in Local Council Courts, this had been to no avail. The Councillors in the court usually rejected cases of land disputes where rural women had reported their husbands to the courts. Issues of transparency and clarity or detail were not considered in the delivering of rulings related to the cases. This has made the whole process of the cases take so long leaving women sidelined and excluded in court hearings; the final rulings are rarely in their favour.

One allegation made during fieldwork is that for a woman to win a case, or for her case to reach the final stage, a lot of money needs to be paid. The Local Council Court Act 2006, clearly indicates that the amount of money to be paid as court fees is 2,500 or 3,000 Uganda shillings. Yet most women in the FGDs, and most of the men, shared the view mentioned, that there were frequent demands of money from the LC Courts. Local Courts were said always to ask for money before settling cases in this community but the issues of justice are given less attention in the courts. In effect, the intended goal of the LCCs as a trusted and easy system for local justice has been compromised. From the findings, the demand of money from men and women in the LC courts breeds corruption tendencies limiting women's access to justice. According to Deininger and Mpuga (2005:178), Ugandans find local council officials even more corrupt than central government officials, perhaps because the visibility of corruption increases as one moves downwards from district to village level.

Busia rural women's participation goes unrecognised in most cases during LCC meetings. This is due to the male dominance in the discussions and presentations in the LCCs. The attendance in high numbers of men in these courts also earns them respect causing fear in women representatives in the courts. (Tamale 1999) observed that male dominated electoral colleges responsible for selecting representatives tended to favour socially conservative women, leaving observers to doubt whether they represented women's interests. Even in the decision-making men's voices are stronger than the women's. Women attendance in these courts is low. This can be attributed to the gender roles they play as women making them act more as observers in LC Courts. That is to say, mainly to fill in the gender gap as provided for in the Local Council Court Act 2006. This makes women's impact very little or invisible and men's views override in the final rulings of the court, thus undermining women's access to justice and land rights.

Identifying the key Obstacles: Inheritance

Customs in Uganda promote patrilineal inheritance in case of intestacy (where no will is written). Widows have usage rights over the matrimonial home upon death of the husband, but not over the land, ownership and control which revert to the family of the husband. The eldest son in most cases also becomes the legal owner of the matrimonial home, at least in the context of Busia. Although Article 31 (2) of the Constitution gives parliament the capacity to make appropriate laws to protect the rights of widows and widowers in inheriting the property of their deceased spouses, these provisions tend to be ignored at local level. In one case, of Law Advocacy for Women in Uganda V Attorney General,[31] the court held that provisions in the Succession Act in respect to Sections 27 and 43, which provided for inheritance male intestate only, discriminated against women. Stating that women did not own property and that at their death, they could not leave behind anything to be inherited as female intestate, was viewed by the court as a discriminatory provision. Furthermore, the Court held that the

31 Constitutional Petition No.13/2005

Act was discriminatory since it did not provide for a woman to appoint guardians for her children in the event of her death.

There are signs that provisions of the Constitution for gender equality have enabled some customary and statutory legal forms of discrimination against women's land rights and inheritance, to be challenged in the Ugandan courts. Such provisions were found in the case cited above of Law Advocacy for Women in Uganda v Attorney General, to be in contradiction with Article 33 of the Constitution, and specifically Article 33 (6) which prohibits law, cultures, customs or traditions that violate the dignity, welfare and the interests of women, as we noted earlier.

Similarly, in the case of Best Kemigisa v Mabel Komuntale[32] Article 33 (6) was cited, and the custom in Toro prohibiting women from inheriting their deceased husband's property was declared null and void. The court granted Best Kemigisa (Queen of Toro) the capacity to inherit her deceased husband's estate. Unfortunately, little more has been achieved so far, and the impact of the Constitution's provisions on courts remains quite limited. Law reforms have been recommended in the Constitutional Court's decision following, the Law Advocacy for Women Uganda v Attorney General case. This leaves a dire need for law reform if women's land rights are to be realised in future. The prevalent tendency remains for often unjust and discriminatory, and sometimes quite repugnant customary provisions, to remain in force, so that women continue to be deprived of their basic constitutional rights.

---

32 Supra, note 5, p.

Married women in Africa are subjected to customs that are repugnant to human rights and this needs significant change. The land ownership rights of women are restricted and their control of land is at minimal levels. Since men assume the responsibility of being family heads, they have the full authority to control their families including the resources. This is partly attributed to the patriarchal nature of African societies. As noted by Land and Equity Movement (2011:5) a man becomes a family head on marriage, and his new family is allocated land by his parents on their marriage, though it is possible for parents to allocate land to their children before they marry. This implies that a man assumes the responsibility of being a family head because of the patriarchal nature of most African societies.

Decisions on land ownership are made in accordance with customary laws, customs and practices that in most cases discriminate against women and other marginalised groups. Unmarried women, on the other hand, who continue to stay at their parents' homes merely enjoy user rights on the land but still have no ownership rights. For instance in Busia where the research was carried out, feedback was that all women do not own land under customary tenure. This leaves a big question lingering. Despite the existence of Section 27 of the Land Act which grants women equal rights of ownership and access to land, women in rural areas remain marginalised in terms of land rights. This illustrates how so little is being done regarding effective enforcement and implementation by the custodians of the law (local councillors).

A divorced woman equally remains in a vulnerable position concerning her rights to ownership of land. According to LEMU (2012:1) a woman becomes vulnerable once she is divorced. When a woman divorces she leaves her marital home and joins her parents' family. In most cases the bride price that was paid to her family when she got married is used by her brothers to pay bride price to marry girls from different clans. The brothers would ordinarily be expected to share part of their land with their divorced sister, but this is never the case. Research carried out by Land Equity Movement reveals that almost all divorcees and separated women are denied land by their own brothers, and often have to support their children under difficult circumstances (LEMU, 2012). At best, the divorced woman retains user rights over the land, but not ownership.

The unmarried women, on the other hand, continue to stay at their parents' homes and also enjoy user rights on the land. Just in case such a woman opted to get married, she would forfeit these rights. However, in case her parents die, the unmarried woman becomes vulnerable. Her brothers will tend to share the land among themselves, and exclude her since according to most customary arrangements, women are expected to leave the community, and this expectation is used to explain that they cannot own land.

All of this sits uneasily with the Constitution of Uganda, especially Article 126 (2), which provides that judicial power is derived from the people and shall be exercised by the courts established under the Constitution in the name of the people, and in conformity with law and with the values, norms and aspirations of the people (and on the basis of non-discrimination, as provided for elsewhere in the Constitution). It is worth noting that the Land Act under Section 88 empowers the traditional authorities to also determine disputes over customary tenure or act as a mediator between persons who are in dispute over any matters arising over customary tenure.

As Aili Mari Tripp notes, the formal recognition of customary law is something relatively new on the African continent, and in Tanzania, where:

> ...one of the most dramatic changes in land tenure reform today is that, for the first time since the pre-colonial period, states are giving legal recognition to existing African tenure regimes, which are being treated on par with the freehold/ leasehold systems.

Or in the case of Tanzania, on par with statutory arrangements for land use (Tripp 2014:2). Whilst some organisations, like the World Bank, propose that reliance on customary arrangements should be a means to improve the status of women in the community, experience tends to suggest quite the opposite – that customary arrangements serve to exclude and discriminate against women.

International Alert (2012:40) asserts that despite the increased importance of women's roles in community structures, they remain widely excluded from local decision-making. The indication from the table above holds water because very few women are members of the local government and their per centage in local assemblies does not exceed the 30 per cent female representation quota (ibid). Due to the small number of women in structures of power, the missing gap between implementation and realisation of women rights to land is the biggest problem.

Most studies show that the rural women continue to face challenges with local council courts meant to safeguard and guarantee women's social justice in land rights enforcement. The women's interviewed observed that most local courts are not well facilitated. They lack proper structures to hold sittings and often times lack even stationery. If LC courts were better facilitated, perhaps they could start to ensure that women were more aware of their land rights, and then what? Respect and clan justice can only be seen to prevail when women can enjoy their land rights. Women should not hesitate to consult the Local Council Courts when they have a land dispute, and this would help women to trust the local judicial systems.

Whereas the LCCs have handled a number of cases involving complainants amidst tensions of customary norms and cultural values, members of the community in focus group discussions revealed that the poor find it difficult to access justice in the local council court system because they cannot afford the cost of litigation. The challenge is worse still for women who do not have control over family resources and are denied decision-making powers because of their marginalised status in the households. The Local Council Act provides that the plaintiff to the case in a local council court shall pay to the local council a court fee in accordance with regulations made by the minister, but the minister shall take into account indigent persons when making the regulations.[33] In reality this does not happen in the rural areas because the poor are tasked to pay in order for the sittings to take place.

33 S.41(1)

It was found during research that the Local Council Courts in Busia district lacked a comprehensive and functional information management system. This caused delays in the appeal process, such that documentation of court proceedings could even be incomplete due to the lack of stationery or materials with which to write. There was lack of relevant legislations for public reference, and not all laws were translated into local languages (for a discussion of a similar situation in Tanzania, see Munzerere's chapter in this volume). There was a general concern that Government and the respective key agencies were not committing enough resources to support access to justice at the local level.

It is my view that full conceptualisation of justice can only be realised when both women and men access justice from the Local Council Courts concerning ownership of rights on land on an equal basis. Ritu's assertion that the land administration system has failed to challenge pre-existing gender biases in implementation seems a fair one, under the circumstances (Ritu, 2007:35). This finding is also evident in the case of Busia, where women have continued to face difficulties in acquiring land rights and access to justice.

Signs of hope for reform

There is, however, some good news in this generally depressing picture. Thus, in the legal case of Best Kemigisa v Mabel Komuntale, the Toro custom of denying the queen of Toro inheritance of her husband's estate which included land and other property, was declared by the court to be unconstitutional, since it was contrary to Article 33 of the Constitution. This case was reinforced by Article 2 of the

Constitution which explicitly stipulates that customs and traditions that discriminate against women are prohibited. A number of other constitutional legal cases have also tested customs and laws that historically have discriminated against women, including the cases of Uganda Association of Women Lawyers v Attorney General Constitutional Petition (2003), Mifumi v Attorney General (a Constitutional Petition of 2007).

The Land Act Cap. 227 is another piece of statutory legislation that explicitly defines rights attached to land, and contains specific provisions to protect women's land rights and those of other marginalised persons. The Land Amendment Act of 2010 also provides for security of occupancy of those on family land. The security of occupancy provision implies the right to have access to, and to live on land that is used for family sustenance. This Act allows a spouse to use the family land and to give or withhold consent to any transaction that affects his or her land rights. The experience of implementing provisions under Section 39 of the Land Amendment Act, on family property, shows that on several occasions women have been excluded from giving consent, when it comes to transactions that concern land (for a similar case in urban Mbeya in Tanzania, see chapter by Munzerere in this volume). The principle that all transactions require equal voice and decision-making from both partners, is contained in the Land Amendment Act, Section 39, which restricts sale, exchange, mortgage, lease, pledge and any other transaction in respect to family land, without the explicit consultation and approval of both the man and the woman.

Local Council Courts have also registered some positive outcomes concerning women's land rights. There have been some collective efforts of different duty bearers, some in the state and from NGOs who have established programmes of community sensitization which, through gradual engagement with LCCs in rural Busia District, was starting during the research period in 2012, to shape some apparently sustainable solutions to women's quest for equal rights with men. In one interview with Kyomukama, the assistant commissioner for the Ministry of Gender and Social Development, he reported that:

> Much as women face various challenges, the Ministry of Gender and Social Development tries its best, by carrying out sensitisation campaigns, networking with other partners like Uganda Land Alliance to enable women to overcome these challenges through male engagement and participation activities like music and dance in the local language (Interview on 29 July 2012).

Although it was not quite clear how musical and dancing activities could tackle patriarchal attitudes among the men, or address customary (mis)use of rules that discriminated against women, an interview with Magdale received, she was quite a keen member of staff who ran the Rural Uganda Land Alliance, a national NGO that has been heavily involved in advocacy, including for women's land rights. From this perspective, Magdale reported that:

> Most of our work is to sensitise both men and women about the importance of ensuring that the land rights of women to possess, access and own land are protected. We promote joint access and ownership of land because of the benefits that come along with it, for the chance to make and write wills as a couple.The pride of John Okuku comes through the help of

> Local Council Court which sensitised him on the importance of women's land rights. This court enabled him to fully give his wife her rights to land but the wife opted for a joint registration of the land (Interview 12 August 2012).

And there were occasionally men who went against the patriarchal type of decision-making, exploring a more cooperative view on male-female relations, for a change. One such was John Okuku, who said during one of the Focus Group Discussions, that he was:

> Very proud that after registering our family property with my wife this has enabled us to work together and also live in harmony and our incomes have been increasing for some time now and we have registered all the children under the family property. My wife is also the manager of the family estates.

What Okuku's example shows, is that patriarchal forms of customary allocation may not even be the most effective from a self-interested standpoint for men. Enlightened self-interest and a more cooperative approach can reduce the gender discrimination that can be associated with customary law.

Unfortunately, such examples remain the exception, and all too often, implementation and respect for the law is overridden by customary practices. Thus it is not unusual to come across cases where the family head has simply transferred a title unilaterally, even where land was acquired through the joint efforts of husband and wife, into his own name. This process can lead to the male household head obtaining exclusive title, and then enables him to execute a land sale agreement, without the woman's consent or even her knowledge. Or the property may be pledged for the purposes of obtaining a mortgage, without the woman's consent or knowledge. Examples of this were also found in Busia, through anecdotal evidence from research informants, who know of such cases. Women can be displaced from family land, without notice, because a bank has decided to sell the security once the man defaults on mortgage payments. If a man has secured a loan on the land, on his own, with the bank, then the woman, children and local authorities can all be taken by surprise.

In theory, constitutional provisions and land law recognise and protect the interests of women, children and other vulnerable groups, such as the disabled, in relation to land rights. These legal protections apply even if land is held under customary rules, since such land is considered family land, and is formally protected. Legal provisions explicitly prohibit decisions about such land which deny women '... access to ownership, occupation or use of any land including conditions which violate articles 33, 34 and 35 of the constitution'. Unfortunately, these excellent protections are not always enforced in practice. What would be required to make these provisions more effective is heightened support from government and NGOs to ensure full practical compliance, and some provision for sanctions in cases of violation by individual men. This could enable more women to benefit from the protective intent of the provisions around family land, and thus to enjoy more equal rights of land ownership and use, as enshrined under the law.

Conclusion

In the context of the Uganda National Gender Policy (2007:13), which establishes a clear framework for identification, implementation and coordination of intervention designed to achieve gender equality and women's empowerment in Uganda, hopes among women's land rights advocates were raised in recent years. Yet what this study in rural Busia suggests is that women are reasonably aware of their land rights, and that the suggestion of Cotula et al (2007:1) that 'rural women always lack knowledge about the law', is wrong. Yet even though many rural women had a knowledge of provisions for equal land rights, the findings also made it clear that knowing about the law and its provisions for gender equality in relation to land, does not imply that women themselves, through Local Council Courts or some other means, actually believe they can do something about their unequal status, by challenging patriarchal norms in relation to the use, allocation and inheritance of land, especially customary land.

As Odeny (2013:25) elucidates, effective land administration eventually requires women's full participation in policy formulation and at an equal level with men, if an overall gender-equitable land tenure system is to be ensured. Participation of women in local land management and administration committees including land dispute resolution and management committees is essential for women's empowerment, since it enables them to take part in community-level decision-making. To ensure that land rights become more equal between men and women, and to ensure that women's legal rights do not remain only in their imagination, and on the statute books and conventions, the role of women in Local Council Courts needs to be placed back on track. Their knowledge of land rights is not always the problem; government can ensure, through requiring women's meaningful representation, alongside men, that this will form an important step towards more active means of helping women gain access to established rights. It is not just a matter of placing women in a certain position to add to the numbers on the committee. It is vital to ensure that these women's voices are then also heard.

When women in rural Busia demanded land rights, it was usually found that this was because they were concerned to ensure their family's food security, the family's bargaining power within the wider community, and the welfare and respect of the wider group. The Uganda government enacted laws that have shown that women's rights to land can be fully realised and protected through Local Council Courts in rural areas, if the political will exists to do so. However, it should be noted that these Local Council Courts do change and they vary, depending on their location and also over time, due to leadership changes with the election of new leaders. There are a range of duty bearers involved in supporting the capacities of Local Council Courts to enable women to realise their land rights. How and when are women's rights to land acquired? Is it necessary to start when girls are still young, or can rights battles still be continued after marriage in relation to husbands and the authorities? Who or what ultimately determines whether women obtain justice – or some degree of justice – regarding their land rights? Unavoidably both women and men, in different ways, have a responsibility to become an integral part of the implementation of land laws and land reform in Uganda (Odeny, 2013). Their efforts can be productive of change, provided that they are supported by the central, as well as local, government authorities.

References

Abel, R, L. (1982) 'Introduction'; in Richard L. Abel (Ed.) 'Politics of Informal Justice', *The American Experience*, 1:1-13. New York: Academic Press.

Adoko, J., Akin, J., and Knight, R. (2012) 'Understanding and; Strengthening Women's Land Rights under Customary Tenure in Uganda'.

Bakyawa, J. (2000) 'Women Threaten To Vote against Movement Over Land,' *Monitor* 22 (February):1

Behrman, J., Billings, L., and Peterman, A. (2013) 'Evaluation of Grassroots Community–Based Legal Aid Activities In Uganda And Tanzania: Strengthening Women's Legal Knowledge and Land Rights', Capri Working Paper No. 108. Washington, D. C.: International Food Policy Research Institute. Http://Dx.Doi. Org/10.2499/Capriwp108.

Bomuhangi, A., Doss, C., & Meinzen-Dick, R. (2011). 'Who Owns The Land?: Perspectives From Rural Ugandans' in Bomuhangi, A., Doss C., and Meinzen-Dick, R. (eds). *Who Owns The Land: Perspectives From Rural Ugandans And Implications For Land Acquisitions*. (No. 1136). International Food Policy Research Institute (IFPRI)

Cotula, L. (ed.) (2007) P.1-2 Changes In Customary Land Tenure Systems In Africa. London: DFID/IIED/FAO.

Daley, E., Dore-Weeks, R., and Umuhoza, C. (2010), 'Ahead of The Game: Land Tenure Reform In Rwanda and the Process of Securing Women's Land Rights', *Journal of Eastern African Studies*, 4(1), 131-152.

Daley, E., and Englert, B. (2010) Securing Land Rights for Women – Changing Customary Land Tenure and Implementing Land

Tenure Reform in Eastern Africa, African Studies Association UK Meeting, September 16 – 19.

Deininger, K., and Mpuga, P. (2005). 'Does Greater Accountability Improve the Quality of Public Service Delivery? Evidence from Uganda', *World Development*, 33(1): 171-91.

Doss, C., Meinzen-Dick, R., and Bomuhangi, A. (2013) 'Who Owns The Land? Perspectives from Rural Ugandans and Implications for Large-Scale Land Acquisitions', *Feminist Economics*, (Ahead-of Print), 1-25.

FHRI and HIVOS (2009) 'Promoting Access to Justice For Socially Deprived Women And Children In Uganda', Baseline Survey. Foundation for Human Rights Initiative and Humanist Institute for Development Cooperation Netherlands. Available at http://Www. Preventgbvafrica.Org/Sites/Default/Files/Resources/BusiaDistrict Baseline Survey. (Accessed on 20 October 2013)

Francis, P., and James, R. (2003), 'Balancing Rural Poverty Reduction And Citizen Participation: The Contradictions Of Uganda's Decentralisation Program', *World Development*, 31(2), 325-337.

Goetz, A. M., and Hassim, S. (2003), 'Introduction: Women in Power in Uganda And South Africa', in No Shortcuts to Power: African Women in Politics and Policy Making, Anne Marie Goetz, A. and Hassims (eds.) (1-28). London, UK: Zed Books Ltd.

Hunt, D. (2004). Unintended Consequences of Land Rights Reform: The Case Of The 1998 Uganda Land Act, *Development Policy Review*, 22. (2) 173-191.

International Alert (2012) 'Women's Political Participation and Economic Empowerment in Post-Conflict Countries: Lessons From Great Lakes Region In Africa', Accessed 19 February 2014 <Http://Www.International-Alert.Org >

International Centre For Research On Women, Human Sciences Research Council, Associates For Development (2008) 'Women's Property Rights, HIV And AIDS, And Domestic Violence: Research Findings From Two District In South Africa and Uganda'. Cape Town: HSRC Press

Khadiagala, L. (2001) 'The Failure of Popular Justice In Uganda: Local Councils And Women's Property Rights', *Development And Change* 32(1): 55-76.

Kigula, J. (1992) 'Land dispute in Uganda: An Overview of the Types of Land disputes and the Dispute Settlement Fora'. Kampala: Makerere Institute of social research and Madison: Land Tenure Centre.

Klaus, D., and Ayalew, A., D. (2007). 'Do Overlapping Land Rights Reduce Agricultural Investment? Evidence from Uganda'. World Bank Policy Research Working Paper 4310.

Kodhek, E., (2010) 'The Gap Between Policy And Practice: The Centre On Housing Rights And Evictions' (COHRE).

Land and Equity Movement Uganda (LEMU)(2012)

Manji, A. (2006) *'The Politics of Land Reform in Africa: From Communal Tenure to Free Markets*. London, UK: Zed Books Ltd.

Mugambwa, J.T. (2002) *Principles of Land Law in Uganda*. Fountain Publishers Limited: Kampala.

Museveni, Y. (1987) 'Why Our Laws Should Be Reformed,' *New Vision*, 3 March -7.

Nsibambi, A. (1998) *'Decentralisation and Civil Society in Uganda'*. Kampala: Fountain Publishers.

Nyamu M., C. (1999) 'Achieving Gender Equality in A Plural Legal Context: Custom and Women's Access to and Control of Land in Kenya,' *Third World Legal Studies*: 15, (3), available at: http://scholar.valpo.edu/twls/vol15/iss1/3 [Accessed 14 May 2014].

Odeny, M., (2013) 'Improving Access to Land and Strengthening Women's Land Rights in Africa'. Annual World Bank Conference on Land and Poverty 'The World Bank - Washington DC, April 8-11, 2013

Ottemoeller, D. J. (1991) 'Institutionalization and Democratization: The Case of The Uganda Resistance Councils.' Phd Dissertation, University of Florida.

Pedersen, R. H. (2010) 'Tanzania's Land Law Reform: The Implementation Challenge'. 2010: 37. Diis Working Paper.

Peters, P. (2004) 'Inequality and Social Conflict over Land in Africa', *Journal of Agrarian Change*, 4 (3): 269-314.

Ravnborg, H. M., Bashaasha, B., Pedersen, R. H., Spichiger, R., and Turinawe, A. (2013) 'Land Tenure Under Transition: Tenure Security, Land Institutions and Economic Activity In Uganda'. DIIS Working Paper 2013: 03. Copenhagen, Denmark: Danish Institute for International Studies.

Ravnborg H.M (Hmr@Diis.Dk); Bashaasha, B., Pedersen, R.H.S., and Spichiger, R. (2013) 'Working Paper', 30.

Rurangwa, E. (2013). 'Land Tenure Reform: The Case Study of Rwanda', *Conference On Land Divided: Land And South African Society.*

Schreck, C. (2012). 'Land Tenure, Agricultural Investment, and Sustainable Land Management: A Ugandan Case Study'.

Spichiger, R., Broegaard, R. B., Hundsbæk, R. P., and Ravnborg, H. M. (2013). 'Report on land tenure', Danish Institute for International Studies, (DIIS).

Tamale, S. (1999) *When Hens Begin To Crow: Gender And Parliamentary Politics In Uganda*. Boulder, Co: West View Press.

Tideman, P. (1994) 'New Local State Forms and "Popular Participation" In Buganda, Uganda'; in Gibbonr P. (ed.) '*The New Local Level Politics In East African: Studies on Uganda, Tanzania and Kenya*', 22-49.Uppsala: Scandinavian Institute Of African Studies.

Toulmin, C. (2006) 'Securing Land Rights For the Poor in Africa - Key to Growth, Peace and Sustainable Development'

Tripp, A. M. (2014) 'Women's Movements, Customary Law, and Land Rights in Africa: The Case of Uganda', *African Studies Quarterly*, 7 (4), available on-line: http://asq.africa.ufl.edu/files/Tripp-Vol-7-Issue-4.pdf [accessed 10 May 2014].

Tsikata, D. (2003). 'Securing Women's Interests within Land Tenure Reforms: Recent Debates in Tanzania', *Journal of Agrarian Change, 3* (1 And 2): 149-183.

Toulmin, C., and Quan,J. (eds), (2000). 'Evolving Land Rights, Policy and Tenure in Africa'.IIED, NRI and DFID, London.

UBO (2002) 'Uganda Demographic and Health Survey'. Kampala, Uganda: Uganda Bureau Of Statistics. Accessed 20 January /2014<Htt://Www.Ubos.Org_PDF.>

United Nations (UN) Habitat, (2006) 'Progress Report on Removing Discrimination Against Women in Respect Of Property and Inheritance: Tools on Improving Women's Secure Tenure', Series 1, Number 2.

Verma, R. (2014) 'Land Grabs, Power, and Gender in East and Southern Africa: So, What's New?' *Feminist Economics*, 20 (1): 52-75.

Verma, R. (2007) 'Without Land You Are Nobody,' Critical Dimensions of Women's Access To Land And Relations In Tenure In East Africa: 31

Villaden, S., and Lubanga, F. (eds) (1996) *'Democratic Decentralisation in Uganda: A New Approach To Local Governance'*. Kampala: Fountain Publishers.

Wily, L. A., (2003) '*Governance and Land Relations: A Review of Decentralisation of Land Administration And Management In Africa*'. London, UK: IIED.

Chapter 6

Land Rights in the Context of Post-War Northern Uganda: The Case of Amuru District, Uganda

Grace Angeline Chelimo

Introduction

Much academic and policy thinking about post-war reconstruction has stressed the importance of resolving land disputes as part of a wider resettlement process of formerly displaced people. This is to ensure that conflicts over this basic resource do not trigger violence, and are instead resolved through the law. According to a report by United Nations Human Settlements Programme (UNHABITAT) and United Nations High Commissioner for Refugees (UNHCR) (2004:1) housing, land and property rights are most crucial components especially during post-war peace building and an important aspect of democracy in state institutions which enhance economic growth. For mainly agrarian societies, access and entitlement to land plays a key role in the resettlement process and in enabling vulnerable rural returnees to derive a more secure livelihood. This study selected the case of Amuru Sub-county in northern Uganda (formerly part of Gulu district), an area in which land disputes are rampant, in order to focus on how existing legal and institutional frameworks are handling land disputes.

The factors behind different types of land disputes are identified, and how these were handled is discussed. Findings revealed that Local Council Courts were vital to resolving land disputes, though the process was characterised by a number of irregularities, which sometimes led to miscarriage of justice. Finally, the study found that the magistrate's courts play a vital role, and if speeded up, could be more important in future. The magistrate's courts were slowed down by the overwhelming work burden on their staff; yet people respect decisions by this court. Especially in the case of more vulnerable complainants, specific challenges were identified in addressing land disputes; perhaps the most significant obstacle was the high cost of accessing justice. The study concludes that in future, attention that is more critical could be paid to specific land tenure arrangements, land boundaries and registration, land ownership, user rights especially in relation to poorer households and harmonisation of the formal and informal justice systems. Within a post-war district like Amuru and within other, similar settings, land claims of large numbers of formerly displaced people will continue to pose a challenge in realising secure and just land rights for the near future.

Just as was the case in an earlier phase of history, the well-being of citizens and the state depend largely on a country's land law (Searle 1944:1). In Uganda, every citizen is guaranteed the right to own property under Article 26 of the Constitution (Government of Uganda 1995). However, prior to the enactment of the 1995 Constitution, in 1975, land was nationalised and vested in the Uganda Land Commission and it was only held in form of leases by people but this was later overturned (Mugambwa 2002:5). Currently in Uganda people own land according to four tenure systems, which are: leasehold, mailo, freehold and customary as provided for under Article 237 (3) of the Constitution (Government of Uganda 1995).

The Great Lakes Region in Africa has experienced armed conflict and political strife, which have consequently led to forced displacements with different humanitarian consequences (Huggins et al. 2005:1). Uganda underwent a series of episodes of violent rule, during the establishment of colonial rule, and the regimes of Obote and Amin (Dolan 2009:39). Northern and north eastern Uganda experienced civil war and insecurity for two decades from 1986 to 2006. The principal perpetrator in the war was a rebel group of a militia called the Lord's Resistance Army (LRA). This rebel group was led by Joseph Kony and waged a brutal campaign against the government of Uganda and the civilian population leading to massive displacements and a consistent pattern of Human Rights violations (evidence from HURIPEC (2003), IRIN (2005), UHRC (2001-2002), OCHA and IRIN (2004), UHRC (2003), cited in Ssenyonjo 2005:406).

The war forced people out of their homes because the entire region was under attack and it became very difficult for government to effectively protect its citizens. When rebel activities intensified, the government moved civilians from their homes into 'protected villages' during the mid-1990s. From 2002, larger numbers of people were forced into camps by an increase in rebel activities and by a government decree (Pham et al 2007:16). The 21 years of war were characterised by the destruction and displacement of more than one and a half million people (1.5m) forced to live in camps and settlements. Northern Uganda had been turned into a large-scale humanitarian disaster (Pham, 2007:1).

In 2005, the Lord's Resistance Army withdrew its forces from northern Uganda to the southern Sudan State of Eastern Equatoria (Pham, 2007). Rugadya observes that from 2007 to early 2008, there were improvements in the security situation in northern Uganda, after the Cessation of Hostilities Agreement was signed between the Government of Uganda and the LRA. Soon, people began to return home from the camps (Rugadya 2008:1). Since then northern Uganda has enjoyed relative peace. With assistance from international agencies such as the United Nations High Commission for Refugees (UNHCR) and the Norwegian Refugee Council (NRC), decongestion of camps began, and there was mass resettlement and reconstruction.

The return and decongestion of camps resulted in setbacks including growing numbers of disputes over land ownership and use, following the end of the war. Such land disputes resulted from most people, who had been forced off their land due to the insecurity, which kept them away from their land for many years. Many people found when they returned from the refugee camps, that other people, including some who had also returned from the camps, now occupied the land they had used and owned prior to the war. In some areas, a peaceful way of resolving these conflicting land ownership claims was found, but in other cases people returning from the camps found it difficult to settle down peacefully, and without dispute on the land they previously had owned or used before the conflict began. Thus, upon return various land disputes needed to be resolved, perhaps through a combination of traditional and statutory legal systems.

Given that land disputes became rampant in Amuru, it is important to study how these conflicts are being resolved, since this has implications for the enjoyment of land rights by parties to land disputes, as guaranteed under Article 17 of the UDHR and Article 26 of the Constitution (UN General Assembly 1948 and Government of Uganda 1995). Such disputes can also affect other crosscutting human rights provisions, such as the right to privacy, to a decent home, a fair hearing, and equal treatment from discrimination as provided in the International Covenant on Civil and Political Rights and the Constitution (UN General Assembly 1966 and Government of Uganda 1995).

This study is concerned with land disputes because they prevent some people from securing their livelihoods, render some people in northern Uganda very vulnerable and undermine successful post-war recovery. This study will inform various stakeholders on existing land disputes in Amuru Sub-county, and how they are being handled by local legal institutions in place, and identify some challenges faced in the land dispute resolution process, especially where the mix of customary and statutory legal arrangements is concerned.

Land Rights and Land Tenure Systems

Land rights, the 'inalienable ability of individuals and groups of individuals to obtain, possess and utilise land at their discretion, so long as their activities on land do not violate the inalienable human rights of others', have been outlined in numerous international human rights instruments agreements, including the Universal Declaration of Human Rights (Nneamaka 2009:16). Land rights entail the inherent ability of people to own, use, alienate, obtain and possess land without interfering with other people's rights (IIED 2006:1). The right to own property either individually or in association with others is provided for under Article 17 of the UDHR and Article 26 of the Constitution of the Republic of Uganda (UN General Assembly 1948 and Government of Uganda 1995).

As in most parts of Africa, in Uganda land tenure is either customary/traditional or statutory (Cotula et al 2004:2). Colonialism introduced different types of land tenure systems which are based on statute law which have very little to do with customary practices and laws of land use and ownership (IIED 2006:1). This greatly influenced land tenure systems, even if many systems were changed after independence to better fit local community needs and aspirations (Adams and Turner, 2005).

One school of thought sees the replacement of customary tenure systems in Africa with private property as enhancing capitalist economic growth, on the grounds that enterprising individuals and families who own land titles will be more likely to invest (Quan and Toulmin 2004:5). However, in line with the arguments of legal pluralists, in most parts of Africa research confirms that people aim to strike a balance by using both customary and formal land tenure systems (Platteau 2000, Coulibaly and Hilhorst 1994, as cited in Quan and Toulmin 2004:4). Each is resorted to, in a strategic way, if it can help to strengthen a family or community's claims over specific areas of land for both use and ownership.

In general, it seems that in practice, people's land rights strongly depend on the tenure systems. Land tenure systems take different forms but indicate the rights of different individuals to use land, the free and open access to land either consecutively or in a serial way. The problem is that the customary user rights over land are sometimes overlapping in a particular area or piece of land (Mabikke 2011:8). In the Ugandan context, on 9 October 1962 when Uganda became an independent state the land tenure systems were freehold, mailo, customary and leasehold that are provided for in the Constitution (Mugambwa 2002:2, Government of Uganda, 1995). The Constitution of Uganda, under Article 237 vests land in the people of Uganda who hold it according to the four land tenure systems (Government of Uganda 1995). Much has been achieved both at Constitutional and legislative levels in as far as integrating communal ownership of land and statutory tenure system though there are still some challenges in institutional management of land especially in war-affected areas like Amuru (Mwebaza 1999:3 and 4).

Among the different tenure systems in Uganda, mailo tenure is a system of land ownership which is said to originate from the 1900 Buganda agreement where the King of Buganda together with notables and protectorate government were given land in square miles (hence the name Mailo) (Barrows and Kisamba-Mugerwa 1989:6). This tenure system is unique to the Buganda Kingdom (Mugambwa 2002:2). On the other hand, the Freehold land tenure system was introduced during the Toro agreement of 1900, the Ankole agreement of 1901 and the Bunyoro agreement of 1933, when land was granted due to requests from various religious organisations (Barrows and Kisamba-Mugerwa 1989:6). This tenure system was common in Western and Eastern regions of Uganda (Barrows and Kisamba-Mugerwa, 1989). For some, freehold tenure of land offers more secure and hassle-free possibilities for transfer of property rights (Quan and Toulmin 2004:5). Another option is Leasehold land tenure which is a system under which a person gives to another an exclusive right to use land for a specific period of time, in return for a payment which can be periodic or paid in a lump sum (Mugambwa 2002:8, Government of Uganda 1998).

Customary tenure is a system where land is owned and organised according to customary laws and regulations and sometimes it is referred to as communal land ownership (Barrows and Kisamba-Mugerwa 1989:4). This tenure system is dominant in many parts of Uganda, mainly where mailo land is not the norm. Customary land tenure system is more flexible to the extent that it can better address the challenges of land scarcity and can enable agricultural commercialisation in some communities (Quan and Toulmin 2004:3). Customary tenure system has been seen by some researches as a means of enabling weaker groups to access land for use (Colin 1995, as cited in Quan and Toulmin 2004:3-4). However, one possible problem with customary land tenure system is that it cannot provide absolute rights, since some clan chiefs in some counties turn against their subjects and sell land commercially. This problem is not confined to northern Uganda or a post-conflict setting per se but it is common to areas in which customary land tenure is a norm. (Woodhouse et al. 2000, Berry 2001 and Amanor 1991; as cited in Quan and Toulmin 2004:4).

In Amuru district and more generally in northern Uganda most of the land is held under customary land tenure. This is confirmed by Rugadya who observed that over 90 per cent of the land holding system in northern Uganda is still under customary land tenure systems which are governed and administered through customary laws which are implemented/enforced by chiefs, and formal justice systems (Rugadya 2008:21). Customary land tenure system poses a challenge in that there is no documented evidence of proof of ownership of customary land other than oral evidence and boundary marks, if at all they are there.

Legitimate land rights are different and overlap in different countries and societies (IIED 2006:1). IIED further highlights that in some communities, individuals or groups of people can have a right to cultivate land, build a house or even donate it but have no right to sell or dispose of that same piece of land (IIED 2006:2). According to the principles and practices of Customary land tenure in Acholi which is the major tenure system in Amuru the universal land rights which accrue to all clan members are much hinged on utilisation and accessibility rights which include right to live on land, graze animals and hunt other than ownership rights (Kwaro Acholi 2008:18).

Between statutory and customary law

Various reforms took place in post-war in Amuru and other areas in northern Uganda. The first major decision was the creation of a Grade One Magisterial Court in Amuru District and appointment of a Grade One Magistrate to handle cases originating from Amuru district, who started work in October 2010 (Interview, Grade One Magistrate, Amuru on 23 July 2011). This was very important, as it enabled land disputes to be resolved within the district, so that not all complainants would have to travel to Gulu to file their cases (something the vast majority could not afford, given transport costs). What has proven daunting for this Magistrate's Court and for other legal institutions involved has been the problem of enforcing property rights, and resolving land disputes, given the sheer number of complaints (International Network to Promote Rule of Law (INPROL) 2009:1).

The Norwegian Refugee Council (NRC) and Internal Displacement Monitoring Centre (IDMC) observed that the Uganda government's plans for promoting durable solutions for returnees did not explicitly address the question of how returnees could obtain land in areas they formerly owned, which was now occupied by others. Apart from providing some supporting transit sites and camps, not much was done to smoothen the transition, sometimes leading to new disputes and forms of violence arising (NRC and IDMC 2010:10). The legal reforms undertaken by government to address the rapid increase in land disputes in post-war Amuru were not sufficient to resolve land disputes so that they would diminish.

To explain the different levels of formal justice systems, there is a short Appendix to this chapter (Appendix 1).

Besides the courts, the main institutions actively involved in mediating land disputes in northern Uganda include traditional leaders, religious leaders, Norwegian Refugee Council (NRC), Uganda Land Alliance (ULA), Uganda Human Rights Commission, Legal Aid Project of Uganda Law Society, Acholi Religious Peace Initiative (ALPI), and the Resident District Commissioner's (RDC) Office. Traditional leaders include clan leaders, chiefs and elders, who in various communities continue to play a very important role in resolving land disputes. This applies across areas in Uganda where land is held under customary tenure, and especially in northern Uganda.

One study conducted by Mwebaza (1999:5) indicated that Section 88 of the Land Act of 1998 permits traditional authorities and leaders to settle land disputes when these arise from customary tenure. Another study indicates that both Acholi and Lango have traditional mechanisms of resolving land disputes though the researcher considers the Acholi traditional system more elaborated than that in Lango (Rugadya 2008:12). The most important characteristics of such systems is their respect for principles of equity, promoting harmony and restoring social relationships between parties to land disputes (*Ker Kwaro Acholi* 2008:16). All these qualities make customary land dispute resolution mechanisms a vital part of any hybrid legal approach to land in a post-conflict setting and any other setting.

The resolution of land disputes in the traditional manner in Gulu was executed by the Rwodi Kweri (chief of hoes), and his authority is independent of the land administration system in the District (Mwebaza 1999:9). However, with long spells of displacement, the mechanisms that worked in the past, and had legitimacy have been massively eroded, and traditional leaders are no longer entrusted with full powers in resolving land disputes in the region. There has been a profound distortion of the purposes and meanings of customary laws and rights, expressed in their widespread misuse by certain families and clans for their own benefit (Rugadya 2008:10). Despite this, traditional authorities still play a vital role in the resolution of land disputes in Amuru, and even in their prevention.

There are also mediators, who move between parties to a land dispute with a view to helping them resolve disputes amicably and without formal recourse to the court system. This can be a very much faster (and less costly) way of resolving land disputes, and can also promote reconciliation between the parties, so that after land disputes are settled, the two parties can return to society and live together, side by side, as it were. Section 89 (1) of the Land Act (amended by section 36 of The Land (Amendment) Act 2004) provides for the employment of a mediator in each district (Government of Uganda 2004). However, in practical terms, mediators have not been employed by government, and are usually working on a voluntary basis, if they operate at all.

Finally, Uganda Human Rights Commission (UHRC) is also involved in the resolution of some land disputes. The Commission keeps a close watch on the property rights of Ugandans in cases where government moved to compulsorily acquire land from people, and for instance fails to compensate them adequately, as provided for under Articles 26 (2) and 52 (1) (a) of the Constitution (Government of Uganda, 1995). The Uganda Human Rights Commission Northern Regional offices are in Gulu, and people involved in land disputes with the government, often go for advice at the Commission offices.

Challenges in Securing Land Rights

Two key elements are necessary for rights to land and property to be secured by individuals. The first is that the rights should be legitimate, in the sense of being recognised as such by the local community. The second is that the state too must recognise and endorse the legality of those land rights (Toulmin 2006:4). Large chunks of land under customary ownership may thus be insecure because although the community recognises it, government may not legally recognise it (Toulmin, 2006). It is also observed that securing tenure and land rights for local people will tend to be highly dependent on the reliability and strength of institutions that intervene in the resolution of land disputes, including informal and formal justice systems, and civil society institutions (IIED 2006:3).

Unregistered interests in land

In practice, following displacement and civil war, it becomes very difficult to protect land ownership and user rights, since there is no documentation about ownership and little proof of ownership through boundary markings. In northern Uganda, as in other regions such as West Africa, the lack of documentation means that most land rights have to be claimed without any documentation, since as little as 2 per cent of the land is formally documented (Toulmin 2006:2). This research similarly revealed that many people in Amuru Sub-county have interests in customary land that is unregistered, and for which there is no written evidence. This makes it extremely difficult for these people to protect their land rights when they encounter land disputes given the fact that boundary marks were destroyed over time during the 20-year war and some people who knew who owned what died (Interview with staff of ULA in Amuru on 7 July 2011). This poses a serious challenge to securing and promoting land rights.

Thus, for example, under customary tenure system, land is owned communally, and most individuals and families do not register their individual plots of land, when it comes to subdivision of land among families or clans; this is done through agreement, and informally. According to NRC and IDMC, land in northern Uganda that was held under customary law, has mostly been held without the formal registration of any boundaries between the land owned by different persons. The problems of boundary disputes were bound to rise, however, with reduced respect for customary authorities and the loss of memory on the part of returnees to northern Uganda (NRC 2010:2). The customary tenure system thus served to create a form of vacuum in the land ownership system in post-war northern Uganda. In a normal situation, as before the war, informality was not a problem as there were many people in the community who would agree about the visible 'dividing lines' between properties of different households, clans and communities. Land disputes did arise, of course, prior to the war, especially on customary land given the informality of allocation practices. However there is no doubt that at least in Amuru, the two decades of war has considerably worsened the overall picture, and led to a significant rise in the number of land disputes, both those handled in formal courts, and by customary authorities.

One way of securing land rights is by registering the people's interests in land in a formal way. Toulmin indicates several different ways of registering rights to land, including through short-term certificates of occupancy, to formal registers and titling processes (Toulmin 2006:5). She emphasises that the state has the responsibility to manage and facilitate the whole process of acquiring land rights and should ensure that land rights at all levels are secured by the government going into partnership with local institutions in checking and validating land claims right from the grassroots (Toulmin, 2006). However, it is also very costly to establish such comprehensive and formalised registers of property rights. Besides, in most cases, given that resources are not sufficient, the pressure to define rights cannot be met through formal legal means alone, but must consider customary institutions and informal processes of dispute resolution as well (Alchian and Demsetz 1973, as cited in Meinzein-Dick and Nkonya 2005:8-1). Therefore government, Land Equity Movement in Uganda, northern Uganda Land Platform and other stakeholders should encourage customary land owners to register their land and acquire certificates of customary land ownership.

Breakdown in customary norms and values

Furthermore, for land rights to be totally recognised; the institutions that issue them have to be legitimate and socially accepted by the people (IIED 2006:3). Thus, to secure land rights there is need for people to know their rights and the state through its actors should then be willing to ensure that the rights and claims of people over land are legitimised. The findings reveal that cultural values and norms have deteriorated due to migration, with many years spent in camps, the death of many elders, and the current perceived lack of respect for elders among the younger generation (Interview with staff of ALPI on 4 July 2011). Another respondent observed that:

> War caused a breakdown in the customary values and norms which support the mainstream legal systems and traditional systems of justice...The young people no longer respect the elders who used to resolve land disputes...because they all underwent similar experiences in the camps and their authority and power could not change the situation (Interview with staff from ULA in Amuru on 7 July 2011).

According to Mabikke prior to the 23-year LRA war, cultural norms, rules and regulations which were administered by the traditional leaders used to provide security of tenure mostly for the elderly, children, disabled, widows and many other people. But due to forced displacement the cultural values have been eroded due to the death of most elders who were the custodians of customary practices and instruments before passing them on to the young generation which has resulted to the rapid transformation of Acholi culture (Mabikke 2011: 9). The current generation in Acholi Land is mostly composed of young people who grew up in the camps and are ignorant or have little knowledge of their customary land rights, never having seen how they operate in customary practice (Mabikke 2011:7). This poses a challenge in the resolution of land disputes and leads to inadequacy of evidence to prove ownership.

Competing claims/interests on land

Land grabbing, as it is sometimes called, or forcible acquisition of land, has been identified as another problem exacerbating land disputes in northern Uganda. One respondent during an interview revealed that the land which he had owned prior to the LRA war had been taken from him, and that he was never adequately compensated (Interview with a resident of Amuru sub-county on 7 July 2011). Land that was left vacant for many years, whilst the population was forced to live in camps, in northern Uganda, became vulnerable to being captured by elites illegally. This includes those who were in government, especially in contexts where people are unable to farm or even fail to return to their home areas. When they are finally able to return, they find that the land has been taken over, in some cases for investment purposes and the value has greatly appreciated (Alden Wiley, 2009; Foley, 2009; Pantuliano n.d.: 3).

In post-war northern Uganda, land grabbing is existent and it takes different forms which may include: borrowing of land, grabbing by force and intimidation, grabbing through gradual encroachment which has flourished because the people who were displaced lived away from their land for many years hence making them vulnerable and falling prey to entry of their land by people without their permission (Mabikke 2011: 16-17). Though unlawful entry of land and use is a common practice, the surrounding circumstance in northern Uganda are exceptional because people were not in actual physical possession of their land for many years following the LRA war.

The findings revealed that whilst the Land Board had granted leases to some people under the Constitution of 1995, they had not always completed the procedures (Interview with Judicial Officer, in Gulu, on 8 July 2011). People had applied for leases and were granted lease offers but did not complete the procedure due to the war. Subsequently, other people also applied for leases on the same land and were offered, and then concluded the leasing procedures (Interview with Judicial Officer, Gulu 8 July 2011). According to this informant, there were also customary ownership claims over the same land, in addition to clashing lease claims. Another respondent mentioned that:

> Some land was leased since the 1970s, the lease offers have since then expired, and the owners of the land would like to renew the leases. However, the challenge is that the land in question has been occupied by communities who claim customary ownership over the same land... (Interview with staff of UHRC, Gulu Regional Office on 8 July 2011).

Another problem that resulted in competing claims to the same land was that most boundaries on land were unclear or unknown, given the length of time such land had stood either uncultivated or unoccupied. This loss of markings and knowledge about the limits of land plots has contributed to a great increase in the number of boundary disputes between neighbours, and even among family and clan members. In some cases, those who had customary ownership have come into dispute with those who have purchased the land, which has been demarcated in title deeds. One respondent reported that:

> Most people are uncertain of their boundary demarcations because some of the people who knew the boundaries died during the war and most boundary demarcations were destroyed or have disappeared. Children who were born in captivity or whose parents died are not sure of where their parents' land is located and some know where the land is but may not know boundary demarcations (Interview with a staff of ALPI in Gulu on 4 July 2011).

Other respondents also stated that young people generally did not learn, or no longer knew the precise boundary demarcations of their family land, and sometimes elders did tell them, but they still claimed not to know, and then encroached on the land of other, weaker, or more elderly relatives. Sometimes, the elderly who know what the limits and demarcations of the boundaries were before the war, fear to insist on expressing this truth because they receive threats from the youth (Interview with Parish Chief in Amuru Sub-county on 6 July 2011). This problem of loss of historical memory and knowledge on land ownership is thus closely tied in with the problems mentioned earlier, associated with the loss of respect for elders which is linked to greed, corruption and loss of trust for elders by the younger generation who survived the camps.

Other challenges for land dispute resolution

The researcher inquired into the main challenges confronting conflicting parties in relation to how land cases were handled by formal and informal legal institutions. Findings revealed that in relation to the formal sector in particular, there were several problems, many of them related to accessibility and costs of accessing formal justice processes which are discussed hereunder.

The interviews conducted with some stakeholders revealed that some land disputes arose due to misunderstanding of the directive government gave to IDPs to return to where they were displaced from first. Since many people had moved several times, fleeing from one place to another in different phases of the war, some have returned to places where they had temporarily settled even though for many years, but were not their original homelands at the start of the war (Interviews with staff of NGOs and government in Amuru and Gulu July 2011). This fuelled some land conflicts in that different people have an interest in the same pieces of land, where some were settlers during displacement.

In addition, resources are a problem even for those who have a strong legal position. Thus, most complainants lack the money to facilitate the process of following up cases and for travel by witnesses to attend hearings, as well as for legal representation and court fees (Interviews with parties to land disputes in Amuru camp, ULA staff and Magistrate Grade One of Amuru on 6, 7 and 23 July 2011). It was revealed by the Magistrate that mainly due to financial constraints, when parties to a case fail to attend the court hearing on the appointed day, this led to adjournments of hearings, further delaying resolution of land disputes (Interview with Magistrate Grade One of Amuru in Kampala on 23 July 2011).

Moreover, it is worth noting that the High Court and Chief Magistrates Court are both located in Gulu, the Regional Centre. The distance from Amuru Sub-county to Gulu town is approximately 96 km and the cost of transport is approximately shs16,000/= (Sixteen thousand Uganda shillings), which is too high to be affordable by people without a regular source of income. Accessing justice through the formal judicial system is thus quite expensive and this reinforces the view that the informal (traditional) system of resolving land disputes is relatively easy to access, compared to the statutory court system (Pimentel 2011:64). It is worth appreciating the efforts of the Norwegian Refugee Council in offering legal services to complainants in land cases and facilitating their transport for court sessions in Gulu town (Interview with NRC staff in Gulu on 4 November 2011).

Furthermore, the research findings confirmed that some Local Council Court officials charged large amounts of money in order to resolve land disputes and to visit the locus. One party to a land dispute stated that in a particular case the Local Council Court committee members demanded one million Uganda shillings from each of the two parties before they visited the disputed land (Interview with party to a land dispute in Amuru, on 6 July 2011). From the researcher's point of view, even asking for such exorbitant amounts of money is illegal; such practices are clearly a major bottleneck to the realisation of justice in land matters, and should be subject to investigation because people are being robbed of money in the name of accessing justice. One of the respondents from the category of stakeholders argued that the fees provided by law, for those working in Local Council Courts are very low, and that this has made them more likely to be corrupt (Interview with staff of ULA on 6 July 2011).

Another challenge, which parties to land disputes encounter is that some Local Council Court officials are biased, and side with one or the other of the parties to the land dispute, irrespective of the relative merits of each case. For instance, one respondent said he did not contact the Chairperson of the Local Council Court because the person concerned who grabbed his land works with the Chairperson, and indeed is his nephew (Interview with a party to a land dispute in Amuru Camp on 7 July 2011). So given the close personal or family ties that LC Court officials may have, they will not be expected by the public to act fairly or in a just manner when such a land dispute is brought to their attention. Findings also revealed that in some land cases, for instance those involving land grabbing, occupants, and defendants may refuse to appear before court, whilst continuing to occupy the disputed land (Interview with party to land dispute in Amuru Sub-county on 6 July 2011). These kinds of challenges continue to delay resolution of land disputes in Amuru Sub-county and many other rural communities majority of whom are poor and vulnerable persons, yet justice delayed is justice denied.

Equally, for orphans, land disputes are difficult to follow up. One respondent, a young boy, said that it is very challenging for him to follow up on the land case since his parents died during the war and he had no income or anyone to support him in his claim to inherit their land (Interview with a party to a land dispute in Amuru Sub-county on 7 July 2011). Besides, he had no memory of living in the area. According to him, when he was summoned to court, sometimes he was unable to answer questions put to him, especially those related to boundaries, former neighbours or the size of the land he should inherit from his parents (Interview with a party to a land dispute in Amuru Sub-county on 7 July 2011).

Also in some of the courts, clerks try to extort money from the litigants, justifying this corrupt practice in the name of expediting the resolution of cases (Interview with a party to a land dispute on 5 July 2013). This appears to be a relatively common practice in Uganda, and is one of the informal costs of using the formal process. It is a great challenge to resist such demands for payments, especially since the clerks tend to be the ones who keep the case files, the ones who summon parties to disputes to attend hearings, and so on.

It is always especially difficult to identify boundaries because during the war, boundary markers like trees and fences were destroyed, and some witnesses died (Interview with a party to land dispute in Amuru Sub-county on 6 July 2013). This makes it very complex to prove ownership and boundary demarcations on disputed land. Findings revealed that the High Court does not provide timely and adequate funding for visiting the location, although it is a requirement that the location be visited before a decision is made. This also leads to delays in the dispensation of some land matters (Interview with a judicial officer in Kampala on 23 July 2011).

Findings also revealed that Local Council Courts are faced with several challenges and limitations which include lack of technical capacity to handle legal matters because most of them have limited technical (legal) knowledge and reference materials which curtails the victim's right to be heard by a competent court in accordance with Article 14(1) of the International Covenant of the International Covenant on Civil and Political Rights (ICCPR) and other legal provisions.

In conclusion, it is very clear that parties to land disputes seek for justice in different forums thus from the traditional institutions, religious leaders, mediators, Local Council Courts and Magistrates Courts among others. This is a clear indication that forum shopping is very common because parties to land disputes are always searching for a forum which can expeditiously dispose their cases without cost implications and technicalities.

Analysis of a Hybrid Post-War Context

This research has shown how a multitude of parallel, interconnected and overlapping legal systems can combine to form a hybrid form of legal pluralism that can help to understand the way land rights are determined under the specific land tenure systems that operate in a post-war setting. Combining legal reforms and institutional changes, the notion of hybrid legal pluralism helps to provide a broader perspective on how customary and 'modern' statutory systems of law inter-connect where land disputes are concerned. Since resolving land disputes is vital to the prevention of a recurrence of violence in the northern region of Uganda, the combination of the various components and levels involved in this flexible and hybrid system of legal pluralism, becomes the way that local justice processes are embedded and given social meaning.

Legal pluralism is a highly contested concept, originating in legal anthropology (Tamanaha 1993:192), and can be defined as a situation in which two or more legal systems operate together, in some way, within a society (Popsil 1971, Griffiths 1982a, Moore 1986a, as cited in Merry 1988:870).

In line with this definition, Griffiths defines legal pluralism as: 'the presence in a social field of more than one legal order'; we have clearly seen that this situation exists in northern Uganda and can be viewed as both a strength and a complicating factor in promoting and protecting post-conflict land justice (Griffiths 1986:1). From a longer-term historical perspective, legal pluralism arises from '...circumstances in the contemporary world which have resulted from the transfer of whole legal systems across cultural boundaries', and especially through colonial rule (Hooker 1975:1 cited in Merry 1988:871). According to Merry, legal pluralism arose from situations where colonisers sought to accommodate their own, imposed laws with a range of customary mechanisms they found in place, developed over generations by different communities (Merry 1988:869). In Uganda and the wider East African context, this study understands legal pluralism as a combination of statutory and customary systems. The concept of hybrid legal pluralism can be useful, since it does convey how customary and statutory law do not operate separately, in water-tight containers, but are inter-twined, combining perfectly the formal and informal.

Legal pluralism and hybrid legal pluralism can help to look beyond an either/or approach to legal institutions; merging of European forms of law with customary forms of law can provide better prospects for the future. Since customary laws can be seen in northern Uganda no longer to operate as they once did prior to the war, indigenous law needs to be rethought as well, given how it has been shaped not only by centuries of conquest, migration and extraversion, but also by decades of a brutal civil war and massive displacement (Merry

1988:870). Where once Europeans imposed their own law in Africa, grafting it onto indigenous law, today something else is needed (Merry 1988:870). Diversity means that hybridity may be a useful concept to add to legal pluralism, since as Popisil states: 'every functioning sub-group in a society has its own legal system which is necessarily different in some respects from those of other groups' (Popisil 1971:107, as cited in Merry 1988:870). This diversity is even more apparent today in the post-war communities of northern Uganda, than it was, say 30 years ago.

On the other hand, legal pluralism is viewed in the 'juristic' view as a particular problem of dual legal systems which was created as a result of European countries' establishment of colonies and the act of them imposing their systems on pre-existing systems (Ibid). When the British introduced a new legal order in Uganda, the customary system of resolving land disputes and tenure was not interfered with in northern Uganda, where resistance to British occupation was fierce and prolonged (Mabikke 2011:8). The two-decade war following independence weakened the customary system, however, and the dual legal system emerged as the norm, and was not viewed as a problem.

For the society, it could be argued that various hybrid forms of dispute resolution around land in northern Uganda could be an asset for the region in future. It allows different legal processes to be matched with varying tenure systems, and to attain coverage uniformity may not even be desirable, under such conditions. The emergence of hybrid and more complex property rights systems, and the fact that statutory orders can be enforced legally unlike the outcomes of a land dispute resolved by the customary system, may justify a more complex understanding of how different legal orders coincide to produce a hybrid set of institutions and practices combining formal and informal powers.

Many legal anthropologists are interested in how different types of law coexist in society; with legal pluralism, being the norm especially in tribally organised or highly segmented societies (Berry 1993; Meinzen-Dick and Nkonya 2005:8-11). More than one legal system is relevant in most domains of social settings and social life (Meinzein-Dick and Pradhan 2002:3). A legal system which is sound and stable must reflect the rule of law which covers broadly different values which include equity, security, justice and basic human rights protection (Pimentel 2011:63). In addition, even where it is possible to fit customary law within the ambit of state law, legal anthropologists argue for other, hybrid forms of legal pluralism. Thus for example, Pimentel recognises that when post-war independent countries struggle to preserve their cultures and norms, such struggles can be reflected in how customary law and institutions persist, intertwined with the functions of a modern constitutional state and legal system (Pimentel 2011:61).

In northern Uganda too, local authorities resolve land disputes in rural areas through relying on custom, and use formal legal institutions to back up land rights in various ways. The state apparatus can be used, but solely relying on formal institutions can mean high costs and a lack of enforcement of decisions, especially in rural areas (Meinzen-Dick and Nkonya 2005:8-11).

Although public access to justice institutions is integral to the rule of law, in most countries statutory courts are in the town centres, whilst most people with land disputes, almost by definition live in the rural areas. They may travel to the town centre and most of them cannot afford to pay for legal advice or representation. Studies done in Mozambique, for example, suggest that in practice, if land disputes cannot be decided in their villages then their claims may never be heard at all; they will resort to traditional institutions, provided they are still operating (Pimentel 2011:64).

Land Equity and Management in Uganda, an NGO, suggests that legal pluralism as it exists in northern Uganda involves the coexistence of two legal orders in which actors tend to try out different systems in order to find something that works best for them (LEMU 2011:4). People have at their disposal parallel judicial paths, which erode power of the customary courts. The source of power of the customary courts is derived from their authority, which comes from the respect they command. Such respect keeps customary norms and practices alive since their decisions are not legally binding (LEMU, 2011).

Conclusions and Some Modest Proposals

In conclusion, a combination of various factors has contributed to the conflict over land in Amuru Sub-county notably: breakdown in customary values and norms, and forcible acquisition of land by mostly rich people and government institutions, unregistered interests in the customary tenure system, contested leases, and unclear boundary demarcations upon return, among others. The appreciating value of land has created high demand for land since the start of the return process. Equally, expansion of families and death of family members have contributed to land conflicts. The other factor which has played a role is the misunderstanding of government directive for people to return to where they came from first. All these factors, which have contributed to existing land disputes in Amuru Sub-county, also apply to the wider northern Uganda region, including some areas less affected by war.

Land disputes in Amuru Sub-county are mainly resolved by traditional leaders, the Local Council Court II, sub-county Court, Magistrate's Court, Chief Magistrates' Court and in a few cases, even by the High Court in Gulu. It is often only once people fail to mutually settle a land dispute with the traditional leaders, who are both cheaper to access and more knowledgeable on boundaries, that they will resort to formal justice systems, starting with the Local Council Court II. Thereafter, if they remain dissatisfied, appeals can be filed in other courts at a higher level (as discussed in Appendix 1). Insofar as Local Council Courts play a vital role in the resolution of land disputes, sometimes cases are not resolved through the proper procedures, or in a just and ethical manner. This is because of widespread irregularities noted in the Local Council Courts, including bias, bribery, corruption, abuse of office, failure to cross examine, failure to pass decisions, failure to visit the locations where land disputes arise from, and following wrong procedures in court. Sometimes the court records are poorly maintained, and sometimes it is noted that both parties have won in Local Council Courts – a nice idea in theory, but not reflective of reality.

The Magistrates' Courts play an important role in resolution of land disputes despite the fact that they are overwhelmed with many cases of different nature. The study recommends that judicial officers consider handling the rising land disputes expeditiously, and that there is an urgent need to establish more specialised Land Courts at the Chief Magisterial Court level; as well as recruit more judicial officers, specifically to handle land cases in the specialised courts and in different districts, though the researcher is aware that this is a costly venture for government. In the alternative, operationalisation of the District Land Tribunals which are provided for in the National Land Policy 2013 is very appropriate, but they should be effective and efficient in handling land cases in a bid to enhance access to justice.

This study concludes that parties to land disputes and judicial officers, who try to resolve such disputes, encounter various challenges in the process of trying to resolve land disputes. Poor and vulnerable rural people, especially those who have returned from the camps after many years of absence, find it very difficult to access justice, due to the associated costs of travel, and the risk that money may be demanded by court officials, in addition to court fees, and fees for legal representation among others. Loss of historical memory related to land holdings and boundaries is another challenge, especially for the younger generation and those orphaned.

The state bears an obligation to protect the land rights of its citizens and ensure that they access justice cheaply and without undue delay. The government should establish partnerships and collaborate more closely with the community and NGOs to strengthen existing institutions that handle land dispute resolution, so that they can resolve land cases in a fair and just manner, protecting people's rights. Although the government may be working hard through existing institutions, much more is needed to effectively address the rising number of land disputes in Amuru Sub-county, and to better protect land rights the area and elsewhere.

Legal pluralism exists in post-war Amuru and other parts of Uganda through the different systems of resolving land disputes and the land tenure systems, which have developed over time. Amidst the rampant land disputes in Amuru Sub-county customary systems of resolving land disputes are weak and the legal system too is characterised with some irregularities, therefore the two systems ought to be strengthened and harmonised to better address the existing post-war land disputes. Moreover, considering the loopholes of customary tenure systems with regard to security of tenure there is need for massive boundary demarcation and registration to be done by government with the support of community and other stakeholders. Based on experience in Amuru sub-county, this could make for more clarity regarding historical boundary demarcations before the war, and can reduce the number of boundary-related land disputes arising in northern Uganda.

Finally, a number of modest recommendations can be made, so informal justice systems for resolving land disputes can become more integrated with formal justice systems. Already, the laws of Uganda recognise traditional leaders, but their decisions are not legally binding.

A widespread campaign of sensitising people about land ownership upon return, land rights, access to justice, customary practices and norms, registration of customary land, tenure systems and appropriate channels for resolving disputes, could be undertaken by government and supported by NGOs, elites, elected leaders, educated persons and councillors among others. These different awareness-raising activities should be harmonised, so that the different institutions work together effectively and improve their impact in terms of the protection, and promotion of the land rights of the most vulnerable community members. This calls for an active land rights platform or forum in which different institutions can meet and discuss various issues, lay down strategies and even review ways of working together. Further, government, traditional leaders, Land Equity Movement in Uganda and other stakeholders should continue raising awareness on acquisition of certificates of customary land ownership.

If more legal aid providers can offer free legal services to persons with land disputes, this would help greatly. Meanwhile, on their own, the Norwegian Refugee Council, Justice Centres and Legal Aid Project of Uganda Law society provisions are insufficient. They barely cover the entire northern region and the respective offices are located in Gulu. In any case, more legal aid provision needs to be planned, in case NRC withdraws or closes down its legal aid services in future; NRC remains the major legal aid services provider for returning refugees in the northern region. I strongly recommend that the state rolls out a legal aid scheme country wide which will enhance access to justice most especially for the poor and vulnerable category of citizens.

Conducting a baseline survey and establishing firm statistics about existing land disputes in Amuru would help establish data that are more accurate. The number of disputes reported to courts excludes very many people who do not report their land disputes, given that they cannot afford to pursue their cases, or lack confidence in the impartiality of Local Council Courts (LCCs). Most LCCs and customary institutions lack proper records of disputes handled. The Local Council Court system should cease to be politicised and court officials should be appointed based on merit. Perhaps retired civil servants could be considered for appointment to serve in Local Council Courts, which should be obliged to maintain proper court records so that cases can easily be tracked back during appeals. In addition, Chief Magistrates Court services should be extended closer to the people because those who wish to enforce decisions of lower courts or to appeal against decisions of the Sub-county courts from Amuru Sub-county now have to travel to Gulu which is expensive in terms of transport costs, hence hindering some poor people from accessing justice.

Another priority should be to create a system of mediation at the local level that could try to settle matters out of court, especially between relatives such as brothers, uncles, sisters and husbands and wives, as well as inter-clan disputes among others. This should happen if possible before cases are taken to court and parties to land cases should utilise the alternative dispute resolution mechanisms which are available in Court.

All Local Council Court members should be thoroughly trained in land laws and procedures, land rights, human rights, ethics, gender, legal interpretation and professionalism, and there should be closer supervision and monitoring of Local Council Court members, perhaps by Local Government, Chief Magistrates or Grade One Magistrates. I commend government for trainings that are ongoing but there is an urgent need to train all the LCC members.

Finally, laws governing land and land rights need to be translated into local languages so people can read the laws themselves. In a way they will better understand their land rights and procedures. Translation can have the additional advantage of reducing levels of mistrust and speculation by local people about the government and other elites intending to grab their land, or occupy it illegally. Courts of law should play a reconciliatory role, bringing parties to a dispute together, and making it possible for them to live harmoniously together, within the local community.

References

Adams, M., and Turner, S. (n.d) 'Legal dualism and land policy in Eastern and Southern Africa', UNDP International land coalition, land rights for Africa Development: From knowledge to action Nairobi, 31 October - 3 November 2005 (proceedings) www:undp/drylands.

Adoko,J., and Levine,S. (2009) 'How can we turn legal anarchy into harmonious pluralism? Why integration is the key to legal pluralism in Northern Uganda', Conference Proceedings Customary Justice and Legal Pluralism in Post-Conflict and Fragile Societies, US Institute of Peace, George Washington University, World Bank, Washington.

Barrows, R., and Kisamba-Mugerwa, W. (1989) 'Land Tenure, Access to land and Agricultural Development in Uganda'.

Available at: <http://pdf.usaid.gov/pdf_docs/PNABF246.pdf> (Accessed on 10 October 2011)

Cortula, L., Toulmin, C., and Hesse, C. (2004) 'Land Tenure and Administration in Africa: Lessons of Experiences and Emerging issues', International Institute for Environment and Development, London. Available at: <http://pubs.iied.org/pdfs/9305IIED.pdf> (Accessed on 15 October 2011)

Pimentel, D. (2011) 'Legal pluralism in post-colonial Africa: linking statutory adjudication in Mozambique', *Yale human rights and development law journal*, 14; 50. Available at: <heinonlinelawjournallibrary>. (Accessed on 11 October 2011)

Dolan, C. (2009) *Social Torture: The Case of Northern Uganda, 1986-2006*. Berghahn Books: New York Oxford.

Foley, C. (2009) 'Land rights in Angola: Poverty and Plenty' in Pantuliano S. (ed.), *Unchartered Territory: Land, Conflict and Humanitarian Action*. Rugby: Practical Action.

Foley, C. (2007) 'Land Rights in Angola: Poverty and Plenty', HPG Working Paper, London: ODI (Overseas Development Group). Available at: <http://www.odi.org.uk/resources>. (Accessed on 4 April 2011)

Griffiths, J. (1986) 'What is Legal Pluralism', *Journal of Legal Pluralism,* 1986 24. Available at: http://law.gsu.edu/jjuergensmeyer/spring08/bonilla_session1_Griffiths.pdf. (Accessed on 30 September 2011)

Government of Uganda, (1995) 'Constitution of the Republic of Uganda', Uganda Printing and Publishing Corporation: Entebbe.

Government of Uganda, (1998) 'Land Act', Uganda printing and Publishing Corporation: Entebbe.

Government of Uganda, 'Local Council Courts Act' No: 1 2006', Uganda Printing and Publishing Corporation: Entebbe.

Government of Uganda, 'Land (Amendment)' Act No: 1 of 2004)', Uganda Printing and Publishing Corporation Entebbe.

Government of Uganda, 'Magistrates Courts Act Cap 16'. Available at: <www.ulii.org/ug/legis/consol_act/mca232l>. (Accessed on 5 November 2011)

Hamre, J., and Sullivan, R. G. (2002) 'Towards Post Conflict Reconstruction', Centre for Strategic and International Studies and the Massachusetts Institute of Technology: The Washington Quarterly. Available at: <http://www.twq.com/02autumn/hamre.pdf>. (Accessed on 30 September 2011)

Huggins, C. (2009) 'Land in Return, Reintegration and Recovery Processes: Some lessons from the Great Lakes region of Africa', Unchartered territory: land, conflict and humanitarian action, Rugby: Practical Action. Available at: <http: //www.odi.org.>. (Accessed on 2 April 2011)

Huggins, C., Musahara, H., Kamungi, P. M., Oketcho, J. S., and Vlassenroot, K. (2005) 'Conflict in the Great Lakes Region-How is it linked with land and migration?' *Natural resource perspectives*, number 96, March. Available at: www.odi.org.uk. (Accessed on 30th october 2011)

International Institute for Environment and Development (2006) 'Innovation in Securing Land Rights in Africa: Lessons from experience'.

International Network to Promote the Rule of Law (2009) 'Forced Displacement and Housing, Land, and Property Ownership Challenges in Post Conflict and Reconstruction', INPROL consolidated response.

Jamii Ya Kupatanisha (Fellowship for Reconciliation), (2008) Framework for expanding the capacity to prevent and mitigate land conflicts in Uganda. Fellowship of Reconciliation: Kampala, Uganda.

Justice and Peace Commission (2011) 'Land disputes in Amuru District', *Justice and Peace* News. Monthly Newsletter, 1:2.

Ker Kwaro, Acholi (2008) 'Principles and Practices of Customary Tenure in Acholiland', Ker Kwaro, Acholi, Gulu. Report available on-line: http://www.land-in-uganda.org/assets/Acholi-PPRR.pdf [accessed 7 August 2015].

Klaus, D., and Raffaella, C. (2006) 'Incidence and Impact of Land Conflict in Uganda', *Journal of Economic Behaviour & Organization,* 60 : 321-343.

Land and Equity Movement in Uganda (2011) 'How we can turn legal anarchy into harmonious pluralism? Why integration is key to legal pluralism in Northern and Eastern Uganda'.

Mabikke, S.B. (2011) 'Escalating Land Grabbing in Post-conflict Regions of Northern Uganda: A need for strengthening Good Land Governance in Acholi Region', Paper presented at the International Conference on Global Land Grabbing 6-8 April 2011.

Meinzen-Dick, R., and Nkonya, L. (2005) 'Understanding legal pluralism in water rights: lessons from Africa and Asia', paper presented in International workshop on 'African Water Laws: Plural Legislative Frameworks for Rural Water Management in Africa', Johannesburg, South Africa (26 – 28 January 2005).

Meinzen-Dick, R. S., and Pradhan, R. (2002) 'Legal Pluralism and Dynamic Property Rights', CAPRi Working Paper No.22. Accessed on 13 October 2011 http://www.capri.cgiar.org.

Merry, E. S. (1988) 'Legal Pluralism', *Law, and Society Review*, Volume 22, Number 5. Accessed on 13 November 2011 http://heinonline.org/HOL/Page?handle=hein.journals/lwsocrw22&div=51&g_sent=1&collection=journals.

Mugambwa, J. T. (2002) '*Principles of Land Law in Uganda*'. Kampala: Fountain Publishers Limited.

Mwebaza, R. (1999) 'How to Integrate Statutory and Customary tenure? The Uganda Case', DFID workshop on Land Rights and Sustainable Development in Sub-Saharan Africa at Sunningdale Park Conference Centre: Berkshire, UK.

Nneamaka, A.D. C. (2009) '*Critical Mass Representation in Uganda*. Kampala, Uganda.

Norwegian Refugee Council and International Displacement Monitoring Centre (2010) 'Peace, Recovery and Development: Challenges in Northern Uganda'.

Okot, S.M. (2009) 'Comparative Analysis of the Traditional Alternative Dispute Resolution and Fomal/Legal Dispute Resolution Process in Land Claims and Allocations for the Indigenous Displaced Returnees in Amuru District, Northern Uganda', Phd thesis Preview: Royal Roads University, Canada. Available at: <http://search.proquest.com>. (Accessed on 7 May 2011)

Pham, P., Vinck, P., Stover, E., Moss A., Wierda, M. and Bailey, R. (2007) 'A Population Based Survey on Attitudes about Peace, Justice, and Social Reconstruction in Northern Uganda'. Available at: <http://papers.ssrn.com>. (Accessed on 26 February 2011)

Pantuliano, S. (n.d) 'Integrating Land Issues into Post Conflict Response: Case Study evidence and implications'. Available at: http://siteresources.worldbank.org/extard/resources. (Accessed on 14 March 2011)

Quan, J., and Toulmin, C., (2004) 'Formalising and securing Land Rights in Africa', Land in Africa: Market Asset, or Secure Livelihood?Church House, Westminster, London. Available at: <pubs.iied.org/pdf/G00166.pdf.> (Accessed on 10 August 2011)

Rugadya, A. M. (2008),'Unveiling Gender, Land and Property Rights in Post Conflict Northern Uganda', Associates Research

Occasional Paper No.4, November 2008. Available at: <http://www.oxfam.org.uk>. (Accessed on 4 April 2011)

Searle, W. (1871-1944), '*An historical introduction to the land law.* The Clarendon Press.

Ssenyonjo, M. (2005) 'Accountability of Non-state Actors in Uganda for War Crimes and Human Rights Violations: Between Amnesty and the International Criminal Court', *Journal of Conflict and Security Law,* 10 (3): 404-434. Accessed on 19 October 2011.< jcl.oxfordjournal.org>.

Tamanaha, B. Z. (1993) 'The Folly of the 'Social Scientific' Concept of Legal Pluralism', *Journal of Law and Society*, 20, Number 2. Available at: <http://heineonline.org>. (Accessed on 13 October 2011)

Toulmin, C. (2006) 'Securing Land Rights for the Poor in Africa - Key to Growth, Peace and Sustainable Development', International Institute for Environment and Development New York.

United Nations Human Settlements Programme and United Nations High Commissioner for Refugees (2004) 'Housing, Land and Property Rights in Post-Conflict Societies: Proposals for their Integration into UN Policy and Operational Frameworks', Expert Meeting: Geneva, Switzerland.

Unruh, J.D. (2008) 'Catalyzing the socio-legal space for armed conflict: land and legal pluralism in pre-war Liberia', *Journal of legal pluralism*, 58

United States Agency for International Development (2008) 'Geographical Assessment, Stability, Peace and Reconciliation in Northern Uganda' (Spring) Project.

World Bank Report (2008) 'Analysis of Post-Conflict and Land Administration: A survey of the Internally Displaced People Return and Resettlement Issues and Lessons (Acholi and Lango

Regions)', Available at: <http://www.oxfam.org.uk>. (Accessed on 20 February 2011).

Zina, O. (2010) *Essential Guide to doing your Research Project.* London: SAGE publications.

Part Three

Health Justice and Disability Rights in Uganda

Chapter 7

Health Justice and Gender Justice: the Role of Traditional Birth Attendants (TBAs) in Uganda

Florence Nyakaisiki

Introducing the Case Study

In Mpigi district, Traditional Birth Attendants (TBAs) were trained starting in the 1980s, first by Mpigi Health Centre IV, with support from the Ministry of Health, from World Vision and from Strides for Family Health-Uganda, the latter two being NGOs. TBAs continue to work in the District, but from 2009, the Ministry of Health has come up with plans to ban their work and not allow them to help mothers giving birth. Since TBAs are often seen as the only option for mothers in rural settings, especially those women who cannot access formal health facilities, the proposal to make TBAs illegal caused distress and concern (Katine, 2010). The District Director of Health Services (DDHS), however, revealed to the researcher that this decision to prevent TBAs from operating has not been fully implemented. Some TBAs thus continue to render services to women, and especially to those who cannot easily reach formal health care providers such as clinics, doctors and hospitals, during their pregnancy, labour and delivery. The DDHS further explained that, in the past, health workers used to supervise and monitor TBAs' activities but that they no longer do this because of the decision of the government that TBAs would be banned. Current uncertainty as to the status of TBAs, and the gap between their informal support during delivery and formal medical services may make safe and healthy delivery more difficult, rather than improving the situation for poor, rural women, especially in remote areas.

The Legal Framework and Health Justice

Health as a social justice issue emphasises the social and ethical aspects of health care and health status. Availability, accessibility, acceptability, affordability and quality of health care are vital in attaining health justice (UN 2000: Article 12). The Committee on Economic, Social and Cultural Rights came up with a general comment (Number 14) on the right to health. It explains that observing this right requires that 'operating medical care facilities, goods and services' be sufficiently available, accessible and acceptable. Accordingly, if governments do not meet these standards in basic motherhood services with existing resources, they are mandated to address the violations of women's right to health (Fathalla 2006: 416). Thus, the government of Uganda has domesticated the international laws into the national legal instruments like the

1995 Uganda Constitution which also guarantees the right to safe and healthy delivery for all women (Article 33).

Rights and duty holders, their entitlements and corresponding duties can be identified using the human rights-based approach (HRB) (Arbour 2006:15). Preventing, morbidity and extension of suitable services to pregnant mothers is a human rights obligation of governments (Boama & Arulkumaran 2009:126). As stipulated in CEDAW, Article 12: 'states parties shall ensure to women appropriate services in connection with pregnancy, confinement and post natal period, granting free services where necessary, as well as adequate nutrition during pregnancy and lactation' (Banning et al 2004:21). Article 12 of CEDAW tasks states to remove discrimination and injustices experienced by women when seeking to access health care facilities, whether during pregnancy, delivery, childbirth or in post-natal stages. In this wider context, what role can TBAs play in helping to achieve this set of outcomes? Paragraph 17 of the General Recommendation No. 24 of CEDAW, states that: 'the duty to fulfill rights places an obligation on states parties to take appropriate legislature, judicial, administrative, budgetary, economic and other measures to the maximum extent of their available resources to ensure that women realise their rights to health care'. Ideally this could include the skills and resources embodied in TBAs themselves.

Demographic and Health Surveys indicate that in many other countries with poor, rural populations, it is mainly family members, neighbours, community health workers (CHWs) and TBAs who provide assistance to mothers during delivery (Rouleau et al 2012:9). Such people are usually preferred to professional medical workers, who may be seen as strangers or outsiders in what is viewed as intimate and personal, rather than a medical event; medical staff are not usually considered part and parcel of local birth culture in Uganda (Kyomuhendo 2003: 20). In many other parts of rural Africa, TBAs are officially recognised as the first line of care for the rural population, and are even viewed as able to successfully implement official safe motherhood policies, including assisting in the prevention of mother-to-child HIV/AIDS transmission, for example (Homsy et al 2004:1723; Walraven and Weeks, 1999).

Taking TBAs Seriously

Whereas some countries have continued with training of TBAs, in Uganda the policies have varied, alternating between training and abolition. As Kamal suggests, all too often the role of TBAs has simply been ignored, or not taken seriously, in terms of providing them with support and training, and recognising them as informal health practitioners. The most important support they need, in his view, is: 'access to emergency obstetric care [so that they can] conduct deliveries and immediately seek help from the modern health workers when they suspect serious delivery complications' (Kamal 1998:45).

Additionally, whilst TBAs are sometimes viewed as providing birthing services and little else, Walraven and Weeks (1999) and Izgubara et al (2009) show that TBAs perform many other important tasks as well as actually delivering babies. TBAs usually pay several visits to mothers both before and after the birth, and may even help with household tasks (Izugbara et al 2009:43). Their research suggests TBAs also provide advice, including about family planning, food and nutrition, as well as providing help with breastfeeding, neo-natal care and occasionally treatment for minor childhood illnesses. TBAs can also encourage mothers to take their babies for immunisation, but only if TBAs are neither criminalised by the government, nor dismissed by the healthcare profession. However, the picture is not entirely rosy. As reported by Carr & White (2012:13), research on TBAs' role in Uganda has also found some evidence of harmful neo-natal practices, for example due to poor hygiene in TBAs' working practices during childbirth. Sometimes things go dramatically wrong, and the lack of back-up for TBAs and deficiencies in emergency services become very apparent as Nabagala explains during a focus group discussion conducted on the 10 August 2012 in Buwama S/C).

> I used to have a lot of pain in my stomach throughout my pregnancy. I visited the Health Centre III and I was told the baby was very tall and was given medicine to reduce the pain. When I was due, my husband called the TBA since she was nearby and we had no means of transport at night. But she was not able to help because I had hypertension and was bleeding, thus she refered us the nearest Health Centre IV in Mpigi Town Concil. Reaching the hospital there was no Doctor or Midwife to attend to me immediately and I lost my baby in the process.

Nabagala's case clearly shows what rural women in Mpigi district and Uganda in general can go through in trying to access formal maternal health services. Health workers are rarely to be found in health facilities, which are understaffed, and there is no ambulance service to transport emergency cases to the nearest health facilities. Any transport that is available is very expensive in terms of fuel. From one of the

Focus Group Discussions conducted for this study, one mother in Buwama sub-county of Mpigi District explained: 'The TBAs assist women in labour instead of women walking all the way to Mpigi Health Centre IV. Women used to die in labour but now each LCI (Local Council 1) has at least two TBAs (FGD, Buwama S/C, 10 July 2012).

Figure 6.1 shows some features of the present system, with key constraints on government, TBAs and local health services indicated, since all three are key actors in achieving safe, healthy and happy delivery for mothers. According to Figure 1, until these constraints on government, local health centres and TBAs are addressed, mothers will not enjoy the range of reproductive rights required for health justice to be attained.

For the TBAs to be relevant and address women's needs requires cooperation and teamwork with health workers to promote women's health justice. Thus the comprehensive role the TBAs can play in countering the discrimination and injustices rural mothers go through in health facilities whenever there is need for maternal services.

Traditional birth attendants should be looked at as duty bearers because at times they ensure the safety of rural mothers during delivery where medical facilities are inadequate and when the mothers persistently seek their services. And as rights holders, they also have their rights which are supposed to be promoted and protected by providing them with the necessary requirements like gloves, cotton wool, razor blades and others which they can use to help the mothers during delivery. If TBAs' roles and responsibilities are clear, the medical personnel develop a positive relationship with them, their rights are protected and respected, good results can be expected at the end of it all (Hoope-Bender et al 2011:10), and health justice would be realised by mothers.

Figure 6.1: Constraints on duty bearers involved in ensuring health justice for mothers

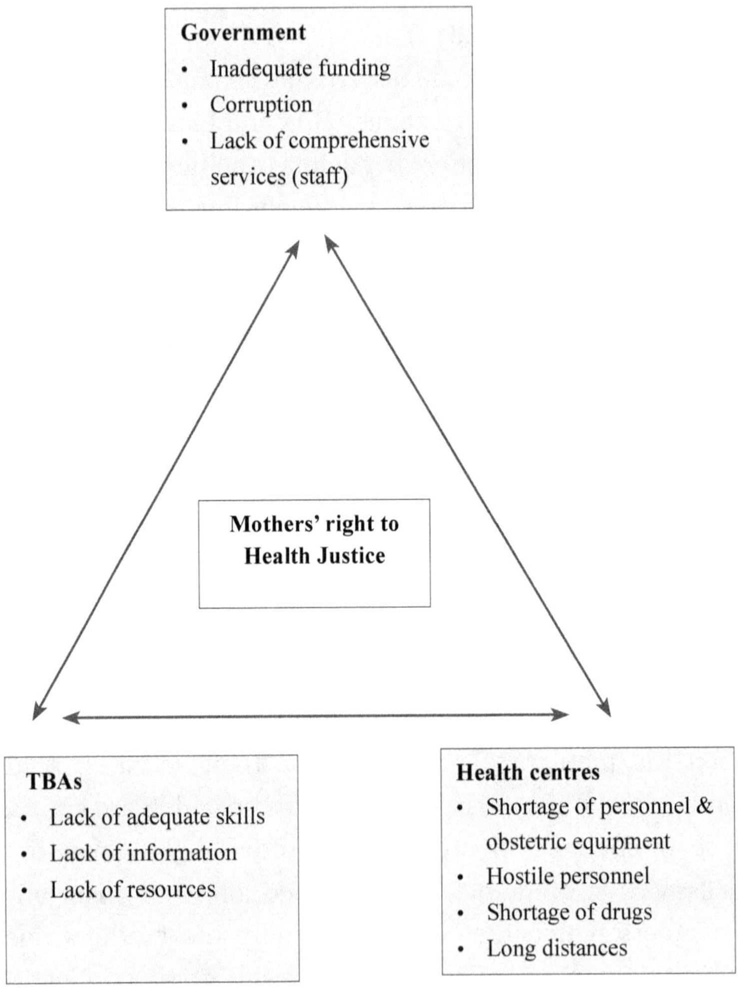

Source: Author's own design

Many believe that TBAs can be a vital link between women and the health system, giving advice, encouraging women to go to the clinic to deliver, detecting simple complications and accompanying mothers to provide them with moral support. While a qualified, fully equipped midwife at every birth is ideal, when they are not available the option of supporting and providing basic training to TBAs is vital to spot dangerous signs of child birth and refer women to health centres which can make incredible changes in communities (Rawe et al 2011: 5). This kind of strategy means empowering the community to be able to identify and handle their own problems whenever necessary.

The World over-promised an improvement towards maternal health within the Millennium Development Goals (MDG 5) – in order to bring down the ratio of maternal mortality by 75 per cent and provide global access to reproductive health by 2015 (Byrne & Morgan 2011:127, Khan 2009:123). In 2010, the health of women and children featured prominently at the World Health Assembly, the G8 Summit, the Pacific Health Summit, African Union Summit and other high level events. This global concern culminated in the Secretary General of the United Nations launching the global strategy for women's and children's health in September 2010 (Banning et al 2004:3). But still women globally, especially the poor and marginalised in both rural and urban settings continue to perish because they cannot access functioning health facilities or qualified health professionals (Hoope-Bender et al 2011:vii).

Uganda is no exception, and despite the existence of good policies on reproductive health, decentralisation of health services and collective efforts to improve the quality and delivery of maternity care services, inadequate resources and lack of skilled staff still make it difficult for many rural women to access effective healthcare in government hospitals and health units, especially during delivery. Despite such problems, Uganda's maternal mortality rate dropped from 600 in 1990 to 530 in 2000 and 410 by 2010 (WHO website, 2013), even though this is almost three times the MDG (Millennium Development Goal) target of 150 per 100,000 by 2015. Many thousands of Ugandan women die avoidably every year (Kyomuhendo 2003:16). Health Justice is a right for rural women and is also a highly sensitive issue since it relates directly to the lives of women, who form the backbone of the local community, underpinning economic and social development. Women play different vital roles within the family, community and at national level. In terms of giving birth, their priority, and the priority of a rights-based approach, is for women to have a safe and healthy delivery.

Maternal ill-health and deaths are attributed to a number of factors, such as limited access to blood and inadequate medical supplies, few qualified medical personnel, low quality of maternal care services, few health facilities characterised by inaccessibility, limited mobility as a result of societal gender norms and inadequate involvement of men in reproductive health issues (EASSI 2010: vii & 3). Because of the above prevailing conditions in most health facilities, many rural mothers resort to TBAs in their efforts to attain health justice in relation to a safe and healthy delivery. In short, this study sought to analyse the role played by Traditional Birth Attendants and how to formalise and reform their services other than by banning them completely. To ensure that rural women enjoy health justice irrespective of their economic, cultural and social status, reforms may be needed that bring TBAs into the formal medical system, rather than locking them out.

Mpigi District: Situational Analysis

The research on which this chapter is based was conducted in Mpigi district, around 50 km from Kampala, the capital city of Uganda. Mpigi is among the districts where inadequate health facilities, human resource and maternal health care are a significant problem. Specifically, Mpigi suffers from shortage of midwives and doctors, frequent stock shortages of essential drugs and the lack of any Emergency Obstetric Care (EMOC) services in Health Centres II, III and IV.[34] A qualitative study was conducted in two rural sub-counties, Kamengo and Buwama, and in the urban area of Mpigi Town Council, following consultations with the District Director of Health Services. The Annual Report (2012), Mpigi District Local Government indicates a significant increase in population which was estimated to be at 656,892 people. Mpigi district has only one referral hospital where women have to pay for maternal health care services since it is a missionary hospital owned by the Catholic Church located in Nkozi. Free medical care in case of complications would only be many miles away at Mulago Hospital located in the city centre, more than an hour

34 Health Centre IIs are found at the parish, treat common illnesses like malaria and provide antenatal care. The centre is headed by an enrolled nurse. Health Centre IIIs are found at every sub-county, led by a clinical officer who runs a general outpatient clinic, maternity ward and a functioning laboratory. Health Centre IV are found at the county, it is a mini hospital and should have wards for all categories of people. It is headed by a senior medical officer and there is a theatre for emergency operations.

away from Mpigi town. This means that other health services such as obstetric care services which are very important to women giving birth in Mpigi are at times difficult to attain.

The Tasks of TBAs

Most TBAs in Uganda, known in Luganda as *mulerwa*, learn the business of assisting women to give birth through apprenticeship or sometimes through more formal training. In Uganda, however, formal training is the exception rather than the rule, since traditional midwives tend to stay within their local communities and are well known to most of their clients (the mothers). As in general, worldwide, with medical midwives, TBAs are looked at as the immediate providers of assistance during pregnancy, labour and delivery. Given this, it would seem that phasing out TBAs' services without providing an alternative would mean social injustice that would impinge on the lives of the many – especially poorer and more remote – rural women who usually seek TBAs' services. Since health facilities may be malfunctioning or may not even exist, social justice implies that for health justice to be achieved by mothers in Uganda, the support of TBAs may presently still be needed.

Culturally it is a must for every pregnant Muganda woman to take herbal medicines. There are a variety of preparations used in different stages of pregnancy and delivery, which can provide relief from discomfort, restore appetite and treat ailments like dizziness, vomiting and body pain. Local medicines are also said to help women's bones to remain firm (the medicines probably contain chalk and calcium); the mothers interacted with included those who had already sought the services of TBAs, as well as those who had never gone to TBAs at all. This group had information about TBAs, however.

When I interviewed rural mothers in Mpigi district, they were full of praises for TBAs, and said within their respective communities TBAs played a vital role; indeed many vital roles. Among their main tasks was to assist with preparing herbal medicine for bathing and also for drinking, including *bombo* and *emmumbwa*, the latter which widens the birth canals to help faster and more successful delivery. Such preparations were also to clean babies and make their skins softer. Other local herbs TBAs provided for mothers are used for a variety of purposes like iron supplement, treating a ruptured uterus and all other kinds of ailments associated with pregnancy, delivery and post-partum recovery.

Some TBAs I interviewed for this study argued that most formal sector health workers and medical staff despise herbal medicine. Yet TBAs say there are some conditions which can only be handled in this way, and gave as examples the use of herbs to treat '*kamuli*' (jaundice or yellow skin in new babies). That is why mothers continue to seek TBAs' services in such situations. Some health workers also seek TBAs' services, as one of the TBAs interviewed reported: 'medical workers from Nkozi Hospital and Buwama Health Centre III refer women to me for herbal medicine and even midwives from Nkozi Hospital come and get *emmumbwa* from me', and she displayed the different types of *emmumbwa*. She then went on to explain:

> 'Our parents did not tell us the names of some of the herbs but we consult each other. We have *nabuguma* which works when the woman feels much temperature in the stomach, express

> (*emmenya*) which softens the pelvic bones during the delivery process and quickens delivery and *kigalanda* which protects women from being operated and helps them deliver through the natural way safely and successfully.'

Bukirwa, a mother in Mpigi Town Council who lost her baby from Mpigi Health Centre IV after delivery due to a high fever which was not detected early enough by the midwives, as well as other mothers interviewed and those in focus group discussions gave different reasons for using herbal medicine during pregnancy (FGD, 24 July 2014, Mpigi). These included preventing miscarriages, stomach upsets linked to pregnancy and treating sexually transmitted infections. Bukirwa, who visited both the health centre and a TBA commonly known as Mama Ssemanda, revealed that she went to her to get herbal medicine known as *bombo* to reduce pain in her legs, relieve her of the discomfort in the stomach and speed up the delivery process when it is due. Figure 6.2 shows a TBA who is holding a traditional herbal-mineral compound given to pregnant women: *emmumbwa*.

Figure 6.2: A TBA in Buwama sub-county, Mpigi District displays traditional medicine.

***Source*:** Fieldwork in Buwama sub-county, Focus Group Discussion with TBAs, author's photograph.

In addition to the above, TBAs play the important role of referring mothers to the health facilities because some mothers do not know the importance of giving birth from medical facilities when there are birth complications. They usually do this when they are concerned that the mothers may not otherwise deliver safely. As one TBA in Buwama sub-county explained:

> 'Due to infections we do refer them to the hospitals for medical treatment and even those who are already infected with HIV/ AIDS we help them to seek medical services because we are

> not perfect in controlling the scourge [to infection of] the newly born babies and in case of an emergency we refer the mothers to the hospitals so that they can go through a safe delivery' (FGD, Buwama S/C, 10 August 2012).

Another also narrated; 'For me in case of a rupture of the uterus I always refer them to the hospital,' but the next one said: 'In case of a rupture we have a leaf (*kikoola*) which is put on as a sanitary pad after bathing and it heals with time' (FGD, Buwama S/C, 10 August 2012).

TBAs agreed that there were complicated cases they could not handle. This is why they felt it was important to have a good relationship with medical care givers, including emergency health facilities. These relations are important so that the mothers are not criticised for going to the Traditional Birth Attendants. Also when interviewed, several mothers revealed that TBAs usually refer cases they think they cannot handle like mothers who go beyond the usual nine months of pregnancy, *prime gravidas* (1st pregnancy) and *multi-gravidas* (multiple deliveries) to ensure that likely complications are detected early enough and handled by trained health workers (FGD, Buwama S/C, 10 August 2012).

Another problem: TBAs and inadequate formal health care provision

During fieldwork, mothers who had been to hospital to give birth expressed their serious concerns about the poor hygiene conditions in the labour rooms in the medical centre. Their concerns were confirmed by observation during visits to the health centres. Mothers revealed that there was sometimes just one bed in the room, which women were using in turns.

There was a lack of privacy, an inadequate water supply and frequent load-shedding especially in rural settings, unless there are other sources of power such as solar. The same situation was described by a midwife of Buwama Health Centre III who lamented:

> 'Look at this ward! There is limited privacy and mothers get squeezed in one room. There is poor sanitation and hygiene all around the centre, it is bushy, we do not have solar power and at times we are forced to use candles. The sewage system became blocked a long time ago, there's no water supply and the mothers have to use pit latrines which are far from the ward. The two cleaners we had ran away because of the poor pay by the government and that is why you see the floor is dirty like this. (Interview, Buwama Health Centre III, 13 August 2012).

Given such appalling conditions, it is no surprise that TBAs are looked at by mothers as the best appropriate source of help during the delivery process because they are assured of what they need, namely privacy, humane treatment in terms of support and care, and reasonably hygienic conditions. TBAs in Kamengo sub-county in a focus group discussion at Butoolo Health Centre III mentioned that they usually encourage the pregnant mothers to attend the prenatal sessions at their local health centres within their reach. One confidently stated;

> 'We should make sure that the mothers who come to us have attended antenatal visits at least three times throughout that period. They will learn a lot and this will make our work very easy. Whenever they come to me, I ask them for letters from the health centres to prove that they have been going for antenatal checkups'.

Another TBA in Buwama sub-county said, 'We receive them, but we are only allowed to stay with them for two days. After that we refer them to the health centres' (Buwama Health Centre III, 10 August 2012). And a TBA interviewed in the same sub-county also stated: 'Me, when I receive one at night, I only help her at night, and if by morning she has not yet delivered, I refer her to the nearby health centre'.

However, besides the above contributions made by TBAs, some health workers insisted that much as TBAs tried to help mothers attain successful deliveries, most still lacked essential supplies like gloves, Vitamin K, tetracycline (eye ointment) for newly born babies and octocin drugs to control bleeding after delivery. TBAs also had no means of ensuring women could be transported to the health centres in case of emergencies (Buwama Health Centre III, 10 August 2012). The only available means of transport in rural settings are motor cycles commonly known as 'boda bodas', which are very uncomfortable and even dangerous for a woman who is about to deliver.

To the researcher, there is a basic contradiction in the argument around the role of TBAs. It does seem that given the major challenges facing the entire health sector in Uganda and in Mpigi District in particular, TBAs' care is no worse, and potentially much better. If government hospitals and health centres had ambulances, had reliable drug supplies and no shortages, if they were fully staffed, had plenty of *mama kits* and if mothers did not have to come with their own supplies of basic requirements, like gloves, mackintosh, razor blades and their own medicines, then it could be argued that women should always deliver in medical centres. However, this is simply not the case, at least not in Mpigi District health services.

This may be why some other health workers, especially those in Buwama Health Centre III, strongly supported those mothers who use TBAs at the time of delivery, because they admitted that the Health Centre lacked adequate equipment, including speculums, episiotomy scissors, artery forceps and gloves, catgut (threads), cotton wool and razor blades normally referred to as 'mama kits'. Understaffing is a serious factor, as pointed out more than once when discussing with the staff in Buwama and Butoolo Health Centre IIIs, where there were only two midwives per centre, to handle deliveries, offer antenatal services and carry out immunisations for children. The District Nursing officer lamented that:

> Inadequate staffing is a serious challenge in the district, and yet there are so many activities to be carried out by midwives for example scanning, PMTCT, offering post-natal care services, immunisation and counselling. At times I don't blame mothers who seek TBAs' services since at times we also have no way out', (District Headquarters, 2 August 2012).

The midwife in Butoolo Health Centre III also commented that:

> A health centre like this needs to have two clinical officers, nursing assistants, guards and others. But here we are so overloaded and every time we get visitors on top of our busy schedules' (Butolo Health Centre III, 9 August 2012).

Several health workers also pointed to the lack of drugs like antibiotics, anti-convulsants, octocin drugs and fansidar for prevention of malaria in pregnant women (Butoolo Health Centre III, 9 August 2012).

Many health workers in Mpigi did appreciate the work of TBAs, since they provide basic health education to pregnant mothers, support antenatal care, handle deliveries, and get involved in treatment of minor illnesses related to pregnancy and the newly born, by administering traditional medicines. The District Nursing officer in charge of maternal and child health care at the district clearly stated that:

> TBAs have good care, and the patient-TBA relationship is good. They give them hot water, food, rub their back and soothe them during labour pains, unlike health workers who are always too busy attending to so many mothers with different needs. TBAs normally attend to few and serve them effectively. Mothers have trust in old women and they stay within their localities. They spend less in terms of transport and little time is consumed' (District Headquarters, 2nd August 2012).

The mothers also reported that TBAs' services are effective since they can even work upon a prolonged labour as one mother explained during a focus group discussion at Butoolo Health Centre III:

> I trust the services of TBAs because one time I happened to go through a prolonged labour. The TBA insisted that I go to the health centre and I refused. After a day she gave me some herbal medicine which helped me to deliver immediately and successfully (Kamengo S/C, 9 August 2012).

Another mother gave her own experience as follows:

> Yes I have [once] visited a TBA because the stomach was paining me and when I visited the TBA she told me that the baby was not in a normal position and referred me to the hospital to avoid further complications and also gave me local herbs (*emmumbwa*). When I used the *emmumbwa*, the pain

reduced but the baby remained below the right position. I later went to the hospital'.

A Holistic Care Model: TBAs as Role Models for the Formal Sector

Many mothers pointed out that TBAs assisted them with health education, providing them with information about food and nutrition, sanitation and hygiene, family planning and offering immediate help in case of a sudden sickness before reaching the health centres, or illness of the new-born baby. TBAs are appreciated because they not only help prepare women for the delivery, but they are always welcoming and supportive whilst they do so, as well as during the birth, and in the postpartum period (Kamengo S/C, 9 August 2012).

Focus Groups with TBAs also confirmed that they see it as their responsibility to educate mothers-to-be about antenatal care services available in the hospitals, about effective use of drugs as recommended by health workers, for instance iron tablets, blood supplement tablets, malaria treatment drugs and so on. TBAs also bring mothers food, show them love during the time of labour and use friendly language towards them, avoiding being rough, as is sometimes the case in the formal health sector (Kamengo S/C, 13 August 2012).

After the birth, TBAs conduct follow-up visits to mothers' homes and check how well they are managing to breast feed, encouraging them to keep themselves and the babies clean. TBAs pointed out that mothers prefer their services because of their hospitality, and do not find the staff are able to show them such kindness in hospitals and health centres. TBAs pride themselves on being accessible, and always available, and mothers can also avoid the inadequate and at times very expensive transport to the nearest health centre. In addition, TBAs offer motherly counselling and guidance.

As Betty, a mother in Kamengo sub-county commented during a focus group discussion at Buwama health centre:

> These are people who can talk to us freely, console and comfort us. They help us during troublesome conditions especially at night, they are always available and enable women to deliver safely and successfully' (Buwama Health Centre III, 15 August 2012).

Even so, in spite of all their hard work and care, TBAs still face challenges from uncooperative and hostile attitudes of some medical staff. TBAs also have limited resources and usually lack the requisites such as gloves, scissors, cotton wool, forceps, razor blades and a mackintosh to serve as a water proof sheet. Most homes lack electric power and safe, running water, thus most TBAs will use kerosene lamps which can be expensive and pose a fire hazard for mothers and newly born babies. Some of them lack private rooms where mothers can deliver, and transport for emergencies can be a major challenge.

As citizens of Uganda, who supplement trained health workers, TBAs work almost without pay and are entitled to some appreciation and respect for what they do. They play an important role in expecting mothers' lives, and could at little additional cost be provided with basic requirements such as mama kits, safe water and power, and private rooms so that they could improve their level of health care for mothers. If TBAs were nationally recognised as other workers and could operate freely without threats of criminalisation from government, this could significantly improve rural maternal health service delivery.

Perhaps the key point here is that different duty bearers such as governments, health centres and TBAs can share the overarching responsibility to ensure that women achieve health justice and are able to have a safe and happy delivery. Although government is the primary duty bearer, TBAs' efforts and those of medical workers are how government support is translated into practice. Based on the research that was conducted since completing the first version of this study, I have been able to devise the following model of the overall problems that beset maternal health care in Mpigi District.

TBAs in Uganda: Improvement or Replacement?

Different initiatives have been established as part of building a supportive community network of TBAs, who can supplement the formal maternal health system, detect high risk obstetric complications and act as a localised referral system for health centres (Ssengooba et al. ND:6). Safe motherhood implies not only accessibility to maternal health care, but also protecting women from violence during pregnancy (Khan 2009:134). As Khan argues:

> There's a clear human rights case for safe motherhood. The right to health is well established in International law. Neglect, denial, discrimination and violence that take place before, during and after pregnancy are injustices done on women's lives. An overwhelming majority of countries have ratified International treaties committing themselves to end such injustices. Maternal mortality is not a social problem that 'just happens' - it is a terrible social injustice that must be ended (Khan 2009: 139).

Traditional Birth Attendants extend their services to rural women experiencing such multiple injustices, and TBAs end up providing holistic sexual, maternal and reproductive health advice and what care they can (Nyanzi et al. 2007: 319). In Uganda, the majority of poor, rural women go to TBAs for antenatal care. These women generally give birth in their own homes, with the assistance of TBAs who have very little formal training (Ssengooba et al. ND:26). Some studies have suggested that despite all the interventions put in place by WHO, UNICEF, USAID, UNFPA and by various NGOs, there is still the need for more training, so that skilled birth attendants, adequate medical supplies and emergency obstetric equipments and care are available locally, so that women in Uganda can realise health justice (Mbonye et al, 2007, cited in Carr and White, 2012:13).

Traditional Birth Attendants educate mothers about food and nutrition, family planning, breast feeding, immunisation and prevention of sexually transmitted infections (Kamal 1998: 50). They provide such services to the mothers to ensure that they are not malnourished, develop strong immunity systems to fight complicated ailments during pregnancy and ensure safe and happy delivery without any complications which might be dangerous to their babies as well. In developing countries, the rural population that depends on TBAs needs to be recognised as a reality that will remain acceptable, well-trained, qualified, accessible and economically friendly substitute is availed, not only to urban but also to rural settings. TBAs thus constitute major actors in the overall health care system. Kamal argues that, while other TBAs' practices are positively harmless, there are others which are associated with a lot of risks leading to maternal or infant morbidity and mortality. They are not always deliberate and most of them work with rightful intentions but at times with inadequate understanding (Kamal 1998:45) and lack of immediate support from professional medical personnel in the formal sector, as this study also revealed.

However, the abolitionist approach of the government of Uganda, in trying to ban TBAs' services altogether will probably not help rural women attain health justice, unless the quality of formal maternal health care is significantly improved. Otherwise, the banning policy infringes on expectant and newly delivered women's basic rights to health. If an appropriate substitute for TBAs is not provided, then the result will almost unavoidably be increased maternal mortality levels across the country.

Concluding Recommendations

The main objective of this study was to explore and understand the contribution of Traditional Birth Attendants to health justice for rural mothers in Mpigi District in Uganda. A number of good public policies have been formulated regarding gender equity, UPE (Universal Primary Education), reproductive health and decentralisation of health services. Chronic and longer-term underfunding of the health sector in Uganda has resulted in local problems of drug shortages, a lack of medical equipment, poor infrastructure, inadequate medical personnel in maternal care units and contributed to the increasing rate of maternal mortality which still stood at 410/100,000 live births in 2010, almost three times the MDG goal of 150 per 100,000 by 2015, as noted earlier. In view of this, it is not surprising that Uganda's maternal mortality rate remains high. Despite such a situation, the government of Uganda is trying to ban TBAs' services. If mothers risk criminalisation when they ask for help from TBAs because they cannot access formal health facilities, or do not want to go there during delivery, because of lack of care and hygiene, then this will not improve the overall situation of poor, rural mothers. It would push the attaintment of health justice even further away into the future. TBAs should therefore be taken as role models, and as ideal partners, and be trained. They should not be regarded as competitors or rivals in the maternal health care system. They are also busy working for health justice for rural women, and are a means to enable most expectant mothers to attain an acceptable and safe birth experience, and basic after-care.

The emphasis should not be on training TBAs and providing them with basic essential equipment. Some formal sector health workers should also change their negative attitudes towards TBAs, since these women can help the formal services to improve their own performance, and to meet their responsibilities in terms of health care delivery in emergencies. Offering TBAs the support they require means that at local level, they will be able to provide improved quality services, remaining accessible and acceptable to local mothers and mothers-to-be (Leedam 1985: 259). To improve the quality of care, TBAs themselves are vital to any realistic strategy that aims to further improve the quality of maternal health care. They can even act as informal researchers, since they gather and disseminate information about the maternal health needs and perceptions of local women in the community (UNPF 1996: 8). The government of Uganda therefore should adopt the reformist approach involving equipping and empowering TBAs with medical training to enable them carry out safe and efficient deliveries other than victimising their services, and supervise their activities such that rural women are able to attain health justice.

References

Arbour, L. (2006) 'Frequently Asked Questions on a Human Rights-Based Approach to Development Cooperation', *Office of the UN High Commissioner for Human Rights. Retrieved May* 30: 2007.

Banning, T. R. G., Sepúlveda, M., Gudmundsdóttir, G., and Chamoun C. (2004) *'Human Rights Instruments'*. University of Peace.

Boama, V., and Arulkumaran, S. (2009) 'Safer Childbirth: A Rights-Based Approach', *International Journal of Gynecology & Obstetrics,* 106 (2): 125-127.

Byrne, A., and Morgan, A. (2011) 'How the Integration of Traditional Birth Attendants with Formal Health Systems can Increase Skilled Birth Attendance', *International Journal of Gynecology & Obstetrics,* 115 (2): 127-134.

Carr, K. C., and White R. (2012) 'Focus Group and Health Teaching with Traditional Birth Attendants in Njeru, Uganda', *International Journal of Childbirth,* 2 (1): 12-19.

EASSI (2010) 'Monitoring Maternal Health and Safe Motherhood Policies; Policy Making in Practice: What can be learned from Uganda's National Budget Implementation?' Policy Issue Paper No. 2.

Fathalla, M.F. (2006) 'Human Rights Aspects of Safe Motherhood', *Baillière's best practice & research, Clinical obstetrics & gynaecology,* 20(3): 409-419.

Homsy, J., King, R., Balaba, D., and Kabatesi, D. (2004) 'Traditional Health Practitioners are Key to Scaling Up Comprehensive Care for HIV/AIDS in Sub-Saharan Africa', *Aids,* 18 (12): 1723-1725.

Hoope-Bender, P., Campbell J., Fauveau V., and Matthews, Z. (2011) 'The State of the World's Midwifery 2011: Delivering Health, Saving Lives', *International Journal of Gynecology & Obstetrics,* 114(3): 211-212.

Izugbara, C., Ezeh, A. and Fotso, J. C. (2009) 'The Persistence and Challenges of Homebirths: Perspectives of Traditional Birth Attendants in Urban Kenya', *Health policy and planning,* 24(1): 36-45.

Kamal, I. (1998) 'The Traditional Birth Attendant: A Reality and a Challenge', *International Journal of Gynecology & Obstetrics,* 63: S43-S52.

Katine (2010) 'Should Uganda ban Traditional Birth Attendants'? Katine-Chronicles Blog (Weblog); March 30, 2010, accessed on 27 January 2010. http://www.guardian.co.uk/katine-chronicles-blog/2010/mar/30/traditional-birth-attendants-ban

Khan, I. (2009) *The Unheard Truth: Poverty and Human Rights.* New York: WW Norton & Company.

Kyomuhendo, G.B. (2003) 'Low use of Rural Maternity Services in Uganda: Impact of Women's Status, Traditional Beliefs and Limited Resources', *Reproductive health matters,* 11(21): 16-26.

Leedam, E. (1985) 'Traditional Birth Attendants', *International Journal of Gynecology & Obstetrics,* 23(4): 249-274. Mbaruku, G., B. Msambichaka, S. Galea, P. C. Rockers and M.E. Kruk (2009) 'Dissatisfaction with Traditional Birth Attendants in Rural

Tanzania', *International Journal of Gynecology & Obstetrics* 107 (1): 8-11.

Nyanzi, S., Bah, O., Joof, S., and Walraven G. (2007) 'Ethnography and PRA among Gambian Traditional Birth Attendants: A Methods Discussion', *Qualitative Research,* 7(3): 317-326.

Rawe, K., Kerber, K., Lawn, J., and Williams, S. (2011) 'Missing Midwives'. Save the children UK.

Rouleau, D., Fournier, P., Philibert, A., Mbengue, B., and Dumont, A. (2012) 'The Effects of Midwives' Job Satisfaction on Burnout, Intention to Quit and Turnover: A Longitudinal Study in Senegal', *Human Resources for Health*, 10(1): 9.

'United Nations (2000) 'General Comment no. 14: The Right to the Highest Attainable Standard of Health (Art. 12 of the Covenant)'. Accessed 10 November 2012 <http://www.unhcr.org/cgi-bin/texis/vtx/refworld/rwmain?docid=4538838d0&page=search>.

Weeks, A., Lavender, T., Nazziwa, E., and Mirembe, F. (2005) 'Personal Accounts of 'near-miss' Maternal Mortalities in Kampala, Uganda', *BJOG: An International Journal of Obstetrics & Gynaecology*, 112(9): 1302-1307.

WHO website (2013) 'Global Health Observatory Data Repository', at: http://apps.who.int/gho/data/?theme=country&vid=20300 (accessed 14 Feb 2014).

Chapter 8

Disability and Social Justice: The Role of Refugee Leaders in Enhancing Access to Social Justice by Refugees with Disability.

Jimmy Mugisha Maguru

Introduction

Social justice connotes the recognition of dignity of every human being irrespective of physical capability and requires their inclusion in the social, cultural, and economic life of the community. Respect for principles of equality, human rights, access to services and participation should apply, and international human rights law provides for those rights that should be enjoyed by every individual in order to lead a decent life. These human rights apply to all situations, whether during peace time or war time, and they apply regardless of gender, race, ethnicity, religion, nationality, citizenship, language, sexual orientation, and physical or mental abilities (Lomo, 2000).

The ultimate aim of social justice in relation to refugees with disability is to ensure that they have full and equal access to all mainstream services available, and that these services are accessible and inclusive. As such, agencies concerned with promoting the improvement of their wellbeing should recognise that refugees with disablity have a legitimate claim to life's essentials such as food, water, health care, education, freedom of expression, political participation, and personal security.

The humanitarian approach remains the major focus for the various humanitarian agencies working with refugees in Uganda as opposed to the development oriented approach where refugees' long term needs are considered and planned for by the concerned agencies. This has created challenges for refugees with disabilities and has left them disempowered, dependent on caregivers, and unable to find employment. The attitudinal factors particularly show a disregard for Persons with Disabilities' (PWDs), suggesting that their equal access to services and rights remains a profound social justice challenge.

The aim of this study was to find out whether Persons with Disabilities (PWDs) in a specific refugee settlement in Uganda were enjoying their rights, accessing services and participating in all mainstream activities in their communities, in comparison to other able-bodied refugees. Critical was to find out the role of refugee leaders and stakeholders in helping to make refugees with disabilities more visible as a minority and marginalised group. Similarly, the study establishes leadership issues relating to realising rights of disabled refugees and general access to available services within the settlement. The chapter looks at what has been done – and what has not been done - to improve the wellbeing of refugees with disability. It should be borne in mind that they have unique needs, which are distinct from the needs of other special or vulnerable categories of persons with special needs (PSNs). The concerns of this minority group of refugees are outlined, and ways for them to be empowered through inclusion strategies, are explored.

The article considers the different levels of refugee leadership; known as Refugee Welfare Committees (RWCs) of nine people; elected at village level, sub-zone and zone levels. This is the equivalent to the decentralised local government levels from one to three. This study uses the inclusive approach to assess whether the refugees with disabilities are included in the mainstream settlement activities and, are able to access, and utilise the available services. This study uses mainly qualitative research methods including document review, field observations, focus group discussions, and interviews, to collect data. It is intended that the findings will provide information needed by the Office of the Prime Minister (OPM), refugee leadership in the settlement, and for humanitarian NGOs involved in provision of services to refugees in general and 'Refugee's with Disabilities' (RWDs) in particular. The hope is that with this information, they will be better able to develop mechanisms for integrating user-friendly services for refugees with disabilities and that this can ease the disabled refugees' access to social justice. The study also contributes to scholarly debates around how refugees with disability can be understood and supported, in Uganda in particular and in general.

The first section of the paper introduces the concepts of disability, refugees and social justice and gives a theoretical framework. It then introduces the refugee situation in Uganda and the prevailing legal instruments. This is followed by a discussion on accessibility of PWDs to services, a look at attitudes which hinder their empowerment, and then the challenges associated with enjoyment of human rights by PWDs are pointed out. It concludes that not only is there a need to transform from humanitarian to development oriented approaches in order to increase the participation of PWDs in the mainstream activities, equally, it is vital to recognise the uniqueness of the persons with disabilities in order to tackle their unique needs with the urgency they deserve.

The Refugee situation in Uganda

Under the 1951 Refugee Convention, a refugee is someone who has fled their country 'owing to well-founded fear of being persecuted for reasons of race, religion, nationality, membership of a particular social group or political opinion.' This generally means an individual or group of individuals who have fled their country and received refugee status in another country (Blankenship, 2007).

Uganda has a long history of hosting refugees that dates back to the 1940s, when it first hosted Polish refugees. From the 1950s to date, many other nationalities have been hosted including Rwandese, Sudanese, Congolese and Somalis. According to Office of the Prime Minister (OPM), there were 244,775 refugees and asylum seekers in Uganda as of December

2013; with 43,374 living in Kampala as urban refugees and the rest in eight settlements spread through the country. Specifically, the total number of refugees and asylum seekers living in Nakivale Settlement was 68,029. It is estimated that there were 3,390 persons with special needs (including those with disabilities) in Nakivale Settlement.

The Government of Uganda (GoU) requires that all refugees register with the government authorities on arrival in the country, and that they live in formally gazetted refugee settlements in locations identified by the government. The GoU's local settlement policy, which derives its legal basis from the Control of Alien Refugees Act of 1960 (CARA) and Uganda Refugees Act 2006, requires that the refugees are registered in these settlements and in case one moves out in search of employment or any other reason, then the Settlement Commandant (GoU officer who manages the settlement) has to give authorisation. The Act recognises the right of refugees to work, to move freely within the country and to live in the local community, rather than in settlements (Dathine 2013). In line with the Act, the Ugandan government promotes refugee 'self-reliance' and allocates land to each refugee household in order to facilitate refugees' economic independence through agricultural livelihoods (Omata and Kaplan, 2013).

The policy of placing refugees in gazetted areas close to the local populations led to establishment of settlements such as Nakivale, Oruchinga, Kyaka II in Southwestern Uganda; Rhino Camp, Imvepi and Ikafe in the West Nile region; Achol Pii, Parolinya and Adjumani settlements in northern Uganda; and Kiryandongo and Kyangwali settlements in central Uganda.

Overall, placement in rural settlements was based on an assumption that the refugee problem was temporal and would end as soon as the circumstances that led to their flight had ceased (Pincywa, 1998). However, this has not been the case and the government was not prepared for a protracted refugee situation exacerbated by an increase in the population of both refugees and nationals.

Nakivale Refugee settlement located in Isingiro District is a gazetted settlement, hosting refugees from over 10 nationalities, including people from Rwanda, Democratic Republic of Congo, Burundi, Somalia, Sudan, Ethiopia, Kenya, Liberia, Pakistan, South Sudan and Eritrea. Refugees leave their countries of origin primarily due to political instability, rebel influence and or tribal conflict. Whereas the majority of the refugees have been coming to Uganda after a war or political/tribal conflict, some such as Somalis come continuously. These wars and conflicts have caused stress, trauma and disability to some of the people affected.

Disability Models and Approaches Promoting PWDs' Wellbeing

Historically, PWDs were treated as passive recipients of support based on feelings of pity. During the civil rights era of the 1960s and 1970s, a wide variety of strategies and programmes intended to effect a shift from policies based on exclusion, with targeted charities, towards policies embracing PWDs were introduced worldwide (WHO, 2001; Cook & Burke, 2002), hence a paradigm shift from 'the medical model' to 'the social model' of disability.

The Medical Model of disability implies that what needs to be done is to intervene in the field of disability and provide general rehabilitation and assistive devices to cure all PWDs so that they can adapt to the environment. It ignores society's handicapping effects. It also, ignores society's insensitivity and hostility to minority rights (WHO, 2001; Ndeezi, 2004; Kabue et al., 2010). This model is also oblivious of the fact that it is not the disability, but the social barriers, that handicap the PWDs in achieving full and equal participation in social development aspects such as social justice.

On the other hand, the social model stresses removal or eradication of disabling barriers, prejudices, social stigma and misconception of the concept of disability. The model further stresses that disability should be treated as a social and human rights issue, not charity; it should therefore emphasise solidarity not charity, respect not pity, equal participation and equalisation of opportunities (Ndeezi, 2004). The social model of disability in this regard, considers the Medical Model of disability as ancient, shallow, inadequate and misleading in the understanding of the concept of disability, as it considers disability as a problem to be 'fixed' (Ndeezi, 2004). The medical model's definition of disability tends to lead to negative attitudes towards PWDs, which further denies them access to socially inclusive opportunities on equal basis with others.

In order to remove negative attitudes, there is need to remove social barriers, demystify misconceptions about disability, embrace the social or human rights model of disability and enhance full participation of PWDs in society as well as provide for development of their potential. In this respect, the inclusive approach should be promoted.

This entails that post-conflict recovery and rehabilitation, which provide an important opportunity to emphasise and strengthen social cohesion and resilience to conflict, should be promoted. The inclusion of all partners, including refugees and specifically refugees with disability, into the policy, strategy, planning and management processes will facilitate the development of a more inclusive and equitable refugee society, less prone to conflict. Such an approach to rehabilitation and recovery is an important component of sustainable peace building (Ndeezi, 2004). Efforts should focus on refugee needs directly but also on supporting and promoting their well-being through other means such as employment, access to food, security and livelihoods interventions capitalising on what exists in the communities. For example, skills upgrading and infrastructure reconstruction can improve psychosocial and mental health, enhance livelihoods and capacitate refugees to earn income and hence participate in the mainstream activities of their communities. This promotes development-oriented rehabilitation as opposed to the humanitarian approach which keeps refugees dependent on humanitarian aid and donor funding. In the long run, there is refugee empowerment and capacity building for self reliance. This means that the vulnerable refugee groups would not be forced to employ negative coping strategies, such as getting involved in commercial sex, begging or pursuing small errands, such as delivering bottles of water for petty cash (Omata and Kaplan, 2013). They would be able to meet their basic livelihood needs and develop capacity to diversify their income sources.

The literature reveals that some sections of society regard PWDs as helpless people requiring 'sympathy, charity and pity'. Positivist authors, however, look at a PWD as a person first and their disability later. They advocate for their right to access all opportunities on an equal basis with others. Therefore, inclusion of people with disabilities into all activities in their communties plays an important role in the reduction of stigmatisation, which is one of the main factors affecting persons with impairments. The Convention on the Rights of Persons with Disabilities (CRPD), a landmark achievement, provides a solid framework, one that promotes and ensures a more inclusive approach to emergency, recovery and development, and a more inclusive society, one that can play an important role in building a bridge to sustainable durable solutions.

Legal instruments on the rights of refugees

According to Women's Refugee Commission (2010), an estimated 3.5 million refugees and internally displaced people live with disabilities in refugee settlements and urban slums all around the world. Their disabilities might be physical, mental or sensory. Some displaced people have lived their entire life with a disability. Others have become disabled in the fighting (and conflicts) that led to their fleeing their homes or as they fled to the relative safe refugee camp/settlement or urban area.

Various legal instruments have been made to enable PWDs' access to social justice. The United Nations Convention on the Rights of PWDs (which also applies on refugees in Uganda) indicates: 'States to recognise the right of PWDs, on an equal basis with others'. This implies that all barriers should be broken including access to social justice, as with any other person. PWDs should share the same general rights as other people. It is therefore unlawful for any actor in the settlement to discriminate against PWDs.

It should be noted that while refugees are staying in Uganda, the laws and all relevant legal frameworks apply to them. It is also worth noting that Uganda has a disability policy and planning framework including the People with Disabilities Act (2006) and, has since enacted other legislations such as the Equal Opportunities Act (2007). In addition, Uganda is a signatory to the UN Convention on the Rights of Persons with Disabilities (2006) which calls for protection of the rights of PWDs.

Above all, the 1995 National Constitution of the Republic of Uganda in Article 32 provides for non-discrimination based on disability, and affirmative action for PWDs. Notably, the presence of disabled people in refugee and asylum-seeking communities in Uganda is frequently overlooked and information about their particular experiences is rarely available. For instance, the organisations working with refugees lack information on how they moved from their countries to countries of asylum, how they have settled and are coping, the social network challenges and day-to-day experiences with the settlements.

The 1951 UN Convention and the UN Protocol 1967 relating to the status of refugees, define their rights and duties and contain provision in respect of a variety of matters in day-to-day life, such as the right to work, public assistance, and social security. In many such matters refugees are to receive the same treatment as nationals of their country of settlement or resettlement.

This study established that despite these legal frameworks, little has been done to integrate PWDs in many of the development processes. Because of these limitations, the negative societal attitudes often go with them in many spheres in life including their situation as refugees.

The study was therefore premised on the notion that PWDs, more than able-bodied persons are likely to experience a range of challenges in their refugee status. A PWD will most likely experience restrictions in a bid to access equal rights and social services. Disability may affect the ability to cope with many more challenges than would a non-disabled person (NUDIPU, 2006) particularly as regards social justice.

The researcher was able to examine the extent to which the challenges associated with the refugee status affect PWDs' access to social justice in the refugee settlement in Uganda.

How the study was conducted: methodologies

The study used a cross-sectional, descriptive-survey design, mainly qualitative. Documentary and survey approaches were adopted for purposes of collecting available data from sources and studies that have been done before. The study population comprised 62 people with disabilities in the refugee settlement. The target population included people with hearing, visual and physical disabilities, to ensure that each category is sufficiently represented in the study. The researcher purposely earmarked varying levels of disability, categorised as: mild, moderate or severe. This study also considered eight members of the refugee welfare committees, most of whom were purposively included as key informants by virtue of their wide knowledge and experience in the area of special needs categories and particularly in disability. The majority of the respondents were below the age of 40 years.

The study provides a basis for drawing conclusions as to whether they receive social justice from their leaders and communities or not, and examines the reasons as well as the available response system to their quest for social justice. This is important for policy formulation and management.

The accessibility of PWDs to services

It is common especially in developing countries like Uganda to find PWDs locked out of many spheres of life and activity only because of the accessibility aspect. Various studies done both in Uganda and elsewhere including the study by Sheer, Kroll, Neri & Beaty (2003), Nganwa (2009) and Katende (2010) have revealed that most places and facilities are inaccessible to PWDs. Most of the facilities have not been designed to enable everyone easily access them. It is for this reason that PWDs find it difficult to get to places of need, and even when they struggle to get there, they fail to move freely as they would have if the place and facilities were 'user friendly'. Most public facilities such as buildings (including offices, health centres and schools, which all refugees should be able to access) have no ramps for wheelchair users.

On the other hand, information is equally not in an accessible format like Braille or audio for visually impaired persons. In Nakivale settlement for instance, there are no facilities for teaching or using Braille. Access to information is difficult, since communication is done physically either by community workers or refugee leaders going to villages to talk to people. Sometimes, vital information is instead written and pinned on notice boards especially at food distribution points. The only open public Internet café is at the Youth Centre in Basecamp zone and a refugee with disability staying in Ngarama village in Juru Zone finds it difficult to move for over 18 km to access such a facility. The implication is that if a refugee has a physical disability, then s/he has to hire a motorcycle at 3 US Dollars to take and bring him/her back, which is expensive.

The refugee community based-workers are not trained on how to work with those with disability, meaning they lack the appropriate skills to perform their duties. Besides, they are not motivated to go an extra mile to help. They also look at PWDs as fellow refugees, without much help to offer. The PWDs also consider community-based workers as refugees and most of the time expect help from somewhere else. The majority of PWDs have resigned to their fate and simply stay in their homes. Whenever there is a request for information, it's their care givers that come out, most of the time to complain about the poor state the PWDs live in.

All offices in the settlement do not provide for sign language interpreters for the deaf and generally, do not provide for people who can help those who face challenges in reading, understanding or moving. There is a case of a physically disabled refugee who failed to register with UNHCR because according to him, he failed to raise money for transport as shown in Box 8.1 below:

Box 8.1: Case study one

Kalema is a physically disabled male refugee, aged 24 years. He is not married but lives with his mother, a widow, and younger siblings in Kankingi E. village. He is not registered as a Person with Special Needs (PSN) as he failed to raise money for boda boda to take him to the UNHCR offices in Isangano about 13 km away from his village. He missed registration because of information gaps and transport challenge. He says: '... the community worker did not inform me to go and register when the registration team came to my village and I missed out. The message informing all persons with special needs (PSNs) had been given to refugees who had been at the food distribution point/centre but did not reach me. When I complained, I was told to go to the UNHCR offices about 10 km away and inform them to include me in their data bank. Since I walk with the help of a walking stick, I have to raise UGX 8,000/= (3USD) for boda boda to take me and bring me back. I have since failed to raise the money, and I am not on the list for persons with special needs (PSNs), and hence cannot access food for PSNs. I have complained to the village leaders (RWCs) but they insist that I go to UNHCR myself. No one has helped me, not even the community worker or our leaders'.

Arising particularly from the American Disability Rights and Equality Act (2010) is the Equal Access Policy, which confirms rights of all people regardless of their disability. This Act and its attendant policies recognise that disability is a social and human rights issue and so, PWDs should be treated, accommodated and conceived as rights-holders while governments and society generally are duty-bearers in the field of disability, particularly in the area of social justice.

The various national and international legal frameworks reviewed are expressive of this view. Despite these laws, PWDs still have challenges in accessing social justice especially in developing countries including Uganda. It is, however, clear, that different categories of disabilities face different challenges and that no single challenge can adequately explain why the PWDs are not treated justly in most parts of the universe, particularly in refugee settlements in Uganda.

The majority of the respondents indicated that refugee leaders have not considerably enhanced PWDs' access to social services. The refugee welfare committee members interviewed confirmed that PWDs have the same entitlements and services as any other refugees. The refugees are entitled to security and each one should receive a plot of land where they can settle as a family. Each family is entitled to receive food rations each month (maize, beans, cooking oil and sometimes soya flour). However, it was revealed that PWDs are regarded as 'persons with special needs' alongside the elderly and the sick, and they sometimes fail to be as visible as other refugees. Some PWDs, like other vulnerable groups, such as persons with special needs (PSNs) may receive a special diet such as soya bean or yellow maize flour (Posho). They also get water although the supply is sometimes not constant and have to line up with other able-bodied refugees. One of the respondents commented:

> ...when we do not get water, we have to move to the lake to fetch it. During the dry season, some boreholes get dry and we have to rely on dams with very dirty water. Fetching water is usually difficult for us who have no children to help...they should leave one tap for PWDs so that we can fetch without struggling with others.' (Interview with the PWD, 2013).

Also noted by the same respondent was the fact that constructing their own houses is quite difficult not only during the process of gathering building materials but also the actual construction such as climbing on the roof and moving around. He commented that:

> '...We also get plastic sheeting (tarpaulin) to thatch our houses but building is difficult for us, we cannot climb the house and moving around during construction is a challenge...who will make us visible so that we can be helped?.' (Interview with the PWD, 2013).

Another added:

> '...distribution of plots for agriculture is always a struggle in most cases the disabled lose and others get. Sometimes it requires running from one place (office) to another (office) which may necessitate a PWD to hire a motorcycle for transport and in some cases bribing the RWCs. Yet most of the disabled refugees fail to give a bribe, since, they do not have money' (Interview with member of welfare committee, 2013).

If the PWDs were made a distinct group, they would be looked at separately and holistically and would therefore be able to enjoy the available services. For instance, the commandant's office would put aside plots for crop growing for PWDs and these would be given to them directly much like how plots where PSN houses are built are jointly identified, given out and houses constructed and allocated to selected PSNs without any struggle. This would enable them to engage in crop farming and have supplementary food, since the majority of them currently find this a challenge. The refugee leaders who are directly involved in plot demarcation and distribution have not helped the PWDs access those plots. This has resulted in less food production in PWDs' households; hence dependency on the donor food, which itself has been reducing due to budgetary constraints.

It was presumed that refugee welfare committees had a role to play to enhance PWDs' access to services and hence social justice. Physical impairment in most cases affects the limbs and so, impedes one's mobility and ability to touch or grip. This limits one's functionality and accessibility to the environments such as physical infrastructure, including health centres, schools, places of worship, offices and training centres in the settlements. Visually impaired persons on the other hand, find difficulties in communication and reading since most of the reading materials are not in accessible formats while most equipment is not specialised. This fundamentally eliminates them from participating in activities that may be perceived to require sight. People with a hearing impairment are denied opportunities due to their inability to hear and communicate effectively in a medium understood by all. Within and outside the settlement, sign language (which is used by the deaf) is known by very few people, hence a serious limitation in the social environment. Therefore, the PWDs deserve support as it was noted that the refugee leaders have not considerably enhanced PWDs' access to social services. The findings agreed with various studies done in both Uganda and elsewhere, which revealed that most places and facilities in the settlement are inaccessible to PWDs. The facilities have not been designed to enable everyone access them and for this reason PWDs find it difficult to get to places of need such as offices, health facilities, schools and churches or mosques, and even when they struggle to get there, they fail to move freely as they would have if the places and facilities were accessible. In the settlement, such PWDs find it difficult even to participate and be elected as leaders since moving around the settlement is problematic. They are rarely found with others in sensitisation or counselling sessions and so they have remained not only traumatised but also hopeless. Even when one tries to look for work to earn income or offer casual labour in exchange for alternative types of food (such as bananas (matooke), sweet potatoes and peas from the neighbouring nationals, mobility is always a challenge and hence they have remained dependent on their care takers and other family members.

Attitude of refugee leaders and PWDs' access to social justice

Attitudes may be viewed as feelings based on or expressive of personal or societal judgment about a subject. It is evident that society generally has negative attitudes towards PWDs (Nganwa, 2009). Society's negative attitudes and assumptions can be more disabling than other disabling conditions and so, prevent PWDs from achieving their goals (National Statistics and Labour force Survey, 2009). It is probable that PWDs in refugee settlements are victims of such negative attitudes.

The majority of the respondents indicated that refugee leaders think that PWDs deserve equal consideration for services but not for human rights and do not appreciate the necessity for reasonable accommodation. This implies that refugees with disabilities were also victims of negative attitudes. Therefore in such a setting, society attitudes and assumptions can be more disabling than disabling conditions and so, prevent PWDs from achieving their goals. This has left them isolated, unattended to and vulnerable to social injustices in the settlement such as lack of information, lack of access to services like health and education or participation in activities that would otherwise improve the social wellbeing of the individual refugees including counselling, income generating activities and other programmes. Therefore, the various attitudinal barriers have affected PWDs' access to social justice.

It was clear that despite the fact that various legal instruments have been made to enable PWDs' access to social justice, not much has been achieved, a fact confirmed by Lomo (2000). The PWDs have remained poor, out of work and without any skills, unlike the other refugees who have had some chances of being trained since they are mobile by agencies working in the settlement, such as in business initiation, farming as a business, environmental conservation, hygiene and sanitation improvement and water source management among others. Perhaps there is need to change the strategy from the humanitarian or welfare approach to promotion of developmental and social justice approach, which increases the participation of refugees with disability, hence empowering them to find solutions for the challenges and problems faced.

Enhancement of access to rights of PWDs

The majority of the respondents indicated that refugee leaders have not effectively enhanced PWDs' human rights. The findings further show that PWDs' access to information regarding their rights is limited as indicated by one respondent:

> '...what we know is that UNHCR has a list for all the PSNs, but some of the PWDs are not there. In case these PSNs are needed, they send a community worker specific for the particular villages to go and look for PSNs and inform them, who may not reach all of us and we lose out. There is no known way of receiving and sending information. Sometimes they send messages during food distribution or pin letters on distribution points. If you do not go there, like many of us do not, you will miss the information.' (Interview with female participant, 2013)

The respondent noted that there is a PSN representative on the village committee, elected by the refugees. These representatives are usually old men, who are not disabled naturally except for the old age, and are not responsive to the issues related to disability. It was further noted that in case a PWD has a grievance or case and takes it to the village leadership committee, he or she is required to pay a mandatory 20,000 Uganda shillings like any other refugee. If the PWD does not have that money, then his/her case is not heard. There is no consideration for a person with disability who may not be working and may fail to raise such an amount of money. The fee is charged because the refugee leaders do not get salaries and therefore depend on such money to cater for the committee needs, but this denies the PWDs access to justice. It was revealed that if the representatives were PWDs, then they would consider the needs of their fellow PWDs as after all, they would know how it feels to live with a disability and the challenges associated with it. Thus, poor representation has made some of them reluctant to go to the village welfare committees in case of a problem hence, living unfulfilled lives, dependent on others. Another respondent said:

> '...what is emphasised here in the settlement is not PWDs but PSNs which include those refugees above 60 years, orphans, widowers and widowed and the terminally ill and the disabled people. It is a mixture of all these categories and sometimes we miss out not only on information but also on services. Disabled people should be separated because we have different needs and we are different people.' (Interview with male participant 2013)

Asked about attending meetings regarding PWDs' issues, the same respondent said:

> '... I last went for such a meeting about two years ago, when we were going to Mbarara Hospital where I got a walking shoe for my leg. There has not been any programme for us, not even a training. We cannot even stand to be elected because we cannot move from village to village; it will be expensive on boda boda.' (Interview with male participant, 2013).

No specific meetings for PWDs have been held, the group is not organised, the leaders of PSNs are not disabled, the PWD issues are not urgent and sometimes are not considered hence lagging behind. No particular organisation has been encouraged to take on disability related concerns of the PWDs in the settlement; they are looked at with other PSNs. Who then will think about them?

The surprise in the findings of this study was that some persons with disability are not identified as having special needs, and identification of the disabled is a serious issue that may need more attention in future. Fellow refugees, responsible as community workers for identifying and reporting on refugees, may fail to identify PWDs as they are not trained and have no skills in disability related issues and even overlook some people who are disabled due to their absence when they call, and then the person is not registered. They look at PSNs as the same. There is no systematic way of handling disability. For instance, some PWDs may be registered and others are left out if they do not reach the registration point on time. There are also disparities for UNHCR where all people who are registered as disabled are considered as the same. It goes without saying that people with multiple disabilities need more support than someone who is suffering from other conditions related to old age, prolonged sickness or being a widow. For example, there is a case of a PWD in Kankingi. village who received three wheelchairs while others had none as explained below:

Box 8.2: case study two

Bonny Serunveri is aged 17 years and lives with his mother in Kankingi village. He came to Uganda in 2008. He is severely physically disabled and crawls on the floor. He can only move with the use of a wheelchair. Even then, he needs someone to push him as his arms, hands and fingers are too weak to hold anything. Two years ago, he received a wheelchair and was later added two more. Now he has three wheelchairs.

In the same village, many other PWDs have not received any wheelchairs although they are in need of them. He says he does not know why he was given three wheelchairs, but his mother thinks only his name was registered as in need of it. However, she quickly adds that he has also missed other material support such as mattresses, lamps and used clothes, which were given to others. He is not on the food log for PSNs although others receive their special diet and he does not know why. He says most of the time no explanations are given for certain things. His mother adds that the PSN leaders have no answers to this too.

Their feeling is that the UNHCR database is not properly managed as some PSNs receive things they do not need and miss those they need most. His mother feels that maybe the community-based workers are the ones who take the things brought for PSNs such as clothes, lamps, shoes or and saucepans. Whenever she asks, no one gives her the reasons for the discrepancies.

Given that some PWDs access assistive devices such as wheelchairs and crutches and some others do not, respondents explained that those without such devices find it difficult to participate in community programmes. They have missed services such as trainings, counselling sessions, do not receive food in case of a distribution and do not do daily living activities such as fetching water, washing and bathing themselves like others. Some miss education, including adult literacy classes, and accessing health services is always expensive since they have to use motorcycles (boda bodas) to reach the health centres. When their peers go to attend parties in their communities, the physically disabled who have no wheelchairs remain at home. This has not only left them dependent on others, but also traumatised and lacking self confidence, hence more vulnerable.

This implies therefore that change of attitude towards PWDs as regards realising rights and services as well as enhancement of their access to services will certainly advance PWDs' human rights.

A minority within a minority

The concept of disability is as old as human history itself. Persons with disabilities (PWDs) have always existed although they have always been marginalised by society in all walks of life (Ndeezi, 2004). Disability is a natural and global phenomenon, which occurs in every society and in every generation. In Uganda, the People with Disabilities Act (2006) defines a person with disability (PWD) as anyone who experiences significant limitations in one or several functions because of a physical, sensorial or mental impairment or deficiency. A person is deemed to have a disability if there is evidence of a physical or mental impairment, which has a substantial and long-term adverse effect on one's ability to carry out normal day-to-day activities. Long-term means that the condition must last, or be likely to last, for more than 12 months, or that it is permanent. As a historical and yet global phenomenon, disability has metamorphosed into various categories. Approaches to disability, too, have been significantly shifting.

In order to promote harmonious living of PWDs with other able-bodied persons and reduce on their marginalisation, many national and international legal instruments have been put in place to advocate for the rights of PWDs including their right to social justice. These include the United Nations Convention on the Rights of PWDs (2006) which Uganda ratified in 2008, the Uganda Equal Opportunities Act (2007), and the PWDs Act (2006) and above all, the Constitution of the Republic of Uganda (1995). All these frameworks give affirmative action to PWDs in all lifestyles including refugees in Uganda. Emerging evidence, however, shows that PWDs including those in refugee settlements remain perpetual victims of social injustice.

It is estimated that over a billion people, about 15 per cent of the world's population, have some form of disability (UN, 2011). About 80 per cent of the world's PWDs live in developing countries, making the worldwide population with disabilities, at least collectively, one of the poorest and most marginalised segments of society (ILO, 2007; UN 2006; UNDP, 2006). The lack of accurate statistics makes estimates of the exact number of PWDs, including those in refugee settlements, difficult. Because of lack of accurate numbers of PWDs in different countries, different organisations have working estimates. For instance, UNDP estimates a global proportion of PWDs at 5 per cent, USAID uses 10 per cent while DFID uses 4-7 per cent (Coleridge, 1993).

Further, the World Health Organisation (WHO) estimates that there are more than 600 million persons with disabilities worldwide – between 7 and 10 per cent of the world's population – 80 per cent of whom live in developing countries (IFRC, 2007). It can be assumed, therefore, that between 2.5

and 3.5 million of the world's 35 million displaced persons live with disabilities. Indeed, the number of persons with disabilities among displaced populations may be even higher. Where displaced persons have fled civil conflict and war, a higher proportion of the population may have suffered serious injuries or trauma due to the fighting or land mine accidents, resulting in physical, mental or sensory impairments.

Despite the use of estimates, the figures clearly indicate that PWDs are not a marginal minority, particularly if it is considered that one person's disability seriously affects his own situation and that of the community, especially if this person is a refugee. 'The number of persons directly or indirectly affected by the problem of disability is therefore considerable' (ILO, 2002) and so, they should not be ignored in social development, particularly in the area of social justice.

In Uganda, there are more than 200,000 refugees, out of which more than 65,000 live in Nakivale Settlement. UNHCR estimates that there are about 852 refugees with disabilities in Nakivale alone. Refugees with disabilities (RWDs) find challenges in accessing resources, education, and other opportunities. They are also more vulnerable to poverty, exploitation, and various forms of abuse. Without confidence in and awareness of their own rights, disabled refugees are often socially marginalised and this reinforces barriers to their access to services and limits achievement of their basic rights. For an especially vulnerable group like refugees, the problem may be who is responsible for improving the conditions of such a minority group, within a minority. Is it the United Nations High Commissioner for Refugees (UNHCR) which is mandated to take care of all refugees; do the government,

INGOs and other agencies working with refugees, as well as refugee leaders have a big part to play in improving the welfare of the minority group of refugees with disability?

Conclusion

Social justice is usually understood as related to human rights. When one considers what people who are marginalised are entitled to, and how it can be ensured that they obtain their entitlements, this is both social justice and human rights. If a human rights-based approach is used actively, rights can be claimed 'from below' or 'from above', as with social justice. In relation to persons with disability, the question is whether the PWDs enjoy their human rights.

For instance, in a refugee setting, it means that all refugees are equal and that refugees with disability should be included in the enjoyment of benefits of their community and should be empowered to participate fully in all activities taking place in their communities. They should not be passive members of their community rather should actively participate in leadership, self-reliance drives and programmes, education, physical and psychological rehabilitation and access any form of available assistance.

This study found that Uganda, like many other states, has failed to implement relevant enacted laws or to create institutional frameworks to ensure international human rights protection and good governance. Many refugees and PWDs in particular are uninformed about their rights, are vulnerable, and are thus amenable to duress; they lack basic necessities of life and although they are a unique minority group with unique needs, many of them depend on care givers to accomplish daily living activities. They have activities they can do on their own, but most of the time another person may be needed to organise PWDs, depending on their type of disability. Therefore, long-term programmes meant for refugees should also reach them so that they can be empowered and work on their own. They should be included in the planning and implementation processes as well as the monitoring phase of programmes. These programmes should emphasise equity, accessibility and inclusion and should aim at empowering PWDs economically, so that they can get income; socially so that they can participate in the community activities and; politically so that they can develop the confidence to make decisions and participate in the decision-making processes of their communities. The government and other stakeholders concerned must work towards changing the attitudes of refugee leaders towards the PWDs in the refugee settlements. They must emphasise that PWDs deserve equal consideration for services and human rights and participation, like every other member of the refugee community. The government must be keen on creating awareness about concerns of PWDs and be keener on issues of social justice.

References

American Psychological Association (1994), 'Guidelines to reduce bias in language. *Publication Manual of the American Psychological Association.* 4th ed. Washington: American Psychological Association.

Americans with Disabilities Act of 1990 (ADA) New York.

Blankenship, D., and Nathan, M. (2007). *Resource Guide for Serving Refugees with disabilities*, United States Committee for Refugees and Immigrants, New York.

Coleridge, P. (1993) *Disability, liberation and development*, Oxford, Oxfam Publications.

Employment rights and the Equality Act, 2010 [Online] Available: http://www.direct.gov.uk/en/DisabledPeople/Employmentsupport/YourEmploymentRights/DG4001071 (accessed on June 6, 2013).

Dathine Agriculture Consult (2013) 'Comprehensive livelihoods assessment of Kyangwali and Nakivale', Dathine Agriculture Consult, Kampala.

Ginyera-Pincywa, A.G.G. (ed.) 1998, *Uganda and the Problem of Refugees*. Kampala: Makerere University Press.

Government of Uganda (1995) 'Constitution of the Republic of Uganda', February, 2006, Government of Uganda Printery, Entebbe.

Government of Uganda (2007) '*Equal Opportunities Act, 2000*', Government Printery, Entebbe, Uganda.

Government of Uganda (2006) 'Disability Act, 2006'. Entebbe Government Printery, Entebbe.

Hershey, L. (2000) 'Women with Disabilities: Health, Reproduction, and Sexuality'; International Encyclopedia of Women: Global Women's Issues and Knowledge, 4 volumes, Routledge Press.

International Labour Organisation (2002) 'Disability and poverty reduction strategies'. A discussion paper, Geneva, November 2002.

International Federation of Red Cross and Red Crescent Societies, (2007), 'World Disaster Report – Focus on Discrimination'

(Geneva: IFRC, December 2007) accessed on http://www.ifrc.org/publicat/wdr2007/index.asp?=CJS4iMDAlJICFSDMXgodV4e7g

Kakooza, T. (1996) 'An introduction to Research Methodology'. 2nd Edition, National Adult Education Association.

Katende, J. (2010), 'Disabled lack access to facilities and services'. in *The New Vision*, 26 April 2010.

Kathuri, N.J., and Pals, A.D. (1983), *Introduction to education research in education*. Egerton: Egerton University Education Book Series.

Kabue, S., Mombo, E., Galgalo, J., and Peter, C.B. (2010) *Disability, society and theology: Voices from Africa*. Limulu, Zapf Chancery publishers Africa Ltd.

Kreijcie, R.V. and Morgan, D.W. (1970). 'Determining Sample Size for Research Activities'. *Educational and Psychological Measurement*, 30: 607-610.

LeCompte, M., Schensul,J. (1999) Analysing and Interpreting Ethnographic Data. Alta Mir Press, New Delhi.

Lomo, Z.A. (2000) 'The Struggle for Protection of the Rights of Refugees and IDPs in Africa: Making the Existing International Legal Regime Work'. 18 Berkeley J. Int'l Law. 268. Available: http://scholarship.law.berkeley.edu/bjil/vol18/iss2/8

Metts, R. (2000) *Disabilities: Issues, Trends and Recommendations for the World Bank*. Washington DC, World Bank.

Ministry of Gender, Labour and Social Development (2006) National policy on disability in Uganda. Government Printery, Entebbe.

Ministry of Health, (2009) Ministry of Health statistical abstract 2008/09. Government Printery, Entebbe.

Mugenda, O. M., and Mugenda, A. G. (1999). *Research Methods: Quantitative and qualitative approach*. Acts Press, Nairobi, Kenya.

National Union of Disabled Persons of Uganda (2006) Evaluation Report: Capacity Building Project, NUDIPU, Kampala.

Ndeezi, A. (2004) The disability movement in Uganda: Progress & Challenges, with constitutional and legal provisions on disability. NUDIPU, Kampala.

Nganwa, A. (2009) Improving reproductive health services for women with disabilities: Community Based Rehabilitation. [On line] Available: http://www.afri-can.org. CBR, Africa Network (AfriCAN). Kyambogo University, Kampala (May 24, 2013).

Office for National Statistics (2009) Labour force survey. [Online]

Available: http://www.shaw-trust.org.uk/disability_and_employment_statistics. (March, 2013)

Omata, N., and Kaplan, J. (2013) Refugee livelihoods in Kampala, Nakivale and Kyangwali refugee settlements: Patterns of engagement with the private sector Refugee Studies Centre Working Paper No. 95, Oxford, University of Oxford

Sankaran, K. (2007) 'Labour laws in South Asia: The need for an inclusive approach. Geneva: International Labour Organization, International Institute for Labour Studies.

Sekaran, U. (2003) *Research Methods for Business. A Skill Building Approach*. New York: John Willey and Sons Inc.

Scheer, J., Kroll, T., Neri, M., and Beatty, P. (2003) 'Access barriers for persons with disabilities', *Journal of Disability Policy Studies*. 13(4), 221-230.

Statusberetning (2003) Attitudes toward the Disabled in Denmark; [Online] Available: http://www.dch.dk/publ/holdningereng/doc4.h World Report on Disability. (June 14, 2011)

UNFPA (2006) Emerging issues: sexual and reproductive health of persons with disabilities, WHO/UNFPA guidance note, available at: http://www.unfpa.org/sites/default/files/pub-pdf/srh_for_disabilities.pdf [accessed 7 August 2015].

Uganda Bureau of Statistics (2006) 2002 Uganda population and housing Census: Analytical report. Government, Kampala Uganda.

Walraven, G., and Weeks, A. (1999) 'The role of (traditional) birth attendants with midwifery skills in the reduction of maternal mortality', *Tropical Medicine and International Health journal,* 4:527–529.

WHO (2001) *Rethinking Care from Disabled People's Perspectives.* Geneva: World Health Organisation.

Women's refugee commission, IFRC (2010) Refugees with Disability: A fact sheet. New York.

Yaghmaie, F. (2003). 'Content validity and its estimation *Journal of Medical Education,* Spring, 3.

Yuko, W. O., Onen, D. (2009) *A general guide to writing research proposal and report: A handbook for beginning researchers.* Nairobi: Jomo Kenyatta Foundation.

Part Four

Legal Justice and Social Justice in East Africa

Chapter 9

'Street-level' Bureaucrats in Rwanda: Working for More Just Outcomes of Judicial Reforms

Gervais Twahirwa

Introduction

This chapter is about the reform of the JLOS sector in Rwanda. The focus is on a group of officials too often ignored in scholarly attention – the lower level administrative staff of the judicial services, who form the majority of courts' low-level workers. Lipsky (1980:3) calls them 'street-level bureaucrats' and 'front line workers', since they interact on a daily basis with the general public as part of their normal work. Street-level bureaucrats, as Lipsky suggests, make policy decisions every time they employ different means of coping with high demand. In line with his findings, this study suggests that these front-line workers in the judiciary get few resources allocated for their training and support, and can become frustrated by their difficult working conditions. The public and their supervisors barely understand the constraints and challenges such lower-level workers face when trying to meet demands for judicial services. This study aims to investigate this problem, and modestly to suggest ways to resolve it.

In the context of Rwanda, in particular, there is considerable evidence that judicial service delivery has improved since 2004 because of various reforms introduced. The first change has involved a restructuring of the courts to improve operationalisation and add to professional competence. The fragmentation of the Supreme Court, for instance, has been reduced, as well as reduction of excess courts and staff, resulting in improved resource allocation among courts. Whilst the current structure has solved some problems arising from former fragmentation, the courts 'street-level bureaucrats' behaviour and motivations have not been fully attended to in these reforms. In practice, this study suggests that delays in the delivery of justice are mainly the result of extensive case backlogs, which reinforces the demotivation of administrative staff. A close inter-connection exists between case backlogs in courts and motivational problems among lower and middle-level judicial administrative staff. Various other factors, like obsolete laws, inadequate infrastructure, and lack of familiarity with ICT-related equipment now installed in all judicial institutions, have also constituted hurdles to fully effective reform processes in the judicial system.

Judicial reforms strive for outcomes that are more socially and legally just, but sometimes it is difficult to influence both behaviour and motivation of lower-level staff. Thus, the judicial reforms introduced since 2004 addressed outdated legal and judicial systems, especially by removing obstacles to business opportunities and improving respect for people's citizenship rights. This study examines how reform processes worked out with 'street-level' staff.

The main finding is that for unofficial reasons, street-level bureaucrats in courts were more difficult to influence than formal judicial and legal procedures and provisions. Many street-level bureaucrats in the court system feel they are inadequately resourced and poorly remunerated, and note rising disparities between their own incomes and those of more highly qualified staff recently recruited to the sector. They report that this can be demotivating. When more highly qualified staff were recruited following the 2004 reforms, the position of street-level bureaucrats, the least paid among all staff in the Rwandan judiciary, appears more unjust. In this context, street-level bureaucrats seek various mechanisms to help them cope with their situation. Informal solutions can mean judicial processes are delayed by adjournments, with the result that backlogs hamper the efficient working of various courts, even at Supreme Court level.

The Historical Context of Rwanda's Judiciary

The 1994 genocide against Tutsi affected all aspects of the justice system in Rwanda. It destroyed the socio-economic fabric of the country, and most professionals in the Justice, Law and Order sector either fled or were killed. During the aftermath of genocide, a lack of competent staff, inadequate equipment, and poor infrastructures were widely observed in the justice sector (Magnarella, 2000). Additionally, there were gross violations of human rights, with a great number of people imprisoned without being properly accused, and without trial, for many years. By 2004, policy makers had introduced comprehensive reforms to address various Rwandan judicial issues including case backlogs, creating new courts and restructuring. Gacaca[35] (semi-traditional) courts hearing genocide cases. These reforms helped speed up justice for genocide victims and suspects, although all Rwandan courts were criticised by international human rights organisations like Human Rights Watch and Amnesty International. Gradually after 1994, the Rwandan Government, with support from different stakeholders and justice partners,[36] supported restoration of justice institutions. The judicial reforms of 2004 focused mainly on legal and judicial systems and on enabling reforms that facilitated private sector-led growth. New laws addressed both the consequences of genocide, and on the other hand, addressed obstacles in the legal system that hampered prospects for business growth, as well as improving access to justice. Reforms of institutions and procedures focused on improving the independence, effectiveness and efficiency of the judiciary. From 2004 onwards, this included the measure of integrating the use of ICT in all Rwanda's courts.

Other political, public service, and administrative reforms followed the judicial reforms, as Rwanda began to move towards building a regionally and globally competitive

---

35 'Gacaca' are semi-traditional courts established by Organic Law No 16/2004 of 19 June 2004. They are charged with prosecuting and trying the perpetrators of the crime of genocide and other crime against humanity committed between 1 October 1990 and 31 December 1994.

36 Various partners in justice have financed activities of reforms. These include the Government of Rwanda, the European Union, The Netherlands through PACT, The Belgian Technical Cooperation (BTC), etc.

economy. The legal and judicial system were failing to meet the challenges of supporting economic and social transformation, and their outdated quality was viewed as hampering national reconstruction. The commitment to reforms started when President Paul Kagame announced in November 2002 that, 'transforming Rwanda fundamentally cannot succeed in the absence of a conducive legal framework' (BizICLIR,[37] 2007:1). Constitutional amendments in June 2003 included elements of legal and judicial reforms including the organisation, jurisdiction, and functioning of courts, as expressed in Article 143 of the Constitution.

There have been many case backlogs within the Rwandan Judiciary. According to the Rwandan Judiciary Annual Report 2009, a total of 55,478 cases were pending as of 31 December 2008. Since investors want to invest in a safe and secure environment, where the government guarantees respect for human rights, and speedy resolution of legal disputes, such delays did nothing to improve the economic climate for investment and economic growth.

In line with the Rwandan Vision 2020,[38] one of the main objectives of the Rwandan Government is to set up a judicial system that favours governance and development. However, the success of judicial reforms in Rwanda remains limited as huge backlogs persist (The Rwandan Judiciary Annual Report

---

37 BizCLIR is a multi-year initiative of the United States Agency for International Development with the goal of improving the efficiency and impact of assistance programmes intended to help developing countries improve their business enabling environments.

38 Vision 2020 is a document elaborated by The Rwandan Ministry of Finance and Economic Planning (MINECOFIN) in which government's long-term priorities are explained.

2010). This can partly be explained by lower-level workers' poor motivation. The number of case postponements[39] has been increasing over the last seven years, and yet there has been a gradual decline in the number of pending cases, pointing to the impact of reforms, especially from 2008 to 2010. Table 9.1 below shows the changes over a period of six years.

Table 9.1: Pending land cases for the last six[40] judicial years

Year	Total of adjourned cases	Average monthly cases	Total pending cases
2005	36,545	3,045	46,704
2006	28,365	2,364	47,861
2007	41,981	3,498	54,409
2008	40,046	3,641	55,478
2009	50,011	4,168	44,644
2010	46,043	3,837	36,154

Source: Researcher's own construction adapted from Annual Reports (2004-2010)

The above table shows that the number of cases brought to court increased in 2007 and 2008, and then significantly fell between 2009 and 2010. These reductions appear to have continued after 2010, when the introduction of mediators reduced the number of cases coming to court and helped to settle part of the backlog as well.[41] The reduction overall in

39 According to Article 11 of Law No 18/2004 of 20/06/2004, backlogs are those cases which have lasted for six months in courts without any action on them.

40 The year 2004 is not included in the list as most of it was used for the first judicial reforms. Rwandan judicial reforms were done incrementally but the most important judicial reform was the one of 2004.

41 Address by the Honourable Chief Justice at the Ceremony of the Launching of the Judicial Year 2013-14, at: http://www.judiciary.gov.rw/fileadmin/

the number of pending cases can be attributed to the special efforts of contractual judges and registrars, who between July 2008 and August 2009 handled a total of 17,713 cases from the backlog (The Rwandan Judiciary Annual Report, 2009). Despite judicial reforms and additional contractual staff being hired to deal with backlog cases, case adjournments and backlogs remain problematic even after 2010.

Street-level bureaucrats and New Public management theories

According to Lipsky (1980:3), public service workers who interact directly with citizens in the course of their jobs, and who have substantial discretion in the execution of their work are street-level bureaucrats. Lipsky and his colleagues first introduced the concept of street-level bureaucrats in the 1970s (Lipsky 1971 & 1980; Prottas 1978 & 1979; Weatherly 1979). This concept refers particularly to the frontline public service institutions that present two important facets. First, frontline workers engage directly with the public, on a daily basis, and so have very close interactions with people. Second, they have substantial discretionary powers, in their actions, and sometimes act as those they work with were their clients rather than citizens, including in terms of how they treat people and the kinds of decisions they take. While defining bureaucratic discretion in a broader manner, Adler and Asquith (1993: 399) claim that: 'A public official has discretion whenever the

News_docs/CJ_Speech_-_Launch_of_JY_2013-2014_Eng.pdf (accessed 28 May 2014).

effective limit of his power leaves him free to make a choice among possible courses of action or inaction'.

From Lipsky (1980), we know that service bureaucracies consistently favour some clients at the expense of others, despite official regulations to the contrary. To understand how and why these organisations often perform contrary to their own rules and goals, we need to know how the rules are experienced by workers in the organisation and to what other pressures they are subjects. Street-level bureaucrats include teachers, police officers and other law enforcement personnel, social workers, judges, public lawyers and other court officers, health workers, and many other public employees. The people doing these jobs tend to have much in common, because they experience analytically similar working conditions. However, not every street-level bureaucrat works for a street-level bureaucracy. For example, a relocation specialist (a type of street-level bureaucrat) may work for an urban renewal agency whose employees are mostly planners, builders, and other technicians. Conversely, not all employees of street-level bureaucracies are street-level bureaucrats, for example, file clerks in a welfare department or police officers on routine clerical assignments. For the Rwandan courts case, street-level bureaucrats include the administrative workers, registrars and perhaps even some lower court judges that interact with people in the course of their daily work.

In addition to defining street-level bureaucrats, Lipsky (1980:27-28) points out five key characteristics or conditions of street-level bureaucrats. First, street level bureaucrats usually work in institutions where resources (time and budget) necessary for task achievement are inadequate. Thus, street-level bureaucrats develop particular specific coping mechanisms at individual level to counter such challenges. Second, ambiguous and conflictual policy goals provide working conditions in which street-level bureaucrats operate. Moreover, target objectives are general and ambiguous, thus giving them some discretion to decide as they wish. Third, the problem associated with measuring and controlling the street level performance at work. A fourth important characteristic of street-level work is the structural weakness of clients. Participation of the clients is often non-voluntary; they do not decide to come to the front office on their own neither do they have somewhere to go and get the services they want. The last and most important characteristic of street-level bureaucracy is the use of discretion itself. Thus, a big number of Rwandan Courts of law fulfill all these conditions and with such discretion and working conditions, street-level bureaucrats make and implement policies and generally enjoy a positive information asymmetry. They know more than the public and even their immediate supervisors about the dominant policy regulations and about the relevant bureaucratic rules for providing people with public services. According to Prottas (1978:294), street-level bureaucrats are powerful actors or 'gatekeepers', located at the boundaries between their institutions and the social environment around them. This interface location makes street-level bureaucrats important intermediary actors between public service organisations and clients.

Furthermore, being located in the middle of information flows coming both from the organisation to the clients (rules), and from the clients to organisations (information on clients), low-level workers are in special positions. As such, they are able to master both internal and external information sources (Prottas 1978:294).

Figure 9.1: The traditional explanatory model of street-level bureaucratic behavior

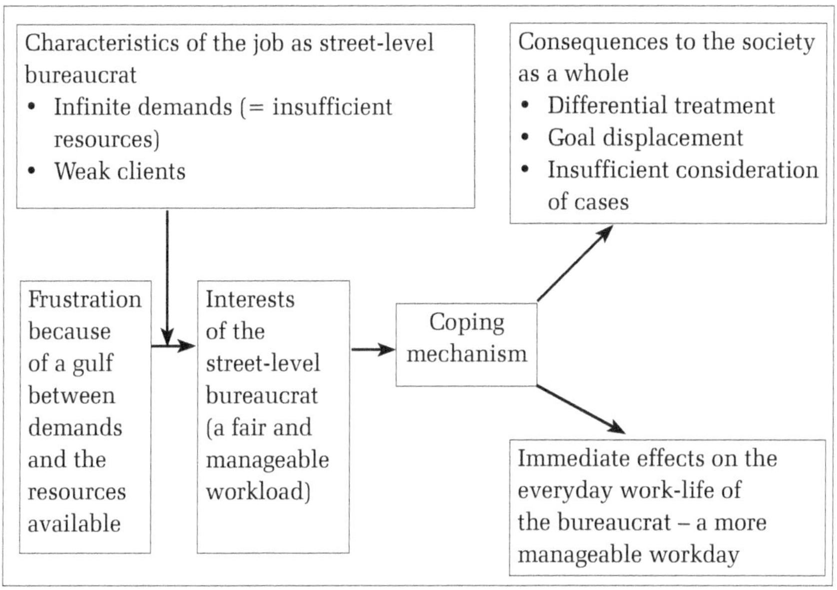

Source: Nielsen (2006:865)

The Figure 9.1, above shows that the conditions under which street level bureaucrats operate have direct consequences on both the society as a whole, and on low-level workers. People may suffer from the way street level bureaucrats behave when coping with difficulties of workload on one hand. On the other hand, street level bureaucrats may have manageable workloads at the end of the day.

Street-Level Bureaucrats in New Public Management Theory

New Public Management (NPM) involves the introduction of private sector practices into public affairs management. Public sector reforms in the Rwandan judiciary have focused on improving service delivery in many ways including motivation of civil servants. As Peters and Pierre (2002:5) argue, 'the reform of public administration over the past several decades has concentrated on managerial aspects of the government, attempting to make government more efficient, effective, and economical'. This has undervalued the peculiar nature of the public service management in government, and the need to think about the values of public service delivery rather than promoting economic efficiency (Stein, 2002). In Rwanda, judicial reforms led to a reduction of a significant number of staff. Currently the structure of the Supreme Court of Rwanda provides for about 663 staff unlike before the 2004 reform, in which Rwandan courts and tribunals had 1,583 staff (Strategic Plan of Judiciary, 2005-2007). However, the reduction has also made it possible for provision of relatively adequate infrastructure. For example there were 146 District Courts in the early 2000s whereas currently the same courts, now under the name of 'Primary Courts' number 60. All this aimed at establishing an efficient, effective, and economical judiciary.

Rwandan judicial reforms exhibit most of the features of NPM discussed by Toonen (2001) and (Pollitt & Bouckaert 2004) including, adapting private management principles into public sector organisation management, public steering by contracts, management and control by results. Before 2004, the Rwandan judiciary was understaffed. Currently, hiring of contractual judges and registrars is to bridge the gaps of understaffing. NPM has brought the idea of public market in the arena of public affairs, but has not necessarily translated into desired results.

While trends in judicial reforms seem to be similar, it remains quite an open issue to know which impacts they have had on street-level bureaucrats' motivation and behaviour. On the one hand, Lipsky (1980) was more interested in explaining that what matters is the insufficient resources availed for street-level bureaucrats rather than the ability street-level bureaucrats have to compensate that gap. On the other hand, the high discretion of street-level bureaucrats was what Hill (2005) focussed on, in linking the theory of street-level bureaucrats to New Public Management theory.

Reforming Rwandan Judiciary before and after 2004

Rwandan judicial reforms have evolved over time since 1961. Before colonial rule, Rwanda was a centralised kingdom with all powers vested in the hands of the king and his close counsellors. The counsellors advised the king on all matters, be it economic or political issues, administration and justice (Mutamba, 2005). The king was above the law, and with all powers in his hands, none could appeal against his decisions.

According to the Strategic Plan of the Rwandan Judiciary (2009-2013), the current Rwandan Judiciary was established first by the Constitution of 28 January 1961 under the ambit of the Supreme Court. Following the 24 November 1962 constitution, the Supreme Court comprised of five sections: the

Department of Courts and Tribunals, the Court of Cessation, the Constitutional Court, the State Council, and the Court of Accounts with judges appointed and dismissed by the President of the Republic. There was no financial and administrative autonomy. Because of the constitution of 28 December 1978, the President remained the Guarantor of Judicial Independence and the President of the High Council of the Judiciary (HCJ). There was no clear separation of powers. Ministry of Justice was second to the President. However, four independent High Courts namely: Cessation Court, State Council, Constitutional Court,[42] and the Public Accounts' Court have replaced the five departments of the Supreme Court. The post-genocide period (1994-2003) adopted the Fundamental Law that established the following ordinary courts: Canton Courts, Courts of the First Instance, Appeal Courts, and the Supreme Court. The constitutional revision of 18 April 2000 added on a sixth level; Department of Gacaca Courts. The President of the Supreme Court was deputised by six people (six Presidents of the six sections). The High Council of the Judiciary was composed of 21 judges. It was given the mandate to manage all court judges with the exception of the Chief Justice and the Deputy Chief Justice.

Given the objectives of the judicial reforms introduced in 2004, several reasons (both official and unofficial) have inspired Rwandan policy makers to introduce judicial reforms including amendments and replacement of obsolete laws. The official grounds for judicial reforms involved court restructuring (The Rwandan Judicial Strategic Plan 2009-2013).

---

42 The Constitutional Court was composed of State Council and Cessation Court.

This is because the former structure of the Supreme Court created weaknesses that led to clashing of different organs, poor resource utilisation, and general poor performance. This contributed towards the restructuring of the Supreme Court and formation of one single unit under the Chief Justice.

However, unofficial reports indicate that judicial reforms were particularly of interest to the ruling political party – Rwandan Patriotic Front (RPF).[43] It was deeply entrenched in RPF's aspirations and priorities as well as government's effort to 'renew' the judicial staff who had served the former regimes and who were perceived as corrupt, especially those prior to 1994.

The idea of changing the symbols associated with the pre-1994 regimes is among the unofficial reasons for Rwandan judicial reforms. As past regimes[44] were accused of having planned and executed the Rwandan genocide against Tutsis in 1994, there was no use for the current government to keep national emblems established prior to 1994 as such symbols were perceived as diversionist. Equally, courts names changed,

43 RPF (The Rwandan Patriotic Front) originated in the late 1980s, and had a military branch called the Rwanda Patriotic Army. It has been in power since July 1994, after stopping the Genocide against Tutsis.

44 Both the 1st and the 2nd Republic are accused of having planned and executed the 1994 Rwandan Genocide against the Tutsis. Many authors on Rwanda History and conflicts wrote about possible reasons for the Rwandan Genocide of 1994. Colonialists came to Rwanda with the idea of 'Divide and Rule'. Under Belgian colonial rule, political discrimination against Hutu was accentuated, and monarchic rule was characterised by repression and economic exploitation. Tutsis were seen as agents of colonisation even more than the Belgians. Belgians introduced various reforms. The introduction of an identity card with ethnic group mention on it reinforced the ethnic ideology among Rwandans (Hintjens 2001).

perhaps with the same ideas, as reiterated by members of one focus group discussion.

In addition to this, there is a problem relating to the quality of decisions rendered by the courts. Unqualified judges could not be able to render better and coherent judgments because of their ignorance of some laws. They were also very corrupt. Lack of competency may often lead to corruption. Subsequently, the new qualified personnel, judges, and registrars had to be recruited and this is one of the positive factors by the winners of reforms. As Klitgaard (1997) puts it, reforms, which are possibly benefiting the whole nation, have great chance of producing winners as well as losers. The latter may resist and when it comes to criticisms, they negatively criticise such reforms.

Moreover, appropriate incentives of public servants in general and judicial staff in particular were lacking in the Rwandan public service before 2004. According to Lienert (1998) in many parts of Africa, the derisory salaries of many public sector staff have resulted in serious consequences, including low staff morale and long-term declining productivity, difficult recruitment and retention of technicians and professionals and unclear systems of remuneration, with nonwage benefits in kind or in cash often outweighing salaries. Finally, there are strong incentives within such structures to accept bribes. This was also the situation in Rwanda before 2004.

Before 2004, the Supreme Court had six separate chambers, each with its own president under the coordination of the President of the Supreme Court. However, the restructuring of the Supreme Court resulted in the formation of one single unit under the Chief Justice with a mandate to oversee the functioning of other courts. To improve coordination of lower courts, one single High Court replaced the former four courts of appeal. In addition, Commercial Courts established in 2008 were to deal specifically with commercial litigations in order to speed up proceedings and therefore enhance the investment climate in the country. Gacaca department soon become a separate entity from the Supreme Court and is in fact now recognised as 'National Service of Gacaca Jurisdictions'. This made Gacaca cases' trials quick and perhaps if Gacaca had remained under the Supreme Court, the number of backlogs would be currently unimaginable.

Furthermore, the High Council of the Judiciary, established by Organic Law of 13 August 2008, is the highest decision-making body for the Rwandan Judiciary and is responsible for judges and registrars' appointment, promotion, and removal from office. Courts supervision and coordination has become easier than under the previous non-unified Supreme Court. As Rhodes (2000:349) puts it, 'Fragmentation constrains the Centre's administrative ability to coordinate and plan'. Thus, the former trends eroded the Supreme Court's capacity to steer the system and its capacity to supervise and coordinate lower courts.

Working conditions of street level bureaucrats in courts

Street-level bureaucrats in Rwanda work under conditions of inadequate resources and are underutilised. Besides, they earn lower salaries that bring about discrepancies in salaries amongst Supreme Court staff. Thus, corruption arising from low salaries is one of the reasons for registrars' dismissals and resignations. In the judicial years 2009 and 2010, more than 20 per cent of the current total number of registrars resigned. The judicial year 2010 alone witnessed dismissals of 23 staff and more than half (12) of these registrars were dismissed due to corruption and other related crimes ranging from changing court decisions to asking bribes from litigants. In fact, all the crimes they committed were corruption related, and caused by the high discretion they have over particular issues (The Rwandan Judiciary Annual Report, 2010:39). The number would probably have been greater if those who resigned due to low salaries were also considered. This negatively affects courts' performance as experienced workers leave the Rwandan judiciary, as one respondent opined:

> It takes time to train new recruits, and too much time is spent on constant trainings of workers who leave only after a short time. Reforms have failed to retain street level bureaucrats because of low incentives, which cause low motivation and high turnover amongst low-level staff. (Interview with a Supreme Court Staff on 19 August, 2011).

Lipsky (1980) argued that with the constraints faced by the street-level bureaucrats, they have broad discretion with respect to the utilisation of resources. In the application of resources to the job, they confront the uncertainty that stems from conflicting or ambiguous goals that unevenly guide their work.

Lower workers from Rwandan courts attempt to do a good job in some circumstances, taking into consideration the available means and the general guidance provided by the system they work in. When asked how they manage to cope with unlimited demand with limited resources, they assert that they are doing what they think is the best they can do. They do not say that they are doing extraordinary things, but they mention that they have been working effectively and properly under the circumstances, they encounter. If they realise that they perform poorly due to the difficult conditions they work in, they are likely to use this as an excuse for their inadequacy. They leave their job and seek other work than to sustain the personal ambivalence that results from that situation of failing to retain a concept of their own inadequacies. Most of the street-level bureaucrats who have not yet resigned seem to be enrolled for capacity building or further education with prospects of seeking better working conditions. They deplore the fact that they face limited resources whereas funds are being returned to the public treasury due to bad planning or/ and inability of the Supreme Court to use fully the allocated resources. In the focus group discussion held with low-level workers, reference was made to fiscal years where 36 per cent of the budget was not utilised in 2006 and thus had to be returned to the public treasurer. This was due to insufficient and inexperienced budget managers. In 2009, the budget allocated to the judiciary was spent up to 89.50 per cent. (Focus Groups Discussions with registrars on 22 July 2011).

Regarding low salaries, Grindle (1997) states that there is no evidence that a better system of pay and less workers leads to higher performance. Recognising these factors as elements of good performance, she further argues that they need to be accompanied by other elements, particularly attitudes, upholding of ethics and organisational culture (Grindle 1997:

481). I do not totally agree with Grindle and Hildebrand about pay because registrars need additional income from salary increase to meet their basic needs. Salary being the foundation element of motivation particularly for low-level workers, productivity might suffer from low salaries, but things get worse when there are unjustified big differences in salary schemes within an organisation.

To illustrate this with regards to courts' street-level bureaucrats, this research has focused on the registrars of Intermediate Courts who earn a monthly salary of 169,000 Rwf (currently, the equivalent of about 200 Euros) and those of the High Court who earn almost double that (329,000 Rwf) per month. This frustrates street-level bureaucrats. Coupled with some other factors, low salaries may lead to corruption among low-level workers as they may be unable to meet their daily basic needs. One of the senior registrars observes:

> Money is a motivator up to a point. It is true that we want salary increase, but we also need to be trained at ILPD[45] like our fellow judges, prosecutors and lawyers. If you look at our job description, you may partly agree on the current registrars' salaries. How can someone do a job which may be done by a high school leaver while they hold bachelor's degrees? We are underutilised and that is why we are the least paid and the most demotivated of our system. (Interview with Registrar Y on 25 July, 2011)

As Lipsky (1980:27) asserts, 'By definition, street level bureaucrats work at jobs characterised by relatively high

45 ILPD is a public institution under MINIJUST, which offers postgraduate training to legal practitioners. It is located in the Southern Province of Rwanda, in Nyanza District where the Supreme Court of Rwanda had its first headquarters.

degrees of discretion and regular interaction with citizens'. Before the 2004 judicial reforms, Rwandan court registrars had high discretion concerning whom to serve and how to serve them. The regular interactions with citizens and the high degree of discretion presented a high probability of corruption in courts. With fewer resources available to former courts' staff, coping mechanisms on behalf of court workers had negative impacts on justice administration. Chief registrars of visited Intermediate Courts unanimously pointed out one of the causes of case adjournments in reference to how registrars cope with limited resources availed to them in the course of their work:

> When registrars have to summon litigants where they should get a mission allowance of three days but are told to come within two days, they make sure that they do not find the litigant at the first place, because they know that going back to summon the litigants will give them additional mission allowances. (Interviews with Chief Registrars of visited Intermediate Courts)

With the advent of ICTs, such levels of discretion and behaviours has been reduced. In addition to this, current instructions on service delivery have changed the ways registrars behaved in the past. Ordinarily, Rwandan courts registrars have been experiencing the following conditions in their daily work:

> First, resources have been chronically inadequate relative to the tasks street-level bureaucrats are asked to perform. The implication is that when they have to summon litigants by themselves, they summon litigants who are in places that are easily accessible while those who are distant are rarely

summoned (Interviews with registrars in Gicumbi on 28 July and on 4 August 2011).

Second, the demand for services tends to increase to meet the supply. This holds in Rwandan courts because when registrars experience declining demand due to population shifts, they encounter different but equal difficulties in relieving caseload pressures. There are more caseloads in urban areas than in rural areas as it is for the population. Ideally, the more improved quality of service delivery, the more demand of services by court clients. Demand in courts may increase either by improved services or other factors like increase in conflicts or consequences of local authorities who have failed to deal with people's conflicts (The Rwandan Judiciary Annual Reports 2010:205).

Third, goal expectations for the agencies in which they work tend to be ambiguous, vague, or conflicting. For registrars, since they do not work independent of the judges, it is difficult to evaluate them individually. They always work with different judges and sometimes do not do their work as they have planned because of the nature of their work, as previously pointed out. Evidences can be found in individual performance appraisals for the last three years (Individual Performance Appraisals for Courts' Street-Level Bureaucrats, 2007-2010).

Fourth, performance oriented towards goal achievement tends to be difficult, if not impossible, to measure. As goals are not clear enough, it is difficult to evaluate performance contracts of street-level bureaucrats in courts (Individual

Performance Appraisals for Courts' Street-Level Bureaucrats, 2007-2010).

Lastly, clients are typically non-voluntary; partly as a result, clients for the most part do not serve as primary bureaucratic reference groups. Justice cannot be realised elsewhere other than in courts. Litigants have nowhere else to go to seek justice; they have to go to courts.

What is strange though in the case of the Rwandan Judiciary is that while street-level bureaucrats suffer from limited means to carry out their duties, money is given back to the National Treasurer because it has not been spent due to bad and/or poor planning. No transfers among different budget lines are allowed. On the other hand, difficulties in service delivery in courts arise because of the fact that demand is very often not predictable. It is not possible to know in advance or to estimate how many cases will enter in courts in a given period. Indeed, a combination of all the above-mentioned issues has variously resulted in case postponements.

Backlogs and service delivery in the judiciary of Rwanda

To start with, case adjournments arising from irregular summons of litigants by registrars and professional court bailiffs contribute to backlogs. Sometimes, cases are adjourned by street-level bureaucrats simply because the second summon may present them with an opportunity to get more mission allowances. Equally, judges may decide to postpone cases because they have not prepared the hearing very well. They may also have indirect or hidden interests in the case they have to judge. As those reasons cannot be put in official reports, they are put under the label of 'Other'. It may be true that some explanations in various reports submitted by registrars to court officials about the reasons for case postponements in reports do not reflect the reality in the field. There are untold reasons and it is difficult to know them.

Registrars may also hide some files or proof of litigants' summons when they have close connections or problems with one or both parties to a judgment. Registrars may not be willing to summon litigants properly because they have been in personal conflicts. They may hide files of one party to the process, which may result in case hearing postponements. A hidden file cannot be easily retrieved. With ICT, this cannot be done any more as all files are scanned and saved in electronic files. This has affected the behaviours of registrars to a certain extent.

According to the Rwandan Judiciary Annual Report (2010), the most ancient pending case at Intermediate Courts' level was introduced on 30 April 1999 and the first hearing was on 16 February 2011 (After 134 months). It is a crucial problem for a case to take more than 10 years without being tried. This is why contractual judges and registrars were hired in 2008 to deal with only backlogs while ordinary judges and registrars are dealing with new cases.

Respondents assume that there are many cases where postponements may be seen as things that lead to corruption. The interviewed litigants see postponement as ways to allow litigants get time to look for what they may offer as bribes. One litigant said:

> If cases are postponed without relevant motives, we assume that it is a warning against the potential loser in a process. The problem is now how to get to the judges in order to corrupt them. Whether you are right or wrong, the judge is the one to take the final decision and once taken, sometimes you cannot appeal against it! (Interview with litigants at The High Court of Musanze on 22 July 2011).

On the one hand, findings showed other reasons for backlogs: inherited backlogs from the period before 2004, a high number of new cases entering the courts, and high number of new cases that begin at appeal courts when compared to the tried cases, and improved service delivery, among others. The last cause is a paradox because improved service delivery should habitually reduce the backlogs. This is partially justified by the fact that now most people believe in the quality of Rwandan Courts' decisions compared to what was done in the past. Therefore, they want to bring every conflict into justice, as they know that they will be given fair justice in a relatively short time.

As mentioned earlier, while the most ancient pending cases at both Intermediate and High Court levels require to be tried after 134 and 85 months, at Commercial and Primary Courts they are tried after 35 and 76 months respectively. This gives a picture of the time it takes for pending cases to be judged if no new case enters the courts. With recent cases, time has reduced down to four, six and eight months for the Commercial Tribunals, the Commercial High Court and Primary Courts (The Rwandan Judiciary Annual Report, 2010:36) respectively. For other courts, time for the first hearing is relatively long if compared to six months for cases to be counted as backlogs but still, this is better when compared to what was happening in the past. This is why improved service delivery has emerged among the causes of backlogs in Rwanda.

Public perspectives on service delivery

Court clients are served according to the principle of 'First In, First Out', with an exception to lawyers and those who represent the public interests. However, most of interviewees said that they are not happy with the way they are served. Courts' clients spend too much time in queues. There are cases where those who come early in the morning are served late at the end of the day. Sometimes, they are told to come another day when it is already late and do not have where to spend the night. They are obliged to spend more money to pay for their accommodation or to look for friends who can host them. As most of them come from far and are peasants, they do not know where to find suitable accommodation, depending on their income. This makes the services they seek very costly. This happens often to those who come to see courts inspectors at the Supreme Court for various reasons. Some respondents stated, 'It is very difficult and rare to get the services the first day you get to court even though there are notices at every court which inform people about their rights while seeking services from courts' (Interviews with litigants who came to see the Inspectors for Courts and Tribunals at the Supreme Court on 20 July, 2011)

When people are told to come another time, they think that those who tell them to come back want to ask for bribes. Other people think that it is a way of making them tired so that they should not return to court. If it is a matter of a case pronouncement, they think that decisions are going to be changed depending on who will be ready to offer bribes. In general, the interviewed people complained about service delivery in courts. The general perception is that the delay in getting services from courts may be associated with corruption. One respondent said in a statement:

> It is the fourth time I am coming here over the same issue. I came here for a case pronouncement. The case hearing was postponed three times. The first day, I was told to go because the judge was in the training. The second time, the judge was sick. The third time, it was a problem of electricity, they said that printing was not possible. Now I am being told again that the judge is on annual recess. How long does it take to write a judgment? Can't those who are here call the judge and ask her the exact time of the pronouncement of my case? I am now suspecting some corruption over this case. The judge may want one of us (litigants), to go and see her. I will not do that because corruption is not good. But if I had another alternative, I would have used it. What I have spent so far in terms of time and money is beyond my imagination. Courts should be sensitive to people's requests or provide with them compensation of incurred losses caused by their staff. (Interviewee J, at Musanze High Court Chamber on 24 July, 2010).

Another lawyer at Musanze High Court, whose client's case was postponed twice, said:

> Before, criminal cases could be heard without prosecutors. Now, they have changed the laws so that no criminal case can be heard in the absence of prosecutors. This will keep for long the people they do not want to be released from prisons on the grounds that prosecutors are not enough to attend all the scheduled criminal cases. Policy makers should think about this crucial issue. Otherwise, people will continue to be kept

> under custody for ever, without being tried (Interview with Lawyer B, on 24 July, 2011).

This reflects the contents of interviews conducted with litigants, which revealed more or less the same thing. There are notices on how people should get services they are seeking, but it is not always the case. As per Lipsky (1980), many laws or instructions may hinder service delivery. What is important is to follow up on how those instructions are being implemented and to take corrective measures in case they are not respected. At the same court, another interviewee complained:

> At least this court registrar tries to ask people what they are looking for before opening his office. When you are mistaken, you know what to do earlier before it gets too late. Other registrars tell us that they are busy. We do not know what is wrong with staff of this court. He has been busy with people since the morning and never complained. You will help us to tell the courts' leadership that we are tired of this kind of service delivery. And sometimes, when you call 3670,[46] it is always busy and if the call goes through, they tell you that they are going to work on your claim but in vain. Maybe it is because calling them is free but replying is costly. However, even if you call back, and maybe they realise that it is the same number which has been calling, they never answer you! What is the use of calling if you do not get answers to your queries? (Interviewee K, at Musanze High Court Chamber on 24 July, 2011)

We can see that people are spending too much time and money on transport to go and get services from courts. Perhaps with

46 3670 is a free line for complaints, suggestions, and anything which may be useful for better service delivery in courts. It is managed under the supervision of the General Inspectorate of Courts and Tribunal.

enhanced ICT, some services like filling in cases, summoning litigants and getting copies of judgments might be done online; hence reducing costs, especially those associated with the distance (transport, meals, accommodation, etc.)

Modernisation of courts by ICTs

In order to enhance service delivery through modernisation, the current Chief Justice constituted the Judicial IT Committee (JITCO) in early 2011. The JITCO oversees, from a non-technical perspective, the work on ICT in the judiciary. The President of the High Court heads it. The committee members, though not all of them technocrats, advise and provide recommendations to the Chief Justice concerning the ICT needs within the judiciary and how these needs can be fully met. While commenting on the prospects of ICT integration one respondent stated:

> With the help of ICT tools, stakeholders and courts' service beneficiaries will get faster delivery of justice to judicial customers while saving time and reducing costs associated with achieving justice. There will be better customer relationships due to increased communications channels. So far, the use of ICT in courts has modified staff behaviours in general and those of Street-Level Bureaucrats in particular. Access to the 'information superhighway' allows the court and counsel to communicate on many matters, the resolution of which can save time and money for all involved parties. By working together, judge and registrars as well as court professional managers promote case flow management, including the creation and maintenance of the records, supporting court management of pre-trials, trials and post dispositional events, conferences and hearings, monitoring cases for staff and judge

> attention and providing needed management information and statistics. (Interview with Top Court Leader B, 29 August, 2011)

As part of its modernisation efforts to improve case management, the judiciary identified ICTs as one of the core components to enable transformation. According to the current Rwandan Judiciary Strategic Plan (2009-2013), the vision of ICTs by senior judiciary leadership is in line with the objectives of judiciary reforms and consistent with the current strategic plan for the judiciary and incorporates the following guiding principles. First, ICT should serve the needs of the judiciary and its constituencies. Second, ICT is essential for the courts to function efficiently for present as well as future operations. Third and last, access to accurate court information is a vital part of the vision for ICT in the judiciary.

According to one of my interviewees on ICT and related issues, the goal of the judiciary in ICTs is, 'To effectively apply technologies that are widely available, using hardware and software which are likely to remain competitive and supported for a reasonable length of time.' (Interview with one of the Top Court Leaders A, on 29 August, 2011). Another Top Court Leader mentioned:

> Our modernisation initiatives have been enabled by active exercise of leadership commitment from key participants to a shared vision, regular and effective communications, assignments of responsibilities and maintenance of accountability, and learning environment (Interview with Top Court Leader B, on 29th August 2011).

Along with various partners, the judiciary of Rwanda now has a system called Electronic Records Management System (ERMS).

Implemented in 22 courts so far, ERMS includes the following functions: Processing and sealing of documents, alerts and statistical reports, retrieval of documents, registration of new cases, scheduling and planners, case management, document tracking and work flows. It is a multi-task system, which brings about efficiency and effectiveness in courts. It makes work a bit easier. Replying to a question on serving legal community in particular and the public as a whole, the following was stated by my other interviewee:

> (An) electronic filing system is one of the solutions to the needs of legal community as a whole and the public. With its implementation, gone are the days where litigants, lawyers and attorneys had to queue at registration counters and travel hundreds of miles to submit documents or to wait to be served just to know if their case is due for hearing. Time is a court's most critical resource. Modernising our courts provides us with opportunities to save on time of both staff and litigants respectively while delivering and seeking justice. (Interview with Top Court Leader B, on 29 August 2011).

This might affect court staff because access to information provided by courts will be done online. The problem is with those who are IT illiterate. In a country like Rwanda where the ordinary illiteracy rate is relatively high, litigants may use people in whom they trust in order get whatever may be got with the help of courts' online services. There will be a relative reduction of discretion over some issues. The researcher observed that in remote courts where ICTs are not yet enhanced, there are still queues of lawyers and litigants when getting services from courts.

Furthermore, there have been other modernisation initiatives in the aspects of ICT such as conducting electronically enabled trials due to cameras and data projectors, rehabilitation of LANs for various court houses, updated website, procurement of new ICT equipment such as printers, photocopiers, desktops etc. The use of ICT has so far tried to positively influence the service delivered by Rwandan courts. Possibly, it will even be improved when all ICT projects are fully implemented.

However, it is important to note that effects may both be intended and unintended, desirable and undesirable. As Norris and Moon (2005:70) argue:

> The evidence available from the literature today suggests that, for the most part, the use of IT in government organisations produces salutary results, although it is not without problems. Among other things, IT improves efficiency, accuracy, timeliness, and effectiveness; enhances jobs; makes work easier and more enjoyable; and extends workers' capacity to work. However, IT also supports existing organisational structures, including structures of power and authority. Typical problems with IT include difficulties with hardware, software, and vendors; poor or non-existent training; and underutilisation of system capabilities. Further, IT is not without costs, and the increased productivity resulting from IT may not be sufficient to offset its costs.

These arguments are very relevant for the case of the Rwandan judiciary where so far the use of IT has resulted into improved productivity especially of street-level bureaucrats. The lack of regular maintenance and training make it difficult to realise the full benefits of IT. The costs of replacing IT tools are very high.

The most part of the current achievements may be attributed to the use of IT in various areas of justice administration. Courts' modernisation needs appropriate infrastructures otherwise equipping small and old court houses would be considered a waste of resources. It may also require demolishing ICT installations when it comes to renovating or constructing new courts. This is the reason ICT installations are done after renovation and construction of new court houses.

As far as equipment is concerned, the following table shows only ICT-related equipment as both service delivery and street-level bureaucrats behaviours have greatly influenced by the use of ICT in Rwandan courts. The following table shows the situation before and after 2004.

Table 9.2: Status of ICT and related equipment

	Before 2004			**After 2004**		
Item	**Needed**	**Available**	**Gaps**	**Needed**	**Available**	**Gaps**
Computer	1,583	78	1,505	830	830	0
Photocopier	162	29	133	124	124	0
Scanner	162	0	162	82	18	64
Generator	162	3	159	82	40	42

Source: Research findings from primary data

Table 9.2 shows the number of needed and available ICT and related equipment. The number of computers is higher than the number of staff (663). This is because there are laptops for court leadership in addition to the desktops they use in their offices. Additional computers are in the Library and documentation centre. Current gaps are on scanners and generators. The current existing infrastructures and equipment would have hardly been availed for courts and their staff if judicial reforms had not taken place and of course if the number of both staff and courts had not been reduced. The researcher has tried to show in various findings to what extent ICT has changed behaviours of judiciary staff, especially the street-level bureaucrats in the course of their daily activities.

Conclusion

As this chapter has shown, the judicial reforms in Rwanda in recent years have failed to effectively meet the challenges that street-level bureaucrats face, and thus to tackle the problem of increasing backlogs through case adjournments. Mainly the research reported on in this chapter found that such backlogs were not being tackled, mainly because of low levels of motivation and inadequate resources and training for lower-level court workers. Inadequate salaries and the previously poor working conditions have all contributed to lowering motivation levels among registrars, for example, resulting in more adjournments. On the other hand, backlogs were found to be the result of new kinds of inheritance and other land disputes entering the Rwandan court system. Even so, the study found evidence of significant improvements in service delivery by Rwandan courts overall, which is starting to increase public trust by Rwandan citizens in Rwanda's court system. This, ironically, can reinforce backlogs since increased confidence means more cases are taken to court in the hope of a just and speedy settlement.

Despite many challenges of computerisation, this reform has made the delivery of judicial services far more efficient. The use of ICT has reduced the discretion levels of street-level bureaucrats, especially recording of details of cases and summoning litigants including online access of services like hearings schedule(s) by the public. This alongside other strategies may enhance proper service delivery in the Rwandan judiciary in the near future, though much still remains to be done. For instance, unnecessary delays, irregular summons, rescheduling and postponement of case hearings including structural challenges as opinioned by most of the respondents in this study. As such, computerisation presents viable options of improving judicial service delivery since it makes recording of details of cases far more efficient. Also, restructuring of the professional tasks of individuals could result into enhanced and legitimate judicial institutions.

References

Adler, M., and Asquith, S. (1993) 'Discretion and Power,' in Hill M. (eds). *The Policy Process: A Reader*, Hemel Hemstead: Harvester Wheatsheaf, 339-406.

Alemika, E.E.O., and Chukwuma, I.C. (2004). 'The Poor and Informal Policing', Nigeria Center for Law Enforcement Education (CLEEN), Lagos.

Bardach, E. (1977) *The Implementation Game: What Happens After a Bill Becomes a Law*. Cambridge/Massachusetts: MIT Press.

Bitner, M.J., Faranda, W.T., Hubbert, A.R., and Zeithaml, V.A. (1997) 'Customer Contributions and Roles in Service Delivery', *International Journal of Service Industry Management,* 8(3): 193-205.

Crook, R., C. (2010) 'Rethinking civil service reform in Africa: 'Islands of effectiveness' and organisational commitment, *Commonwealth & Comparative Politics*, 48:4, 479-504. Online publication of 8 November, 2010 on http://dx.doi.org/10.1080/14662043.2010.522037

De Bono, E. (1995) *Parallel Thinking*. London: Penguin.

Grindle, M.S. (1997) 'Divergent Cultures? When Public Organisations Perform Well in Developing Countries', *World Development*, 25, 481-495.

Grindle, M.S., and Hilderbrand, M.E. (1995) 'Building Sustainable Capacity in the Public Sector: What can be done?' *Public Administration and Development*, 15, 441-463.

Hintjens, H.M. (2001) 'When Identity Becomes a Knife: Reflecting on the Genocide in Rwanda', *Ethnicities,* 1(1):25-55.

Hill, M. (2005) *The Public Policy Process*. Harlow: Pearson/Longman (4th edition).

Hill, M., and Hupe, P.L. (2007) *Public Administration*, 85, (2), 2007: 279-299, Blackwell Publishing Ltd, Oxford, USA.

Klitgaard, R. (1997) 'Cleaning Up and Invigorating the Civil Service, *Public Administration and Development*, 17: 487-509'.

Law, S., Harper, C., and Marcus, R. (2003) *Research for Development: A Practical Guide*. London: Sage &Save the Children.

Lipsky, M. (1971) 'Towards a Theory of Street Level Bureaucracy', *Urban Affair Quarterly*, 6:391-409.

Lipsky, M. (1980) 'Street Level Bureaucracy: Dilemmas of the Individual in Public Services', Russell Sage Foundation, New York.

Lienert, I., and Modi, J. (1998) A Decade of Civil Service Reform in Sub Saharan Africa IMF Working Paper 97/179, Washington, DC: International Monetary Fund.

Magnarella, P.J. (2000) *Justice in Africa: Rwanda's Genocide, Its Courts, and the UN Criminal Tribunal.* Burlington VT, Farnham Ashgate Publishing, Limited.

Manning, N. (2001) The Legacy of The New Public Management in Developing Countries, *International Review of Administrative Sciences*, 67, 297-312.

Mutamba, J. (2005) Strategies for Increasing Women's Participation in Government. Case Study of Rwanda. http://www.un.org/africa/osaa/report (last access on 6th May 2010)

Nielsen, V.L. (2006) 'Are Street-level bureaucrats Compelled or Enticed to cope?', *Public Administration,* 84(4):861-889.

Norris, D.F., and M.J. Moon (2005) 'Advancing E-Government at the Grassroots: Tortoise or Hare?' *Public Administration Review*, 65 (1): 64-76.

O'Leary, Z. (2005) *Researching Real-World Problems: A Guide to Methods of Inquiry*. London: Sage.

O'Leary, Z. (2010) *The Essential Guide to Doing Your Research Project*. London: Sage.

Peters, B.G., and Pierre J. (2002) Introduction: The role of Pubic Administration in Governing, in Peters, B.G. and Pierre J. (eds) *Handbook of Public Administration.* London: Sage.

Pollit, C., and Bouckaert, G. (2004) *Public Management Reform: A Comparative Analysis*. Oxford: Oxford University Press.

Prottas, J.M. (1978) 'The Power of the Street-Level Bureaucrat in Public Service Bureaucracies, *Urban Affairs Review,* 13(3): 285-312.

Prottas, J.M. (1979) *People-processing: The Street-level Bureaucrat in Public Service Bureaucracies.* Lexington, Massachusetts: Lexington Press.

Rainey, H.G. and Chun, Y.H. (2005), 'Public and Private Management Compared', in Ewan Ferlie et al, *The Oxford Handbook of Public Management.* Oxford: Oxford University Press, 72-91.

Rhodes, R.A.W. (2000) 'The governance narrative: key findings and lessons from the ESRC's Whitehall programme', P*ublic Administration*, 78:345-63.

Scott, S. and Lars, W. (2011) *Remaking Rwanda: State Building and Human Rights after Mass Violence.* The University of Wisconsin Press.

Stein, J.G. (2002) *The Cult of efficiency*. Toronto: Ananasi Press.

Toonen, T.A.J. (2001) 'The Comparative Dimension of Administrative Reform: Creating Open Villages and Redesigning the Politics of Administration,' in Peters, B.G. and Pierre J. (eds.) *Politicians, Bureaucrats and Administrative Reform*. London: Routledge, 183-201.

Weatherley, R. (1979) *Reforming Special Education: Policy Implementation from State Level to Street Level.* Massachusetts. MIT Press.

Documents from Rwandan Public Institutions

The Government of Rwanda, The Ministry of Finance, Vision 2020.

The Government of Rwanda, Law No 18/2004 of 20/06/2004.

The Government of Rwanda, Organic Law No 16/2004 of 19 June 2004.

The Rwandan Judiciary Annual Report for 2004

The Rwandan Judiciary Annual Report for 2005

The Rwandan Judiciary Annual Report for 2006

The Rwandan Judiciary Annual Report for 2007

The Rwandan Judiciary Annual Report for 2008

The Rwandan Judiciary Annual Report for 2009

The Rwandan Judiciary Annual Report for 2010

The Rwandan Judiciary (2005), Strategic Plan of the Judiciary 2005-2013.

The Rwandan Judiciary (2008) Strategic Plans of the Judiciary 2005-2013.

The Republic of Rwanda (2003) The Rwandan Constitution of 4 June, 2003.

Websites

http://www.bizclir.com/cs/countries/africa/rwanda accessed on 6th June 2011.

http://www.gov.rw/OPEN-JUSTICE-Q-A-with-Minister-of-Justice-Tharcisse-Karugarama, accessed on 3 June 2011

http://www.supremecourt.gov.rw/document and publications/Laws accessed on 12 November, 2011

http://thinkexist.com/search/searchquotation.asp?search=Justice+delayed+is+justice+denied accessed on 3 June 2011

http://www.cjcr.gov.rw/eng/constitution accessed on 11 October 2011)

Chapter 10

No Justice? Mob Violence, Community Policing and Crime Control in Uganda's Urban Markets

Joshua Mugambwa and Helen Hintjens

'Mob justice perpetuates a cycle of violence, creates a culture of fear, and rejects personal accountability for violent acts that are committed in the name of justice. As we condemn the act of mob justice, it is important to understand the social climate that allows for it to happen.....' (Global Science Initiative, 2011:57)

Introduction

With increasing rates of urbanisation in Uganda, many rural areas are slowly transforming into urban centres, with attendant increases in crime, and more focus on crime prevention systems and services. The Uganda Police Force Operational Policing Review Report 1994 recommended 'community policing' through an area policing approach.

The basic elements of this kind of community policing involve consultation with community groups regarding their security needs; command devolution so that those closest to the community can determine how best to respond to local people's security needs; mobilisation of agencies other than the police to assist in addressing those security needs; and remedying the conditions that generate crime and insecurity through focused problem solving. Although there is no reliable evidence about this, it may be that the unemployed and the poor are more likely to be more vulnerable to accusations of stealing, and thus to become victims of mob justice.

There are some problems that arise when crowds determine the fate of a person suspected of a crime; ethnic 'markers' may be used to police market places, and this chapter asks why mob violence was more common in one of the two markets than in the other, where criminals were more often handed over to the police. Sensitisation on the rule of law, the dignity of human life, and tolerance could be used to enhance social cohesion and reduce mob violence in markets. The aim of such strategies would be to ensure that impunity is overcome for those who perpetrate the crime of mob violence, in the name of cost-benefit and of rapidly punishing crime. The major question for this study is: how does community policing address mob justice or mob violence? Why has community policing sometimes failed to address this problem? Using a mix of historical, qualitative and quantitative data, this study contributes to the literature on mob justice and mob violence, and on popular but violent responses to crime, and the role of the police and of 'community policing' in combating crime.

This study is concerned with mob justice as a form of social violence, which often takes place in markets. It is not only unlawful in being violent to human beings, mob violence also destroys capital assets and leads to loss of business and time. Two markets in Kampala were studied as examples: Nakulabye and Owino. As a form of community-legitimated violence, so-called mob justice may or may not be controlled by the state (Loader and Walker, 2001). History supports the argument that mob violence tends to take place in the absence of judicial justice in the form of fair trials, proper police investigations and fair punishments. In more formal legal justice systems, the accused is usually given the right to defend him or herself. This is not so with mob violence, which reflects different norms of 'justice' and 'social justice'. Where dominant powers in society are in control of the legal and justice systems, which therefore lack independence, groups of 'crime-fighting' actors can arise to fill in the void of ineffective judicial and police structure. When mobs take criminal punishment into their own hands, they often express their loss of faith in a system where a corrupt police or judicial force, not adequately salaried, relies on bribes and releases criminals or finds them not guilty following payment of money. Although this is often a means to survive, it means that formal justice systems are undermined and devalued (Loader and Walker, 2001; Steenkamp, 2011).

Consequently, what may be needed to prevent mob justice or to reduce it, is to improve the image of the police, on law enforcement and of the judicial system as a whole, as this chapter will conclude. Community policing in Uganda being a relatively less focused approach does not feature much in the literature yet. In Tanzania, some literature has examined the *sungu sungu*, which is the rough equivalent of community policing in Uganda or Kenya (UN Habitat, 2000). In fact, no analysis of how mob violence may relate to community policing has been found in the literature; this study thus sought to bridge this gap in the literature. In addition, the chapter also proposes that alongside community policing, the much-needed state response to rising mob violence needs to tackle social inequalities and poverty as well. This applies in Uganda and also more generally across the Eastern African region. In Kenya, for example, there is a fear that 'mob justice' may substitute formal justice at the national level (Sriram and Brown, 2012). In Uganda, community policing has comparatively restrained the mob violence but at a slow rate (CHRI, 2006).

By using specific examples from Kampala city, this chapter looks at how community policing and poverty reduction can help reduce the incidence of mob violence. In the conclusions, the authors tease out some lessons for public control of mob violence in other contexts as well. It is proposed that both community policing and poverty reduction need to be integral parts of any workable solution to the problem of mob violence. The following specific research questions helped to guide this study:

a) What are some of the comparative and historical meanings of 'mob justice' as a form of community-legitimated violence?

b) According to research, what makes 'mob justice' violence escalate or decrease in general?

c) How can we explain how mob justice is manifested and varies between Owino and Nakulabye markets in Kampala?

d) What general lessons can we draw about the state's response to mob violence from these examples?

The word 'mob justice' is used in this study interchangeably with 'mob violence'. The police term is 'mob action', and sometimes the literature refers to 'lynch mobs'. On the one hand are those who consider mob violence to be justified, for example by the lack of justice in formal state justice, law and order institutions like the police, judiciary and prisons. They tend to use the term mob justice to suggest that mobs of citizens can 'take the law into their own hands' when nothing is done to address crime. On the other hand, we take a more critical approach, and tend to prefer the term mob violence, which better describes what is really happening. If mob action included holding a hearing, of evidence, and considering the facts before taking action, then justice might be the right term. Nevertheless, most mob violence is action taken – usually all of a sudden – by a mass vigilante group of people, usually in response to crimes said to be committed within their communities or market places. The unjust character of violent mob action is that it takes place in the absence of any conventional or other form of trial in which the accused can defend themselves and in which evidence can be heard from both sides (Outwater et al, 2013). Instead, under the circumstances of mob justice, the accused is brutally punished and can be sentenced to death within minutes or even seconds of being identified as a thief, or worse (Glad, Stromberg and Westerlund, 2010). The same authors ask in their study of mob justice in Uganda; 'What crime was so awful that the culprits deserved to be sentenced to death without trial? What made all these people choose to take the law into their own hands?' (Glad, Stromberg and Westerlund, 2010:iii). The Uganda Police trains volunteers approved by local leaders on a programme in community policing and have become crime preventers in communities. Therefore, they are referred to as crime preventers or collectively as community police (Interview in Owino, 24 July 2013). The terms crime preventers and community police are used interchangeably in this chapter.

The research for this chapter was carried out between June and July 2013 in Owino and Nakulabye markets, located in Kampala city, where primary data was recorded using open-ended questionnaires and structured interviews. Respondents in both markets totaled to 42 and included six police officers, 20 community crime preventers, 10 members of the public who are familiar with and shop from the markets as well as six market vendors. A three-point Likert scale (three alternatives) was used to describe the dimensions that influence mob violence adopted from Vowell, (2007). The vendors chose from three alternatives in a questionnaire namely: 1-low, 2-moderate, and 3-high. The response with the highest frequency was recorded in Table 10.2 and 10.3. The researchers targeted police officers that worked in the market where crimes are recorded and investigations instituted, as well as community crime preventers (market vendors trained in community policing) and vendors. Secondary sources included documents, manuals, reports and other studies on the subject. The choice of study locations and selection of respondents were based on purposive sampling, implying that territorial locations and fieldwork respondents were selected on the basis of their considered relevance to the study, as well as the logistical convenience of the researchers

Mob violence or mob justice in context

Historically, examples of mob violence have been prevalent in societies all over the world, and are a particular form of the wider problem of vigilantism. Although vigilantism is widespread in the world, mob violence is today strongly associated with African countries, including Uganda, where the police data suggests that since around 2007, lynching of suspected criminals by crowds of 'ordinary' people have been on the increase (Uganda Police, 2008). We will explore this and suggest some causes for it in a later section of this chapter. First, we can consider some evidence of the prevalence of this form of crime.

The evidence suggests that public responses to crime may be changing, with overall violence increasing for less serious crimes. Data collected by the police is not consistent between reports, however. Thus for 2008, 'any other' mob action lynching's data is missing, and this means the overall totals will not be strictly comparable. The comparison between the 2008 and 2011 data in the table below suggests that the increases in mob violence have mainly been in economic crimes, such as theft, robbery and burglary. There has been a decline in mob justice killings for more serious crimes like murder as well as witchcraft. There is gender-disaggregated data for 2011 but not for 2008.

Table 10.1: Comparing 2008 and 2011 data for mob violence

Reasons	**Mob Lynching**		**Female (2011)**
	2008	**2011**	
Theft	232	278	14 Female
Robbery	29	34	0 Female
Murder	59	39	7 Female
Witchcraft	26	22	5 Female
Burglary	22	31	0 Females
Any Other	no data	71	0 Females
Grand Total	368	476	26 Females

Sources: Uganda Police, 2011, Appendix H; Uganda Police, 2008: 26; 28.

Overall, an upward trend is evident, and is reflected in the increase in mob violence cases resulting in deaths through lynchings, from a total of 184 cases reported in 2007 to 368 cases reported in 2008, and 476 cases in 2011 (Uganda Police, 2011: 1). The question is whether, as with the reporting of crimes like sexual violence, this increase and stabilisation has been only as a result of increased mob violence, or also the result of greater willingness to report the crime on the part of the public and the police alike.

According to the 2011 Uganda Crime Report, enhanced intelligence collection among the public has facilitated more intelligence-led forms of policing, and has increased the mobility and visibility of the police in the country, contributing to crime prevention. There was a slight decrease in total crimes and complaints to police from 2010 and 2011, of 3.8 per cent. This is perhaps attributed to the process of bringing Police services nearer to the people by creating more police stations and outposts. Equally, Community Policing increases police accessibility, their mobility and visibility to the public. Perhaps this has resulted in greater public confidence in the Police as well. If the trend continues, the result could be a more stable and peaceful environment for economic, social and political activities in Uganda, which could increase confidence of the international community. However, death cases due to mob action increased in 2011 from 2010 and were 476 and 438 respectively. The police decided to step up their response in situations of mob action, improve on intelligence and investigation capacity, continuous involvement of the public in community policing and sensitisation. Death due to mob justice has been attributed to cases of poisoning, mob action, and domestic violence, land wrangles, dissatisfaction with delayed and or omission of justice, family misunderstandings, and business rivalry (Uganda Police, 2011). Mob violence can be viewed as deep-rooted in human nature or can be viewed as a crisis response to collective threats that lead people to perform group punishment when they feel their 'norms and values' have been violated and when they think the police and courts will not act to punish crime. With modern social constructs such as judicial systems, mob justice can be considered unacceptable and even a barbaric solution to handling petty and more serious crime within the wider society. This calls into question why some societies have higher rates of mob justice, and of crowds taking punishment into their own hands than others (Glad, Stromberg and Westerlund, 2010). At the forefront of analysing what works to prevent mob violence in relation to crime, have been criminologists like Gottfredson,

Mackenzie, Farrington, Sherman, Waller and reputable international organisations and research bodies such as the World Health Organisation (WHO) of the United Nations, and the United States National Research Council (Braga, 2008; Weisburd et al., 2010; Waller, 2006 and Eck, 2006). They propose to include crime prevention within the broader social justice framework to transfer economic and political resources to local institutions and residents, thus empowering communities and to build capacity. This helps to integrate the marginalised youth, enabling them to tackle key community-level risk factors of crime and delinquency. Other structural changes are also proposed such as transparency within the judicial system and improvement of the educational system, as ways of preventing mob justice and increasing awareness of this issue.

It appears that one cause of mob justice is public distrust of formal institutions such as police and law enforcement agencies. These may be accused of corruption and of improper handling of criminal investigations (Sherman et al, 2004). In Uganda and the rest of East Africa, the public has little faith in the police due to their perceived corruption; many accuse the judicial process of being easily manipulated. Experience suggests that many criminals and perpetrators are let off if they can pay a substantial bribe. The public's dissatisfaction with a corrupt system can thus result in people collectively taking the law into their own hands on the streets. This situation enhances public support for what is viewed as 'mob justice' as an alternative form of enforcement and punishment for crime (Uganda Police 2011, Glad et al, 2010).

'If a thief steals, no trial is necessary. He is immediately killed' (HRW, 2010:23). This was noted in a study on the case of Burundi. Mobs were reported to kill individuals who were alleged to have committed a range of offences like adultery, petty theft, armed robbery, rape or murder instead of bringing them to the police. Mob justice here, as in Uganda, seemed to reflect a loss of faith among the public in the police force and judicial system. Corruption, incompetence, and inadequate resources all played their part. Unlike in Burundi, some data on mob justice exists in Uganda, and the crime is now being investigated and punished more often. Since mob violence is taking place in Uganda – as in Burundi – in the context of a country emerging from conflict, one problem is how violence has become normalised. Not prosecuting those responsible implies a tacit acceptance of the practice as a form of 'community crime prevention' by both police and central state authorities, thus encouraging mob violence. Those plagued by desperate poverty themselves are not able to lose anything however small, without fearing destitution. Yet whilst victims of crime have a right to redress, they do not have a right to deprive others, only suspects in any case, of life. The right to due process and to a fair trial is absolute and the state is responsible, ultimately, for ensuring that this right is protected, including for those suspected of serious and petty crimes alike. The state should not be seen to condone, abet or as having failed to investigate murders of alleged criminals through mob violence, since to do so will imply impunity. In Uganda as in Burundi, the police may be thought not to be very effective at protecting the community from crime. Yet as crime statistics fall in Uganda, so too the onus is on the public to hand over suspected criminals, whether petty thieves or murderers, to the police. One of the first critical studies on mob violence in Uganda was Harriet Nalukenge's bachelor's thesis on the subject (Nalukenge, 2001). This reported that mob violence was common because of perceived problems with justice and police effectiveness. As one study on the problem of post-conflict violence noted, vigilante or mob violence: '...is social insofar as it wants to rid society of suspected criminals, but it is also political in that it provides a challenge to the authority of the state, which is seen as incapable of providing safety and security from crime' (Steenkamp, 2011:375). Before considering the causes of mob violence in the Ugandan context, we will consider the issue of community policing and how it relates to crime in general.

Community Policing and Crime in Kampala

As we have suggested, mob violence as a phenomenon is not restricted to Uganda or East Africa. Mob violence also known as mob justice exists in many parts of the world, including formerly in Europe and North America. In Europe today, however, examples of mob violence are relatively rare, as compared to mob violence in other parts of the world such as India, for example (Sundar, 2010). In post-conflict situations, resort to mob violence can arise from a difficult peace process; in Guatemala, public lynchings started after the end of the war in 1996, and escalated thereafter (Steenkamp, 2011:374). Evidence shows crime increases in Uganda and East Africa in recent years, according to available police evidence (see Table 10.1). Knowledge of the phenomenon is still relatively limited and therefore requires further research (Kanaabi,

2004, Wisler and Onwudiwe, 2007). For instance, mob justice was not reported in Kenya as a separate crime until the 2011 Police report; reporting in Uganda started in the early 2000s (Mugunga, 2005).

With increasing rates of urbanisation in Uganda, many rural areas are slowly transforming into urban centres with attendant increases in crime and mob-justice, and there is an urgent need for the police to focus on crime prevention systems and services. In line with this, the Uganda Police Force Operational Policing Review Report of 1994 already recommended 'community policing' through an Area Policing Approach. The basic elements of this kind of community policing would be: improved consultation with community groups regarding their own security needs; command devolution so that those closest to the community could decide how best to respond to local people's security needs; mobilisation of agencies other than the police to assist in addressing locally-felt security needs; and remedying the conditions – especially poverty – that generate crime and insecurity through focused problem-solving within specific locations (Nalunga, 2012). Almost 20 years after this promising start, what has resulted from community policing in Uganda in relation to reducing mob violence incidents?

Article 212 of the Uganda Constitution stipulates that the police force is an important organ of the state. Article 212 also stipulates the police functions as to keep law and order, prevention and detection of crime and cooperation with civilian authorities and with security organs established under the constitution. Cooperation with the population generally is also required. This provision requires the police to cooperate in crime control with other institutions and the public, and this cooperation is what is commonly referred to as community policing (Uganda Constitution, 1995). The Uganda Police Force (UPF) was established to ensure law and order, discipline and allegiance of people to government. Over the years, their operational strategies became almost entirely 'reactive'; taking complaints, conducting investigations and recording statements, with little personal interaction in the form of community and preventative policing. The report of the Commission of Enquiry into the Violation of Human Rights in Uganda from 1962 to January 1986, pointed out that the UPF was one of the state agencies implicated in atrocities during the Idi Amin military junta era and the second UPC-Obote government of 1980-85. For some time afterwards, the resulting fear and mistrust discouraged the public from supporting the police and working together in a partnership against crime. The UPF itself, however, had made little systematic attempt to market its image and solicit public support. The UPF tended to see members of the public's role exclusively in terms of the help they could provide in the combat and prevention of crime and mob justice in particular and so has for some time been pursuing strategies aimed at promoting a partnership against crime. These attitudes have been changing since the 2000's and research has found evidence of improved police discipline and performance. The police's focus has turned to community policing in terms of sensitising the public on their role and what they can do to contain crime. The communities collaborating with police receive elementary military training to enable them serve as alternatives to state policing, providing protection to communities. Participants in the community policing training programme are identified through Resistance Councils (RCs) and Local Defence Units (LDUs) for their later role as local police officers. RCs are grassroots structures for local governance. The participants of the programme become promoters of community policing and popular participation (Omach, 2010, Raleigh et al, 1998 and Nalunga, 2012).

Friedman noted that community policing is a crime reduction tool, a philosophy as well as an organisational strategy, which allows police and community residents to work closely together in new ways to solve problems of crime, social disorder and neighborhood decay. The philosophy of community policing rests on the belief that law-abiding people in the community have a right to have inputs into the policing process at local level. Community policing is based on the idea that finding creative solutions for crime at neighbourhood level involves moving beyond a narrow focus on individual crime incidents and towards more preventative and participatory forms of policing (ICPC, 2005). Some key elements of community policing as a form of community-based crime prevention include proactive servicing, devolution of command responsibility and public participation in the planning and supervision of police operations (Mirsky, 2009).

Background to community policing in Uganda

Community policing programmes began in 1989 in Old Kampala and in Katwe police divisions. Due to a lack of logistics and of proper management, efforts to adopt community policing policies and practices it almost came to a halt in 1993. The programme resumed in October 1993 with the assistance of the British Government through its Department for International

Development (DfID). The programme was centred on the following objectives: to establish an effective and efficient policing system with the assistance of the public to prevent crime; to sensitise communities on crime and its control; to promote open and honest relations between police and members of the public; and to improve the quality of police services and integrate them into public life (Friedman, 1992). The two themes of community policing and mob justice are widely studied in literature, however, they are studied separately, a gap that this study tries to bridge. Community Policing (CP) is very popular in Western democracies; it is an informal policing used by police promoting community participation. Informal policing is also widely practiced especially in Asia, Latin America and Africa. In Africa, Community Policing strategies are relatively new supplements to policing with challenges of an often poorly trained, ill-disciplined and underpaid police force, (CHRI, Uganda Report 2006). Despite efforts to introduce CP in various parts of the world, the problem of mob justice continues to take place. CP is perhaps misinterpreted as vigilantism rather than involving community-based groups in defining how the police at community level should manage public order (Omach, 2010). Examples like Nigeria, Tanzania, and Kenya suggest that this can be a problem, and that vigilantism can become institutionalised under CP. A relatively well-established example of institutionalised vigilantism is Tanzania, where local security patrols have often taken the law into their own hands, resulting in deaths and lynchings. In Nigeria's case there is partial institutionalisation of such groups, and this contrasts with South Africa where there appears to be stronger 'state resilience' to vigilantism becoming entrenched. As Jensen and Burr (2003) argue, state responses to vigilantism oscillate between repression and tolerance, depending on the group level of violence and priorities of the state. There is a need to promote the rights based approach to guide community policing to protect against excesses of vigilantism in Africa (Alemika and Chukwuma, 2004).

In Nigeria, the group that best approximates this typology of vigilantism is the 'Bakassi Boys' that were active in three eastern states of Abia, Anambra and Imo State. They began as an initiative of traders in Aba, the commercial city of Abia State, who were worried about the high rate of violent property crimes in their markets. However, the Bakassi Boys were later hijacked by state governments, which added partisan political ends in their objectives and armed them with dangerous weapons including firearms without police check (Tertsakian, 2002). The Bakassi Boys made routine public spectacles of some of the criminal suspects they captured, who were often paraded naked on the streets and their body parts chopped into pieces and later burnt to the cheering of surging and urging crowds (Chukwuma, 2002; Buur and Steffen, 2003). In the following section, we examine the factors that escalate or reduce mob justice and later compare the mixed relative meaning and interpretations of mob violence.

Factors that tend to escalate or reduce mob violence

Literature has documented a number of mob justice escalating and reducing factors. The mob justice escalating factors include improper crimes investigations and handling by the police and judiciary, for example due to incompetence or corruption. Frustration is obtained from accumulated injustice, and unfair judicial processes and procedures; so direct physical violence or vigilantism is directed to new suspects before they reach Police (Outwater et al (2013) and Nyonyintono, 2009). Rampant crime in an area can lead to mob justice if police are seen to not be doing enough to solve the problem (Human Rights Watch, 2010; Dar es Salaam, 2000; Refugee Law Project, 2009). Research also suggests that a key cause of crime in Africa (and elsewhere) is poverty. In Uganda, in 2008,76 per cent of the population was living on less than $2 a day (Glad, Stromberg and Westerlund, 2010). The Chronic Poverty Research Centre estimated that in 2004 one in five Ugandan households – or just over one quarter of the total population, lived in chronic poverty (poverty that is passed on through generations) (Chronic Poverty Research Centre, 2005). It is therefore no surprise to learn that 63 per cent of recorded mobs have been in reaction to relatively minor thefts of goods and money, for example. In a poor society like Uganda, theft is more likely to occur in situations where people need to feed themselves and where they believe the only way to live is to steal. Therefore, effective poverty reduction in the communities and a fair and effective judicial system are key deterrents of crime and mob justice.

Comparative meanings of 'mob justice' and findings from the study markets

This study involved primary data collection using structured questionnaires and focus group discussions and interviews. Data was collected between June and July 2013. A total of 42 respondents from both Nakulabye market and Owino market contributed to the study, and of these 90 per cent of the respondents viewed 'mob justice' as an unjust practice, an undesirable practice and something used to punish criminals, which can end up killing innocent people. Even those who are on the receiving end of serious injuries require costly medical treatment. Most respondents equated mob justice with mob violence, because it does not give individuals a chance to benefit from a fair justice system or proper police investigation. For most respondents, mob violence incites more violence and it is also noted that growing number of people fall victims to mob violence since they are arrested for being involved in the practice themselves. Escalation of violence by mob violence was witnessed in two weeks of post-election violence in Kenya 2007 in that claimed over 1,000 people (Halakhe, 2013).

Some respondents stated that although mob justice is not desirable, the serious crime situation at hand and a certain mindset is what leads the culprits to engage in mob violence, and mistake it for justice. Ninety per cent of respondents condemned the mob violence. Those who condemned mob violence claimed it was 'taking the law in one's own hands' or rather; a common man's court that does not objectively analyse the evidence' (Focus Group Discussion in Nakulabye Market, 23 July 2013). They emphasised that many people had been innocently killed but only for it to be established later that they were not guilty. The respondents condemned the Police for unnecessary delays or non-reaction in responding to calls from concerned citizens to rescue people from the mob. Human rights Watch, 2010, mentions the same causes of mob justice in Burundi.

10 per cent of respondents disagreed with the vast majority, and said that mob justice was an appropriate practice in the

Ugandan context. *'Netumala tukwata kumubbi tumuttabusi,'* some vendors emphatically said in Luganda. This is translated literally, to mean that if a thief is caught he/she must be killed. Mainly they thought such mob violence was justified because it could give a 'serious lesson' to others who might think twice before risking committing a crime. Those who favoured mob violence also suggested that its occurrence awakens the police to make quicker responses and to be more serious about their work. If there were no mob violence, the police would be less likely to take criminal cases seriously. Although undesirable, this reminds us of Emile Durkheim's theory on social function of deviance (mob justice) and how it facilities social functioning (Douglas and Waksler, 1982). Respondents who favoured mob justice further informed the researchers that the leading motivation that made them get involved in mob justice or mob violence was that the police would release criminals without convicting them. Some of the articles sold in the market are deadly tools such as *pangas* which can be used to violently attack suspects in the market, pointing to the need to deal with mob violence. (Focus Group Discussion, Owino market, 24 July 2013).

In explaining mob violence, even those who disagreed with it – the vast majority – cited issues that can explain the phenomenon. They stated, for example, that police collaborate with criminal gangs, and sometimes take bribes from criminals, and then ignore the crimes committed. There is a great deal of anger at this among respondents, especially among persons who are victims of crimes. They report that the police have been reluctant to heed calls rescue mob violence situations. As some respondents claim, people struggling in poverty who have managed to obtain a little wealth, are not able to tolerate those who steal their wealth instead of working on their own (Focus Group Discussion, Owino Market, 24 July 2013). This means that such people who steal from the poor can be mobbed (Human Rights Watch, 2010).

It was noted from the Owino Market Police Post report that the trend of mob justice has continuously reduced compared to the past two years. The Officer in charge of the Police station estimated that the number of mob justice crimes being committed was still high; 30-50 cases were recorded in a week in the previous year (2012) as compared to 10-20 cases in a week currently in Owino Market (interview with Officer in Charge, Owino Police Post, 22 July 2013). In Nakulabye Market, it is estimated that five cases of crime are reported weekly in the market and about 10-20 cases monthly (Interview with Officer in Charge, Nakulabye Police Post, 25 July 2013). The difference in cases is due to the relative differences in activities; Owino is more active and has a bigger population than Nakulabye. The study was also informed through interviews with vendors that the leadership of Owino Market is marred by politics of intrigue and segregation. This is because some vendors support the ruling NRM government and some do not, thus increasing crime rates in Owino as compared to Nakulabye. This reducing trend of crime is, however, against the police report comparisons of 2008-2011 in Table 10.1, which show an increase in crime and mob lynching. However, the decrease in mob violence can be attributed to the vigilance of community policing officers who are operating in the market community and can report mob violence to police. The police officers interviewed also suggested that the national figures do not show the differences in crimes by location and sector. The police reporting systems do not disaggregate data to direct police focus on particular areas or activities of high crime. It should be noted that community policing officers have not been able to stop mob violence completely. The respondents reported that the crimes which led to mob justice were; theft, assault, inciting violence, failure to pay debts, pick pocketing, insulting the modesty of a woman, and middlemen stealing people's money. All these were said to be a result of high population, market ownership wrangles, unemployed youth, few crime preventers, few law enforcement officers, lack of trust amongst the Police and law enforcers and poverty.

A number of factors were given by the respondents for mob violence in the markets in spite of the presence of community policing namely: that the set-up of the markets especially Owino, does not give room for quick response and most vendors are ignorant about the legal process; the congestion; some vendors are hostile and unfriendly to each other; lack of trust and confidence in police and judiciary, and delay in court procedures yet people are not patient and few police and community police officers and police stations. The same reasons for mob justice were highlighted by Peelo and Soothill et al (2002) in their work 'The Public Construction of Justice'. Owino Police Post has only 15 police officers giving a ratio of 15:10,000 people as estimated. The other issue is Police taking bribes and releasing criminals without punishing them. These factors as informed from the interviews relate to Vowell, 2007's two factors of creation of a situation of a loose social commitment among the market vendors and a growing non-commitment to obey government authority. The factors increase the intensity of mob justice or mob violence, to be more accurate. Tables 10.2 and 10.3 below provide detailed analysis of the factors influencing mob justice in the two Kampala market spaces studied. In the foregoing discussion, we further examine the explanatory issues for differential levels of mob justice between Owino and Nakulabye market as evidenced from the field findings.

The disagreement among market management causes conflict and crime in Owino Market. There are two different factions that are interested in market leadership and always confronting each other. One leadership faction supports the ruling government party (NRM) whereas the other does not. Mob violence sometimes takes place in the confrontations. Owino Market ownership is also a challenge; the vendors many times strike to get a land title and ownership as had been promised by the President. Comparatively, the Kabaka of Buganda owns Nakulabye market. Therefore, this does not cause ownership conflict in any way. Interviews also established that there are some youths in the market who do not have businesses and only wait to exploit the mob violence situation to steal and make a living.

Table 10.2: Nakulabye market survey: factors influencing mob violence/justice

Variables: Factors influencing mob violence	**Perceptions**
Social attachment between market vendors	High
Commitment to obey authority	High
Involvement in market activities	High
Belief in Police and justice system	High
Costs of engagement in mob justice	High
Benefits of engagement in mob justice	High

Data was analysed from 20 total respondents.

Table 10.3. Owino market survey: factors influencing mob violence/justice

Variables: Factors influencing mob violence	**Perception**
Social attachment between market vendors	Moderate
Commitment to obey authority	High
Involvement in market activities	Moderate
Belief in Police and justice system	Low
Costs of engagement in mob justice	Moderate
Benefits of engagement in mob justice	High

Source: Based on data from 20 respondents; variables adapted and revised from Vowell (2007).

In Tables 10.2 and 10.3 above, a three point Likert scale (three alternative choices) was used to describe the dimensions in the study by the vendors in a questionnaire namely: 1-low, 2-moderate, 3-high. The study used 20 respondents who were administered questionnaires in each market. The response concerning the perception on the variable with the highest frequency was recorded. As can be seen from Tables 10.2 and 10.3 above, Nakulabye Market was found to have high frequencies on all the variables recorded and this partly explained the low crime and mob justice cases. Owino Market, on the other hand, had a mix of frequencies in the variables; this also partly explains the relatively higher crime rate than Nakulabye. Other factors that explain the variation in crime and variable differences are that Owino has a bigger population (10,000) whereby 85 per cent are the youths than Nakulabye Market with a population of (6,000) where 20 per cent are youth. On the other hand, Nakulabye managers are able to have few crimes because they are united as compared to politically divided Owino leadership. Nakulabye is smaller to monitor and people are easier to mobilise for a common cause. The stronger bonds in Nakulabye market vendor community as described by the dimensions in Table 10.3 have contributed to the relatively better control of mob violence in that market. The reduced incidence of mob attacks to almost zero in the Nakulabye market area is the outcome of this closer sense of cohesion. In Nakulabye interviews, vendors praised their leadership for liaising with crime preventers to resolve conflicts fast and peacefully. Besides, they give community service as punishment for small offences. Community service helps in the elimination of social exclusion and poverty, which are the main causes of crime (Carlson, 1999). Before we turn to social bonds we comment that it is irregular and against their responsibility for community police to constitute themselves into courts of law.

Social bonds: responding to mob violence

The respondents suggested enforcement of the following strategies to reduce mob justice in the markets in future: Issuing toll-free lines to pass on messages when an incident of crime occurs within the market, sensitisation through community policing, as well as special courts to speed up the handling of cases. These steps would all help build confidence among members of the public in the government services and personnel (Van Der Spuy and Röntsch, 2008). Detaining criminals and charging them fairly; increasing police posts near the markets, and making police officers more visibly on patrol would help to improve the tendency for people at the market to observe the laws and to govern that market without too much effort.

It was noted that urban markets have some characteristics that make crime by mob justice more likely to happen. One of the key concerns was that the markets have so many people who are unemployed and it is difficult to identify them because one may pretend to be working or shopping. The police officer informed this study that it was difficult to monitor the number of vendors in the market because of its size. This factor is intensified by the fact that many people in the market are uneducated and come from different distant places so, the social ties and relationship with others is almost nonexistent. Therefore, there is little fear of being publicised when caught in wrongdoing. Vendors only unite while engaging in mob justice, community cleaning and burials of colleagues. There is little respect for authority in Owino market as compared to Nakulabye because it is believed the authority does not serve the people to reduce crime and mob justice and that police and management serve government interests. One interviewee mentioned that 'mob justice takes place because some people exploit the opportunity to let out their annoyance for loss of property to theft at that moment or in the past. It was noted from the focus group discussions that the costs of engaging in mob justice are low for the perpetuators of mob justice when they are caught because the offenders can corrupt themselves out of the case but benefit from it when they permanently punish the suspect and finally reduce criminals in the market. The returns of mob justice were said to be faster than the justice system. One interviewee noted that 'those who are engaged in mob justice are not taken to police; they are instead praised for being brave and strong' (Focus group discussion, Owino Market, 24 July 2013). There is need to practice and understand the importance of speed, fairness and transparency in the public construction of justice in community policing (Peelo, and Soothill et al (2002).

The community crime preventers informed this study that social bonding in some cases worked negatively to facilitate crime where the vendors did not report criminals who were their colleagues. Some policemen also detested the crime preventers for tracing criminals that had given bribes to the police. So, social cohesion and bonding encourage collusion for and against justice and breeds reluctance among the crime preventers to avert crime (Interview with crime preventers and vendors, 24 July 2013). We now examine the role and structure of community policing in the markets and later draw conclusions and recommendations to improve community policing effectiveness.

Community policing activities in study markets

The Police community liaison officer manages the affairs of community policing. The community crime preventers do weekly reporting to the Police liaison officer. This study was informed that Owino has 25 and Nakulabye five trained crime preventers. These available crime preventers are overwhelmed by the task yet training others is not planned due to the cost implication. Community policing links the community with the police. Respondents informed this research that community policing is useful in dealing with crime by sensitising people on having respect for rule of law rather than taking laws in their hands. It creates awareness about the dangers of mob justice so that offenders are handed to police. Community policing has contributed towards crime control and mob justice since it has raised security awareness and respect of the rule of law. It has reduced on crime rates.

Owino Market radio is very instrumental in sensitisation; however, it was noted it does not reach some areas of the market and some crime preventers feared to use it lest they be misunderstood to be mobilising for political reasons. This study was informed that there were games organised involving vendors like board games and football and these enhanced cohesion. Mobilisation for participation during market activities like market cleaning and burying colleagues also developed collective responsibility and action. They also help in organising the market, by creating walkways that help in rescue missions (Focus group discussion, Owino Market, 27 July 2013). These activities are similar to other community policing activities in East Africa (Safer World, 2008).

Community policing strategy requires more effort in markets because vendors have no time to attend community policing sessions. In addition, the Police do not follow what they teach (Wisler, 2007). Despite the strategy, crimes are being committed because the market vendor community has not given enough attention to community policing instead they concentrate on their businesses. The market vendor community needs to be continuously reminded. The market comprises many categories of people such as the different age groups with various levels of education and backgrounds.

The respondents suggested the following strategies to reduce mob justice; carrying out massive sensitisation; establishing community sensitisation points in the market; focusing on the leaders of the market zones as coordinators; formalise management of the market; and visiting the market radio and interacting with the vendors periodically on issues of mob justice. Reported cases should be handled professionally to build confidence in the public. Police should be facilitated to continue educating members of the market community. The number of police officers should be increased and the people educated on the need to follow laws. It was also noted in the interviews, that the community police officers are not paid officially, as one emphatically stated, 'We are not paid yet we have to patrol this large market. Our homes need food, we are badly off and demotivated. Some of our colleagues have left community policing and engaged in vending to make a living.' This is a weakness since they get handouts from the culprits and may be more likely to engage in crime (Focus group discussion, Owino Market, 27 July 2013).

Conclusion and recommendations

It was noted that social bonds help to ensure that people can escape mob justice (Vowell, 2007). Community Policing does not seem to have much of an impact on the rate of mob violence, since unless market vendors trust one another, they are not willing to invest time and energy in things which may not be necessary for economic survival. Loose social bonds among the market vendors is weakened by unemployment, redundancy, and the need for daily economic survival, and few deliberately organised activities to enhance the social bonds among the market vendor community. Community policing activities are voluntary, vendors cannot forego making money and engage seriously in unpaid community policing. So, government and the local authority should ensure payment of crime preventers. There are no activities deliberately planned in the market for enhancing social bonds amongst the vendors. The visible slow or inaction by police on mob justice offenders increases the benefits of mob justice, and this makes it harder to have the vice permanently eliminated from the markets.

This study recommends that community policing engages the market vendor community in Owino and Nakulabye in activities that can increase the social bond between the vendors, such as game competitions. This will increase the concern for one another and need to report intentions of crime other than being reactive. The Police should also act on the offenders as the law prescribes and give feedback to the vendors using the market radio. The market community should continuously be sensitised on the awareness of, respect for, practice of the rule of law, and the dignity of women while being discouraged from mob justice and encouraged to work hard to reduce poverty and redundancy among the market community. Sensitisation should emphasise community policing as a revival of the traditional African indigenous security systems, which rely on trust, reciprocity, networks and cooperation. Poverty is a key trigger for mob violence (Halakhe, 2013). A number of home-grown practical poverty reduction projects should be initiated for the unemployed youth by the Kampala Capital City Authority with the assistance of the civil society. Future research should study the relationship between activities for enhancing cohesion by community policing and crime rate in the markets.

References

Abdullahi, H.B. (2013) 'R2P in Practice: Ethnic Violence, Elections and Atrocity Prevention in Kenya'. Global Centre for the Responsibility to Protect, Occasional Paper Series, No. 4, December 2013. https://gupea.ub.gu.se/bitstream/2077/23084/1/gupea_2077_23084_1.pdf

Alemika, E.E.O., and Chukwuma, I.C. (2004) '*The Poor and Informal Policing*'.

Braga, A.A. (2006) 'Policing Crime Hot Spots,' in *Preventing Crime: What Works for Children, Offenders, Victims, and Places*, Brandon, C.W., and Farrington, P.D. New York: Springer.

Buur, L., and Jensen, S. (2003) 'Vigilantism and the Policing of Everyday Life in South Africa', paper presented at the workshop at the WISER Law society, South Africa.

Carlson, B. (ed.) (1999) *Social Dimensions of economic development and productivity: Inequality and social performance*. United Nations Publication.

Chronic Poverty Research Centre (2005) 'Chronic Poverty in Uganda - The Policy Challenges', Accessed 3 September 2013 at: http://www.chronicpoverty.org/publications/details/chronic-poverty-in-uganda-the-policy-challenges.

Commonwealth Human Rights Initiative (CHRI) (2006). 'The Police, the People, the Politics: Police Accountability in Uganda', CHRI report.

Dar es Salaam (2000) 'Crime and Policing Issues in Dar es Salaam, Tanzania Focusing On: Community Neighbourhood, Watch Groups' - 'Sungusungu', Presented at the 1st Sub Saharan Executive Policing Conference, International Association of Chiefs of Police (IACP) Durban, South Africa: 27 – 30 August, 2000.

Decker, S.H., and Curry G.D, (2002) 'I am down for my organisation: The rationality of responses to eelinquency, youth crime, and 'gangs' in Piquero, R.A., and Tibbetts, S.G. (eds.) *Rational Choice and Criminal Behavior: Recent Research and Future Challenges*. New York: Routledge.

Douglas J.D., and Waksler, F.C. (1982) *The sociology of deviance: An introduction*. Boston: Little, Brown

Eck, J.E. (2006) 'Preventing Crime at Places, in Sherman L.W., Farrington D.P., Welsh, B.C., and MacKenzie, D.L. (eds.) *Evidence-Based Crime Prevention*, rev. ed., New York: Routledge.

Friedman, R. (1992) *Community policing; Comparative Perspective and Prospects*, New York: Harvestor- Wheatsheaf.

Glad, R., Stromberg. A, and Westerlund A. (2010) 'Mob Justice: a qualitative research regarding vigilante justice in modern Uganda, Bachelor thesis, Social Work, University of Gothenberg. Accessed 3 September 2013:

Global Science Initiative, (2011) 'Combating mob justice, Cameroon and Nigeria, A Report On Poor People's Perceptions and

Priorities on Safety, Security and Informal Policing' in A2j Focal States in Nigeria, Centre For Law Enforcement Education (Cleen), Lagos.

Human Rights Watch (2010) 'Mob justice in Burundi: Official complicity and impunity'. Retrieved from http://www.hrw.org/reports/2010/03/31/mob-justice-burundi.

International Centre for Prevention of Crime (1999) 'Crime prevention Digest 11: Comparative Analysis for Successful community safety', Montreal.

International Centre for Prevention of Crime (ICPC) (2005) 'Urban crime prevention and Youth at Risk: Compendium of promising strategies and programmes from around the World', Montreal.

Kanaabi, M. (2004) *An assessment of the factors responsible for mob justice in the management of public affairs in Kampala District.* Kampala: Makerere University.

Loader, I., and Walker, N. (2001) 'Policing as a Public Good', *Theoretical Criminology*, 5, (1)27

Mirsky, I. (2009), 'Community Oriented Policing Journal of Criminology'. Internet Journal of Criminology, at: http://www.internetjournalofcriminology.com/mirsky_community_oriented_policing.pdf [accessed 7 August 2015].

Mugunga, E. F. (2005) 'Rule of law and access to justice: Eliminating rough justice in Uganda', Unpublished MSc Dissertation, University of Birmingham, Governance and Development Management.

Nalukenge, H.A.(2001) The right to life – A case study of the mob justice 'system in Uganda'. Bachelor's Thesis, Makerere University, Kampala

Nalunga (2012) Women Employees in the Informal Sector, Master's dissertation). Kampala, Uganda.

Nyonyintono, M. (2009) The challenges faced by the police in eliminating mob justice in Kampala: 2005 – 2007, Makerere

University Research Repository Faculty of Arts Theses & Dissertations (Arts) available at www.*dspace.mak.ac.ug*

Omach, P. (2010), Political Violence in Uganda: The Role of Vigilantes and Militias.'Journal of Social, Political and Economic Studies', 35 (4).

Outwater, A. Mgaya, E., Campbell, J.C. (2013) 'Community violence in Dar es Salaam, Tanzania: A mixed methods study', *African Safety Promotion Journal*, 11, 1.

Paternoster, R., Bancman, R., (2001) *Explaining Criminals and Crime*. Los Angeles, California: Roxbury Publishing Company.

Peelo, M., Francis, B., Soothill, K., Pearson, J., and Ackerley, E. (2002) 'The Public Construction of Justice: Homicide Reporting in the Press'. Retrieved from ://www.maths.lancs.ac.uk/~penn/papers/hommeda.pdf.

Piquero A.R., Hickman, M. (2002) 'The Rational Choice Implications of Control Balance Theory', in *Rational choice and Criminal Behavior*, Piquero, A.R., and Tibbetts, S.G. New York: Routledge.

Raleigh, C., Biddle, K., Male, C., and Neema, S. (2011) 'Uganda Police Project Evaluation', DFID, Department For International Development, London.

Refugee Law Project (2009) 'Partial Justice: Formal and Informal Justice Mechanisms in Post Conflict West Nile', Refugee Law Project Working Paper No. 21, Uganda

Safer World (2008) 'Implementing community-based policing in Kenya', Training manual, Kenya.

Sherman, L., Farrrington, D., Welsh, B., Mackenzie, D., (2004) *Evidence Based crime prevention*. New York: Routledge.

Sriram, C.L., and Brown, S. (2012) 'Kenya in the Shadow of the ICC: Complementarity, Gravity and Impact', *International Criminal Law Review*, 12 (2): 219-244.

Steenkamp, C. (2011) 'In the shadows of war and peace: making sense of violence after peace accords', *Conflict, Security & Development*, 11(3): 357-383

Sundar, N., (2010) 'Vigilantism, Culpability and Moral Dilemmas', *Critique of Anthropology* 30: 113-21

Uganda (1995) 'The Constitution of the Republic of Uganda 1995'

Uganda Police (2005) 'Community policing and crime prevention Training Manual for police Trainers and community Liaison officers', Kampala.

Uganda Police (2011) 'Uganda Annual crime report', Kampala.

UN Habitat (2000) http://www.unhabitat.org/downloads/docs/1825_12883_sungusungu.pdf

Van Der Spuy, E. & Röntsch, R. (2008) *Police and crime prevention in Africa: A brief appraisal of structures, policies and practice.* Cape Town, South Africa: International Centre for the Prevention of Crime.

Vowell, P. R. (2007), 'A partial test of an Integrative Control Model: Neighborhood Context', Western Criminology Review. 8(2), 1–15.

Waller, I. (2006) *Less Law, More Order: The Truth about Reducing Crime*. Westport, Conn.: Praeger.

Weisburd, D., Telep, C.W., Hinkle, J.C., and Eck. J.E. 2010. 'Is Problem-Oriented Policing Effective in Reducing Crime and Disorder? Findings from a Campbell Systematic Review, *Criminology and Public Policy*, 9: 139-172.

Wisler, D., and Ihekwoaba, O. (2007) 'Community Policing: A Comparative view'.

World Health Organisation (2005) 'Preventing Violence: A guide to implementing the recommendations of the World Report on Violence and Heath', Geneva: Violence and Injuries prevention.

Chapter 11

Conclusion: The Future of Social Justice across the JLOS Institutions in East Africa

Freda Joyce Apio

Introduction

As this volume's contributors have shown through numerous examples, and using experiences from different sectors, across East African countries, achieving social justice remains central in the legal and justice sectors' agenda, but also in relation to social protection, resource distribution, disability rights and definitions of crime. Since social justice represents the application of justice to an entire society without discrimination, it is also a reflection on the manifestation of human rights in the everyday lives of people at every level of society. The Justice Law and Order Sector (JLOS) institutions are mechanisms through which equal rights should be able to be enjoyed without discrimination for the poor, marginalised and vulnerable people such as the disabled, refugees and the poor rural women, all among the examples considered in this volume.

Conversely, these are the groups perhaps most vulnerable to all forms of crime, coupled with illiteracy and inability to pay for legal services by poor people in East Africa without social protection. The most injurious aspect of the legal and justice sector is the vice of corruption, which works against the struggles for justice of the poor and marginalised, as a last resort. Reform initiatives have, however, attempted to avert this trend in all the East African countries. Indeed, the legal and justice sector reforms that commenced in the 1990s centred on making the poor, marginalised and vulnerable visible in the processes. This is seen in the Poverty Reduction Strategy Plans (PRSP) framework which considers justice as an integral part of people's social being.[47] However, this strategy can only be achieved when effectiveness and efficiency of the justice processes are emphasised. This would advance access to justice, enjoyment of rights and promote good governance.

Inevitably, there are commonalities and differences in the experiences of the East African States in actualising social justice in legal and justice sectors. That notwithstanding, the sector wide approach (SWAP) to development adopted across the region continues to leverage opportunities for greater collaboration and synergies between the different institutions and Non Governmental Organisations (NGOs) involved in legal service provision. The establishment of the East African

47 Poverty Reduction Strategy Papers (PRSPs) were introduced in 1999 by the World Bank and the IMF as a new framework to enhance domestic accountability for poverty reduction reform efforts.

Community (EAC) is also pivotal to coordinate legal and judicial affairs to accentuate the need for regional programmes, moulded to bridge the gap between law and justice in order to cause social change in societies. The EAC integration is crucial to promote and share best practices between the legal and justice sectors in the region.

The EAC and social justice: Legal and institutional framework for the administration of justice in East Africa

The EAC is the regional intergovernmental body of the republic of Burundi, Kenya, Rwanda, Uganda and the United Republic of Tanzania.[48] The EAC integration process is on-going until the final stage of political federation. The EAC structure offers a great opportunity for economic development and social protection of citizens of the region.

The future of social justice before JLOs in EAC Partners States can be envisioned through the available opportunities under the regional and the national structures. The EAC has a wide range legal, policy and institutional framework and mechanisms to promote rule of law which is fundamental to achieve social justice. Through these frameworks and mechanisms, rule of law not only prohibits those in power from abusing it, but also obligates them to act positively and meaningfully for the welfare of the people. This includes the EAC Treaty, the East African Court of Justice (EACJ), the East African Legislative Assembly (EALA) and other non treaty

48 The EAC Treaty was signed on 30 November 1999 and entered into force on 7 July 2000 after ratifaction by the pioneer states.

bodies and institutions such as the East African Law Society (EALS), East African Police Chief Cooperation Organisation (EACPCO), the East African Association of Prosecutors, East African Association of Magistrates and East African Chief Justice Forum.

The EAC Treaty

The Treaty for the establishment of the EAC is affixed on strong pillars of good governance; democracy; rule of law; social justice, observance of human rights; peace and security; mutual trust, cooperation and social and economic development. Specifically, Articles 3(b), 6(d), and 7(2) espouse principles on good governance, democracy and the recognition, promotion and protection of human and people's rights in accordance with the provisions of the African Charter on Human and People's Rights.'[49] The treaty provides for enhancement of the role of women in socio-economic development; providing for women empowerment and gender mainstreaming and prohibiting discrimination and prejudices against women.[50] The political federation is a key aspect of the treaty and the ultimate stage in the integration process. It strides on development and consolidation of democracy; rule of law; respect for human rights and fundamental freedoms; peaceful resolution of disputes and conflicts between and within partner states; and preservation and strengthening of peace and security.[51]

Other features include cooperation on regional peace and security including enhanced strategy on handling of

49 Article 6 (d) of the EAC Treaty.

50 Articles 121 & 122 of the EAC Treaty

51 Article 123 of the EAC Treaty.

cross-border crime; provision of mutual legal assistance in criminal matters; arrest and repatriation of criminal fugitives and exchange of criminal intelligence and other security information for combating criminal activities including counter-terrorism measures.[52] Further, cooperation in legal and judicial affairs is considered. This includes harmonisation of legal training and certification; standardisation of judgments of courts; exchange of legal and judicial knowledge and jurisprudence and harmonisation of national laws to accord with EAC laws, policies and regulations.

The East African Court of Justice (EACJ)

The Court has a critical role to play in the administration of justice and promotion of peaceful resolution of disputes between the EAC Partner States, or between the EAC and its employees as well as in consensual arbitral disputes for the EAC or a Partner State. The EACJ also provides advisory opinions on questions of law arising from the Treaty if requested on request by the appropriate organ. The EACJ issues binding judgments and decisions on the parties to the dispute, whereupon the Partner State or the Council is obliged to ensure implementation of the judgment. In addition, a party may execute an authenticated pecuniary judgment of the Court without the protracted process for recognition and enforcement of foreign judgments.

The EAC Treaty makes provisions for the expansion of the present jurisdiction of the Court to cover human rights and other jurisdiction as the Council of Ministers may determine. Indeed, the Extension of the jurisdiction of the EACJ will

52 Article 124 of the EAC Treaty.

enhance its mandate to administer justice more broadly, effectively and efficiently.

Other constraints and challenges of the EACJ must be urgently addressed. This includes technical capacity and financial constraints. In addition, more campaigns to sensitise the East Africans about the existence, processes and procedures must be undertaken. It must enhance collaboration and cooperate with national judicial authorities of the partner states and other key stakeholders. It should also develop an ICT framework to ensure that its operations are more understandable, accessible and efficient and provide the citizenry with easier access to judicial information and boost judicial cooperation.

The East African Legislative Assembly (EALA)

The Assembly plays an equally important role in the administration of justice and the promotion of the rule of law in East Africa. It has both legislative and oversight functions. Since its inception it has enacted a number of key pieces of legislations of the Community which have binding force in the Partner States. It has the obligation to foster cooperation and build linkages between itself and the national assemblies of the partner states. It is a vital organ in enhancing public awareness on the affairs of the community. It is therefore an indispensable catalyst for the acceleration of integration and in the attainment of the political federation.

Notwithstanding its undoubted achievements, the Assembly, like all the other organs and institutions of the Community, has experienced operational, capacity, financial and other constraints. Moreover, the delays in the domestication of Community legislation by National Assemblies have slowed its work and impaired the harmonisation of national laws with the laws, regulations and policies of the Community.

Other Non-Treaty Bodies and Institutions

Aside from the above mentioned framework, organs and institutions of the EAC, there are a number of non-professional bodies and associations within the region that play a key role in the administration of justice, promotion of good governance, democracy and rule of law and in the promotion and protection of human rights. These include: The East African Law Society; The East Africa Judges and Magistrates Association; The East Africa Association of Prosecutors; The East Africa Association of Anti-corruption Authorities; The Eastern Africa Police Chiefs Cooperation Organisation; The East Africa Chief Justices Forum; and The EAC Heads of Prisons/Correctional Services Forum. These bodies and organisations, contribute immensely to the promotion and enhancement of legal and judicial cooperation and in the exchange and sharing of information; best practices; knowledge and expertise as well as in building synergies between the National and Community institutions and organs.

National Justice Law and Order Sectors: Opportunities for social justice

The JLOs is a key player in the movement towards the realisation of a world where all members of a society, regardless of background have basic human rights and equal access to their community's roles, wealth and resources.

Uganda

JLOS in Uganda is composed of 16 institutions closely working on the administration of justice. Under JLOs frameworks have been designed to achieve social protection. These include the approval of the National Orphans and Other Vulnerable Children Policy and a National Strategic Programme Plan of Interventions for Orphans and Other Vulnerable Children (NSPPI) in 2004 by the Ministry of Gender, Labour and Social Development (MGLSD). These two instruments reflect a commitment to and a context for the fulfillment of the rights of Ugandan children who are orphaned and/or vulnerable. However, Uganda still needs to provide social protection for vulnerable employees, by improving working conditions and instituting a realistic minimum wage. In addition, space and facilities for Labour Courts with capacity to handle labour disputes need to be established. The Labour Court is established by law and it needs to be operationalised urgently. Uganda is the first country in Africa to have established an Equal Opportunities Commission (EOC) that has been empowered to undertake its own investigations and prosecution of discriminatory practices while enforcing affirmative action in Uganda. The EOC needs to be strengthened to offer adequate social protection to vulnerable groups from inequalities in society.

Uganda is on record as the first country in sub-Saharan Africa to enact a comprehensive Person with Disabilities law. Efforts are underway to align it with International Conventions and implement its provisions. The latest innovation is the establishment of the Justice Centres which are a one-stop-shop legal aid service delivery model that seeks to bridge the gap between the supply and demand sides of justice by providing legal aid services across civil and criminal areas of justice to indigent and vulnerable persons, while at the same time empowering individuals and communities to claim their rights and demand for policy and social change.

Uganda has some best practices to share with its partner states in the region which include: gender audit, community service as a punishment to decongest the prisons, powers to hear cases by the Human Rights Commission, establishment of the Equal Opportunities Commission and Electoral Commission's transparency practice of open basin voting. The government involves CSOs in processes of policy formulation and implementation the bulk of CSOs, are involved in policy processes related to service delivery areas as opposed to advocacy let alone in areas of governance and democratisation.

Kenya

The starting point of any future opportunities in Kenya is bound to be the Constitution. Promulgated in 2010, this grand norm presented a fresh beginning for a country that had its fair share of turbulence. This was reinforced by the government-launched Governance, Justice, Law and Order Sector (GJLOS) initiative, which had the core objective of improving the quality of life of all Kenyans and enhancing effectiveness and efficiency in the justice, human rights and governance fields. A number of initiatives have been undertaken to achieve this objective and a host of remarkable achievements have been recorded. These include building partnerships with local police to prevent root causes of crime, development of a community policing framework, increase in police responsiveness and visibility, enhancement of justice for prisoners, prison decongestion through Community Service Orders Programmes and facilitation of humane transport services for prisoners.

The GoK has established the National Gender and Equality Commission (the Commission)[53] aimed at promoting the integration of the principles of equality and freedom from discrimination in national and county policies, laws and administrative regulations. The state commits to ensure equality and freedom from discrimination for all. Women and men shall enjoy equal treatment, including the right to equal opportunities in political, economic, cultural and social spheres.[54] The Commission is mandated to instill a culture of equality and non discrimination in all legal, policy and administrative spheres. It also serves as an advisor in courts of law.

The Commission has undertaken awareness sessions all over the country which has empowered Kenyan citizens on issues of gender and equality. This can be enhanced further with more funding where use of local languages in disseminating relevant information will be adopted. The Republic of Kenya has also ratified the various relevant international instruments which are domestically enforceable since Kenya is now a

53 It was established on 30 August 2011 by an Act of Parliament – The National Gender and Equality Commission Act Cap15 of 2011.

54 In 2010, the Republic of Kenya promulgated a new Constitution which, under articles 2(5) and 2(6), includes as part of the Constitution general international law as well as treaties ratified or acceded to by Kenya Under Article 27 of the Constitution of Kenya (2010).

monist and not a dualist state with regard to international and domestic law.[55]

This shift from dualism to monism, where ratified international treaties automatically become domestic law, is the result of a series of reform efforts in relation to the legal and justice sector, where the system was (re)conceived to serve all people-women, men and children-without discrimination. The creation of new institutions and revamping of old ones with wider mandates is certainly something that the rest of the EAC countries could emulate in future. The coordination of the Law Reform Commission with other agencies with similar mandate is a good example of how to speed up the process of policy reform in crucial areas needing urgent attention. The creation of the National Cohesion and Integration Commission and the Truth, Justice and Reconciliation Commission are other initiatives that could be emulated elsewhere in the EAC. Most crucially, the willingness to respect the constitution and abide by it, especially through the establishment of bodies and institutions with oversight and potential sanctions for non-adherence, is very fundamental. The coming into force of the 2010 Kenya Constitution has shown that Kenyans are willing to breathe life into this fundamental document and give practical meaning to it. This has been managed in a spirit that is admirable and should be replicated elsewhere in the EAC.

55 Under Article 2 (6) Kenya becomes a monist state, which means that instead of a dualist system, where states need to enact national legislation to 'domesticate' international law, there is the assumption that international laws, once ratified will become domestic law automatically.

Rwanda

The Constitution of Rwanda presents excellent opportunities for social justice, especially with regard to women. It provides that representation for women must be at least 30 per cent. This has already translated into Rwanda having the highest number of women in Parliament anywhere in the world. This is coupled with the presence of the Ministry of Gender and Family Promotion whose mission is 'promoting equality and equity for both men and women and [ensuring] empowerment of women through the national development processes of Rwanda.' The ministry has two organs – the National Women's Council and the National Commission for Children. Also in place is a National Gender Policy and Plan of Action which aims at effective gender mainstreaming and full participation of women in the socio-economic development of the country.

Rwanda also has a number of laws aimed at attaining gender equality. These provide, among other things, for separate ownership of property in marriage by women.[56] Furthermore, gender mainstreaming across a number of government programmes and policies is already a reality. Moreover, Rwanda has also put in place some important institutions such as the Law Reform Commission and the National Commission for Human Rights and the Ombudsman's Office. The National Commission for Human Rights has a number of responsibilities of, inter alia, examining violations of human rights committed on Rwandan territory by state organs, including by public officials who may use their functions to cover up their own malpractice. The Commission also examines violations by

56 Republic of Rwanda Law No. 22 of 1999.

organisations and individuals, and can file complaints about those violations with competent Rwandan courts.

Rwanda has made a number of improvements with regard to access to justice. The country has introduced video conferencing, especially in the Supreme Court. The other area is the emphasis on the rights of women and equality for men and women in public life. Institutionalised gender mainstreaming is one of the best practices that should be replicated in other EAC countries. In Rwanda, performance contracts are signed, stating that individuals will execute specific undertakings. This seeks to increase levels of accountability and commitment to work at all levels of the public sector in particular. Perhaps again, this is something that other EAC countries, with the exception of Kenya, have not yet managed. The other initiative that stands out is the National Dialogue Forum, where every year, citizens have a chance to interact with officials and the President to directly question the authorities about their policies and especially about the outcomes of those policies.

Tanzania

Like Uganda and Kenya, Tanzania inherited its legal system from the British. Over the years, it has carried out a number of reforms in this sector, and the country is now in the process of creating a new constitution to replace that of 1977. This presents the United Republic with a unique opportunity to base the new constitution on involving the entire body of citizens in formulating the grand norms and values on which the constitution would be based. None of the previous constitutions was debated in this way by the population so as to generate consensus. The new draft has some novel provisions in a number of areas, including the provision allowing the challenging of presidential election results and the establishment of a Supreme Court as the highest court.

Aware that corruption is one of the hindrances to access to justice, Tanzania put in place a National Anti-Corruption Strategy Action Plan (NACSAP) in 2004-11, in an attempt to combat malpractices across all sectors. Further, there is in place the Prevention and Control of Corruption Bureau (PCCB), which is supposed to oversee prosecution of individual cases. Although there no doubt remains work to be done in the fight against corruption, recognising the problem as a vice, and putting in place measures to combat it, is certainly a step in the right direction.

Tanzania also has in place the Commission for Human Rights and Good Governance. It is the only human rights commission in the region that includes good governance in its mandate. Besides monitoring human rights, this Commission also monitors the implementation of good governance in the country. It presents a unique opportunity for self reflection for Tanzanians. There is also the Law Reform Commission which is tasked with, among other things, reforming outmoded laws in the country. While there is a long way to go, the work of any law reform commission cannot be gainsaid. This is an avenue that can bring about badly needed progress across all areas of the justice, law and order sector.

The Tanzanian Public Reform Programme (PRSP) acknowledges the link between poverty and difficulties in accessing justice. The 2000 PRSP, for instance, notes that the wellbeing of the poor is also dependent on personal security afforded by the state. This presupposes that government should acknowledge the special circumstances of the poor, the marginalised and other vulnerable groups, in relation to access to justice. It may be proper to delve further into how the government of Tanzania has addressed the needs of the poor with regard to access to justice.

Access to Justice for the poor and disadvantaged groups

Access to justice is another objective of the PRSP and an important aspect of social justice. The importance of access to justice is underscored by a number of other factors. The Tanzanian legal system, like that throughout the EAC region, bears all the hallmarks of the impact of colonial laws and policies. It is adversarial and highly technical, with legal provisions couched in language that most poor citizens may not be familiar with. This situation gives a headache to many, including also the lawyers and judges and administrators who are well acquainted with English and French. Combined with the high price of legal services, language barriers conspire to make access to justice difficult for the average Tanzanian (see Chapter 4 by Thomas Munzerere for more details of this). This is not to mention the other problems that hamstring the judiciary in Tanzania and more generally in East Africa. Viewed from this point therefore, it is crucial to examine how far access to justice in Tanzania has improved in recent years.

There have been a number of initiatives that have been undertaken to improve the access of poor Tanzanians to justice. For instance, the Tanzania Network of Legal Aid Providers (TANLAP) has been instrumental in coordinating legal aid services in the country, and brings together legal aid providers throughout the regions of Tanzania. Its work involves: capacity building by promoting legal literacy among legal aid providers in the country; extending and improving legal aid provision across Tanzania's regions; initiating, promoting and supporting proposed legislation and other measures affecting its members; building mutual understanding and coordination amongst legal aid providers and legal aid clients in the country.

As a result of this organisation's coordinating role, there is little doubt that more Tanzanians now have had access to justice. TANLAP even engaged in discussions to enrich the Draft Constitution, which was the work of Non Governmental Organisations (NGOs) and not of government. Funding for these initiatives came from donors and not from the national government. Another aspect of Tanzania's legal system that is distinctive is the role of paralegals, justified as being necessary in a country where access to justice was not assured for the poor. In 2004 the Law Reform Commission of Tanzania noted the need to recognise this cadre and institutionalise its role through the national legal framework.[57] Most paralegal services have been offered in Tanzania from about 1992, mostly by NGOs.[58] Despite the government's acknowledgement of the need to have paralegal service providers, there has not been much work done in terms of operationalising this. This is the

57 Law Reform Commission of Tanzania, Report on the Scheme for Provision of Legal Services by Paralegals, 2004, pg7.

58 See Angela K. Ishengoma Report on the Legal Reform Process for the Recognition of Paralegals in Tanzania, Freiderich Ebert Stfiftung, 2001. Available at http://www.fes-tanzania.org/files/fes/pdf/Report%20on%20the%20Legal%20Reform%20Processes%20-%20Angela%20Ishengoma.pdf. Accessed 15 September 2014.

case despite repeated attempts by key players in the sector to move forward in this respect.

Burundi

Burundi shares common features with its neighbours in the EAC, with 90 per cent of the population engaged in agriculture, which accounts for 30 per cent of its GDP, fitting perfectly the portrait of an impoverished African post-conflict state.[59] The government has put in place a number of institutions aimed at promoting justice, including a Ministry in charge of Good Governance and Privatisation, the Office of the Auditor General, the Special Anti-Corruption Brigade, an Anti-Corruption Court, the Accounts Court and a Tribunal in Charge of Prosecuting Cases of Embezzlement, and over 90 local courts throughout the country that have been upgraded and rehabilitated.[60] All of these initatives were funded by the government, with some support from various donors.

While all the above measures are laudable, especially in the context of the wars that have plagued the country, it ought to be noted that a number of areas need improvement. Given the prevalence of poverty in Burundi,[61] access to justice is a major concern. The country has in total an estimated 200 lawyers.[62] This, moreover, in a country with a population of 8.5 million, is an insufficient number. In such a setting, legal aid would be

59 CIA Factbook, Burundi, https://www.cia.gov/library/publications/the-world-factbook/geos/by.html 20 September 2014.

60 See Report of the East African Assembly Legal Rules Committee of Good Government in Partner States, p5.

61 The country has an estimated GDP of 600 USD, CIA Fact Book, 2014.

62 See Advocates Sans Frontier, 2012, http://www.asf.be/blog/2012/08/12/a-national-legal-aid-strategy-in-burundi-a-first-in-the-great-lakes-region/ Accessed 20 September 2014.

a welcome strategy for improving access to justice, but legal aid in Burundi is still very much in its infancy. A number of legal actors, many of them funded by foreign donors, have been trying to address this problem for some years.

There are some opportunities in Burundi for offering social protection to the poor and marginalised sectors of society, however. A number of laws are in place with very progressive goals. The first, the Constitution of Burundi, has provisions for quotas of women in a number of public institutions.[63] In part because of this, well over 30 per cent of MPs in Burundi are women. This is a figure that many countries the world over would be more than pleased with. Additionally, Burundi has a Ministry of National Solidarity, Human Rights and Gender (MNSHRG) which, among other things, works to end violence against women. This specific provision for women in Burundi presents a special opportunity, especially in the context of the fact that the many years of war left many women widowed and vulnerable. If used to good effect, the opportunities that exist in the law with regard to women's equality and their protection, could well translate into better wellbeing for a large per centage of the population in future.

Like Rwanda, Burundi has created an office of the Ombudsman[64] to, among other things, receive and investigate complaints of managerial shortcomings and violations of civil rights by public officers, make recommendations to the relevant

---

63 Article 164 and 180 provide that a minimum of 30% of all Representatives in the National Assembly and Senate respectively must be women. In 2005, the quota for women was not met; the Independent National Electoral Commission (CENI) allocated the remaining seats to ensure the quota was achieved.

64 Under Article 237 of the 2005 Constitution.

authorities and scrutinise the operations of the administration. The Ombudsman is mandated to present an Annual Report to the National Assembly and to the Senate, a report that is also published in the official Bulletin.[65] This is a step in the right direction for Burundi in increasing levels of accountability. If public officers are aware that their transgressions in office will become public, this may inhibit them from behaving corruptly. Crucially, the fact that violations of rights of citizens by public officers are monitored is a welcome development, especially in the context of the history of civil wars and violations of Burundian citizens' human rights by state officials.

There are a number of best practices from Burundi. These include abolishing the death penalty, something that is still on the statute books of Uganda[66] and Tanzania; the establishment of a ministry specifically responsible for Gender and the Stakeholders' Forum on Justice and Human Rights.

Challenges across the East African region

Discriminatory legislation

There cannot be any move towards human and holistic development when certain specific sections of the population are either targeted by law, or routinely ignored when it comes to protection measures. The very concept of social justice presupposes the aims of including all people and ensuring

---

65 Under Article 238 of the 2005 Constitution.

66 Uganda, while still maintaining the death penalty, has modified its position somewhat. Following Attorney *General v Susan Kigula & 416 Ors.* Cnstitutional Appeal No.03 of 2006, whereas the death penalty is still lawful in Uganda, condemned persons, if not executed within three years from the time of passing the death sentence, will have the penalty commuted to life imprisonment.

betterment of their livelihood. While some countries have, no doubt, made progress in terms of amending legislation that is discriminatory, especially on the basis of sex, other countries in the EAC remain far behind. Moreover, even for countries that have made progress, that progress can sometimes be at the behest of private individuals or organisations and is not always led by the state for the public good of all. A good example is Uganda. While there have been, for example, a number of constitutional decisions that have outlawed numerous forms of legislation in Uganda,[67] some of these illegal laws remain on statute books, even so. In situations where these decisions have not been followed by implementation through repeal or amendment by the legislature, such milestones turn out to be hollow. Moreover, in some countries such as Tanzania, Rwanda and Burundi, there has been very little such litigation. So long as this remains the case, the lack of respect for constitutional principles will continue to cripple access to justice, especially for the poor and socially excluded.

The growing anti-gay movement

The discussion about social justice cannot be complete without mention of homosexuality. Homosexuality is a sexual orientation where same-sex relationships are practiced as opposed to heterosexuality.[68] These are a category of vulnerable groups who

67 One example is the widely publicised Constitutional Court ruling of 2014, which declared the 'Anti-Homosexuality Act' unconstitutional , albeit on a technicality. See W. Helbling (2014) 'Uganda Constitutional Court strikes down anti-gay law', Jurist. 1 August available on-line at: http://jurist.org/paperchase/2014/08/uganda-constiutional-court-strikes-down-anti-gay-law.php [accessed 9 August 2015].

68 See Stephen.O. Murray and Will Roscoe, 'Boy Wives and Female Husbands: Studies in African Homosexualities' (1998) XII and 13.

by their nature, suffer disproportionate prejudice and stigma in times of economic and political crisis. An emerging trend in Africa, in the EAC and also beyond, is legislation that criminalises homosexuality. Most EAC Partner States are not tolerant to the rights of homosexual people, and Uganda has moved to criminalise same-sex relationships. The debate remains fresh in most countries such as Tanzania and especially Kenya, where an anti-homosexuality Bill which proposes a discriminatory sentence of life imprisonment for Kenyan nationals and death by stoning for non-Kenyan nationals was introduced, aimed at persons 'found guilty' of homosexuality. In Uganda, the Anti-Homosexuality Bill was assented into law by the President in March, 2014, and was later annulled by the Constitutional Court in August 2014. This was on the basis of the lack of quorum, and followed a petition from human rights and pro-gay activists. The Bill was likely to be re-tabled, after careful study by a committee from the NRM party appointed by the President of Uganda. The existence of such legislations in the EAC will continuously perpetuate discrimination and thwart social justice before the legal and justice sectors. The only EAC country to have openly excluded the possibility of anti-homosexual criminal sanctions, at the time of writing, is Rwanda.

Donor dependence

In all the countries in the EAC, a key feature is the dependence on donor funding for the justice sector, something that has been made very evident in responses to anti-homosexuality legislation in Uganda from a number of partners and donors. External support is welcome, especially in view of the fact that a number of countries in the EAC have had their fair share of turbulence in the past, making stability difficult to achieve. However, it can be argued that there cannot be sustainable development of justice sectors and access to justice generally where there is a great deal of donor dependence. The outcome of this reality for EAC member states is not difficult to see. Donors have different priorities which are embedded in their strategic plans and the use of any development assistance has to fit into such donor strategies. In essence, the recipient has to fit into the donor box, as it were. The strategies of the donor may not reflect the priorities of the recipient. In Tanzania and Uganda in particular, adapting to donor requirements has involved a growing bias on the part of government towards commercial justice, as seen for example, through such development as, for the cases of Uganda, the setting up of the Commercial Court Division of the High Court and, in the case of Tanzania, the enactment of a number of commercial legislations, both of which reflect a clear bias towards big companies, private investment and trade. This is regardless of the fact that for the majority of the population representation in criminal and civil cases and access to basic needs is of far more importance than protection of the rights of investors and other commercial actors.

Conclusion

This volume started with the case of the uses of history and language as part of the struggle for recognition, connecting this to questions of criminal justice and social justice. In her chapter, Muigei shows how *Mungiki* youth have been criminalised, and she draws parallels with earlier criminalisation of Mau Mau during struggles for Kenyan independence. Odong's chapter reflects on how different actors define justice, analysing content of a radio programme *Facing Justice*. He concludes that legal and rectificatory approaches to justice dominate, and that gender justice and victim-centred justice were the most marginalised perspectives. In relation to land, there are complex questions of gender relations, and ties between customary law and dispute resolution, discussed in different ways in chapters by Munzerere, Cheremoi and Chelimo. Munzerere's chapter on land dispute resolution in urban Mbeya in Tanzania concludes that professional integrity is essential among land officers for robust local leadership to emerge. As Cheremoi noted, demands for land rights by women were generally tied to their obligations to ensure that their families were food secure. Chelimo provided an overview of how local courts operate in post-war northern Uganda, concluding that most poor people do not report land disputes, because of financial constraints and perceptions about Local Council Courts not being impartial.

Gender justice in health was presented as an aspect of wider social justice in the chapter by Nyakaisiki, who suggests that most rural women still prefer traditional birth attendants because they see few alternative care providers available who will support their births without charging higher fees. Maguru's chapter on refugees with disabilities considers them as 'a minority within a minority', and shows how the categorisation of refugees means disabled refugees are to a large extent invisible when it comes to special protection. Cases of mob violence were compared in two Kampala markets in the chapter by Mugambwa and Hintjens, which considered social bonds and greater police responsiveness to be vital for tackling this form of collective violence. Mob justice differed in the two Kampala markets taken as examples in this chapter. This suggests there is still some improvement needed in both our practical and theoretical understanding of such forms of popular 'rectificatory' violence, as in our appreciation of the interconnections between social justice and criminal justice.

The above challenges combine with outdated laws – many already repealed in the former colonial countries from whence they were imported. There is also an implementation gap – which sometimes can be closed, as for the justice sector in Rwanda, as discussed in the chapter by Twahirwa, in this volume. More generally, this gap means that even when specific legislation has been passed, implementation is extremely slow and can be very patchy. Shortages of requisite legal capacity and skilled personnel in key institutions; corruption and limited political will; patriarchy and gender insensitivity and corruption mingle to present gigantic bottlenecks for social justice in East Africa. Finally, the advent of an African prosecutor at the ICC may have opened up the hope that relations between international justice and national justice may in future become less conflictual for EAC member states in future.

References

Ishengoma, A.K. (2001) *Report on the Legal Reform Process for the Recognition of Paralegals in Tanzania*, Freiderich Ebert Stfiftung.

Murray, S, O. and Roscoe W. (1998) 'Boy Wives and Female Husbands' *Studies in African Homosexualities*'.

Appendix 1

Towards Hybrid Justice? Formal courts in Uganda (appendix Chapter 6)

Under Article 129 (1), the Constitution of the Republic of Uganda empowers the Supreme Court, the Court of Appeal, High Courts, and Subordinate Courts, to exercise judicial powers as prescribed by parliament (Government of Uganda, 1995). Land disputes in Uganda are handled and resolved by Local Council Courts II, Sub-county courts, Magistrates Courts, High Court, Court of Appeal, and Supreme Court. Local Council Courts were established quite recently, under Section 3 of the Local Council Court Act No.1 of 2006, a law which provided that Local Council Courts should be established in every village, parish, town, division and sub-county. Section 76A (1) of the Land Act provides that the parish or ward executive committee is the Court of first instance in respect of land disputes (Government of Uganda 2004).

Under Section (9) of the Local Council Courts Act No.1 of 2006 (LCCA), the area of jurisdiction of the Local Council Court is defined, within the territorial areas of the council only on issues for which a party resides within the area (Government of Uganda 2006). The appeals from judgements of a parish local council court are filed at the sub-county or division level, as provided for under section 32 (2) (b) and (c) of the LCCA (Ibid). Section 76 A (2) of the Land Act allows for appeals on land matters, from the sub-county executive committee courts and from divisions, to the respective district tribunal whose operation was stopped by government and from there to the High Court (Government of Uganda 2004, 1998). The National Land Policy re-establishes the District Land Tribunals under Ministry of Housing Lands and Urban Development but they are yet to be operationalised (Government of Uganda, 2013)

Section 207 (1) of MCA (Magistrates Courts Act) makes provision for a Chief Magistrate to have jurisdiction over matters where claims do not exceed 50 million Uganda shillings and unlimited jurisdiction in matters relating to damage of property, conversion of land use or trespass. The Magistrate Grade 1 can handle disputes whose subject matter is not above 20 million Uganda shillings and a Magistrate Grade 2 jurisdiction where subject matter in a dispute is not above 500,000 Uganda shillings (Ibid). However in circumstances under which the matter or cause of a civil nature is governed only by civil customary law then the jurisdiction of the Magistrate Grade 1 and Chief Magistrate is unlimited as provided under Section 207 of the MCA (Government of Uganda 2004, 1998). The Magistrates Courts receive appeals from the Sub-county Local Council Courts. In addition, if parties to various land cases before the Magistrates Court are aggrieved with the court's decision, then they have a right of appeal to a Higher Court (Government of Uganda, Section 220 of MCA).

The High Court is established under Article 138(1) of the Constitution of the Republic of Uganda of 1995, which empowers the Chief Justice in consultation with the Principal Judge to appoint and ensure accessibility of the High Court to people (Government of Uganda 1995). Cases originating from Amuru District can be handled at Gulu High Court. Under

Article 134(2) of the Constitution, appeals against decisions of the High Court lie with the Court of Appeal (Government of Uganda 1995). Therefore, in the context of land cases, the appeals arising from the decisions of Gulu High Court are filed in the Court of Appeal in Kampala.

The Supreme Court is the highest and final court of appeal. Article 132 (1) and (2) of the Constitution stipulate that appeals from decisions of the court of appeal shall lie to the Supreme Court (Ibid). Conclusively, decisions of the Supreme Court are most respected but land matters are mostly resolved at the Magistrates and High Court, and people respect their decisions. Otherwise, appeals from the High Court to the Court of Appeal and Supreme Court mostly arise in contentious matters touching the law or complexities, which the High Court cannot handle.

Index

able-bodied refugees 251, 264
Acholi people 84, 85
Administrative competence 13
affirmative action 151, 259, 274, 365
African Charter on Human and People's Rights 361
Alternative Dispute Resolution (ADR) 20
Amin, Idi 148, 335
Amnesty International 57, 287
Amuru Sub-county 182, 185, 194, 197, 199, 200, 202, 203, 208, 209, 211, 213
Ankole agreement 1901 188
antenatal care services 241
anti-corruption policies 6
anti-gay movement 378
armed
  robbery 332
Armed
  Conflict 61, 92
assistive devices 256, 272
asylum seekers 253, 254
attitudinal barriers 268
audio information 261
awareness-raising activities 212
Bakassi Boys (Nig) 338
boundary demarcations 199, 203, 208, 211
boundary disputes 194, 198
Braille 261
breast feeding 244
Buganda agreement 1900 187
Bunyoro agreement 1933 188
Buwama Health Centre III 233, 237, 238, 239, 242
certificates of occupancy 195
child birth 229
child sacrifice 13
civil disturbances 41
Civil disturbances/violence 41
Civil Wars 60
class conflict 54
Commercial
  High Court 307
  Tribunals 307
communal land ownership 188
community
  -based crime prevention 336
  -based groups 337
  cleaning 347
  crime preventers 327, 348, 349
  -legitimated violence xx, 324, 325
  -level complaints 10
  -level decision making 174
  policing xx, 322, 323, 325, 327, 330, 333-336, 338, 342, 343, 347-352, 367
  policing (CP) xx, 322, 323, 325, 327, 330, 333-336, 338, 342, 343, 347-352, 367
  policing framework 367
  violence 71
Community
  Police. *See* crime preventers
constitutional principles 110, 151, 378
Convention on the Elimination of

all forms of Discrimination against Women (CEDAW) 149
Correctional Services 364
counselling sessions 267, 272
counter-terrorism measures 362
court bailiffs 305
court information 312
crimes
against humanity 77, 78
investigations 331
criminal
fugitives 362
intelligence 362
justice 1, 7, 12, 19, 25, 32, 57, 63, 64, 73, 79, 380, 381
cross-border
crime 362
trade 158
Crown land (Ug) 147
cultural norms 156, 196
customary
courts 208
institutions 195, 213
land practices 109
land tenure 149, 158, 188, 189
law(s) 136, 180
practices 139, 142, 143, 172, 186, 196, 211
property rights 115
values 196, 208
degrading treatment 10, 20
development
assistance 379
initiatives 67
-oriented media 68
disability policy 259
disabled refugees 24, 25, 251, 252, 265, 275, 381
disabling barriers 256
discriminatory
customary practices 139
traditional laws 156
dispute resolution 20, 23, 174, 185, 191, 195, 199, 206, 211, 213, 380
distributive justice xv, 4, 5, 12, 13, 42, 63, 78, 87, 88
District Land and Housing Tribunal (DLHT) 121, 129
District Land Tribunals 210, 384
donor funding 257, 379
drug abuse 13
East African
Association of Prosecutors 361
Community (EAC) xxi, 360
Court of Justice (EACJ) 361, 362
Law Society (EALS) 361
Legislative Assembly (EALA) 361, 363
Police Chief Cooperation Organisation (EACPCO) 361
economic
development goals 4
discrimination. *See* systematic injustices
greed 77
justice 8
electoral colleges 162
Emergency Obstetric Care (EMOC) 231
emmumbwa (traditional herbal-mineral compound) 233, 234, 240
Equal Opportunities Act, 2007 (Ug) 259, 274
ethnic
mobilisation 48

polarisation 40
ethnic identity 38, 49
struggles 38, 49
extrajudicial killings 36, 45, 56
Facing justice radio programme/fj programme 63, 65, 66, 68, 72, 86, 89
Family Health-Uganda 222
family planning 225, 241, 244
Food and agricultural organisation (FAO) 95, 96, 97, 101, 103, 104, 105, 107, 121, 123, 133, 143, 176
food security 139, 151, 175
formal
governance structures 22
health care 223, 236
health facilities 222, 246
judicial system 201
justice infrastructure 4
medical services 223
medical system 231
freedom of expression 251
Freehold land tenure system 188
fundamental freedoms 361
Gacaca courts
(semi-traditional courts) 22
gender
audit 366
dimensions 115, 158
equality 73, 86, 88, 110, 113, 114, 117, 118, 120, 121, 139, 140, 142-146, 149, 152, 155, 164, 174, 369
equity 245
inequalities 139
justice 7, 16, 17, 73, 88, 89, 113, 143, 145, 148, 149, 380
mainstreaming 361, 369, 370
relations 17, 24, 120, 380
gender-
based discrimination 142
based quotas 143
based violence 72
equitable land tenure system 174
sensitive laws 139, 145
genocidal violence 81
genocide victims 287
Gikuyu beliefs 47
global crimes court. *See* ICC
Global/international justice 5, 21, 63, 64, 66, 67, 79, 382
good governance 49, 67, 94, 95, 96, 97, 99, 101, 103, 105, 107, 129, 131, 276, 359, 361, 364, 371
Great Lakes Region 177, 183, 216
group punishment. *See* mob action
health
education 240, 241
facilities 222, 226, 227, 229-232, 235, 236, 246, 267
justice 223, 227, 228, 230, 231, 232, 243-247
services 2, 226, 227, 229, 232, 239, 245, 272, 280
healthy
delivery 223, 224, 230
Herbal medicines/local medicines 232
historical
grievances 48
injustices xiv, 39, 46
justice 23, 35, 39, 40, 42, 43, 58, 59
holistic development 377
homosexuality 378, 379
Bill 2014 378
human

practice 3
rights' obligations 3
sacrifice 13
Human
resource 112
Rights vii, xiv, 1, 2, 9, 18, 20, 28, 29, 35, 49, 61, 90, 91, 137, 177, 183, 186, 191, 192, 193, 219, 247, 248, 287, 320, 335, 339, 353, 354, 366, 370, 371, 376, 377
Rights violations 183
Rights Watch 287, 339, 354
humanitarian
agencies 251
aid 257
hybrid legal pluralism 204, 205
Identity Politics 27, 60
illegal laws 378
illegitimate children 115, 116, 117, 120
income generating activities 268
informal
institutions 14, 15, 22
policing 337
informational medium 81
infrastructure reconstruction 257
Institute for war and peace reporting (IWPR) 65, 66, 67, 68, 72
Institute for War and Peace Reporting (IWPR) 65
institutional framework(s) 360
institutionalised vigilantism 337
inter-generational discourses 42
inter-generational political authority 41
interlocked land conflicts 158
Intermediate Courts 302, 303, 306
internal
displacement 38
security systems 56
Internal Displacement Monitoring Centre IDMC 190, 194
international
justice interventions 21
International
crimes 77
criminal court (ICC) 25, 35, 36, 63, 66, 67, 74, 75, 77, 78, 79, 356, 382
criminal justice 64
Humanitarian Law 77
human rights law 250
International treaties/conventions 243, 365
intra-Kikuyu community 46
intra-state armed conflicts 75
Islamic inheritance 117
Islamic law 115, 116, 117
judicial
cooperation 363, 364
information 363
institutions xx, 87, 285, 317
knowledge 362
service delivery (Rw) 285, 317
judicial cooperation 363, 364
justice
institutions 12, 21, 156, 208, 287
justice initiatives 63
Justice, law and order sector (JLOS) xiv, xvi, xxi, 1, 2, 4, 7-13, 15, 17-19, 22, 25, 26, 284, 358, 365
Justice, Law and Order Sector (JLOS) xiv, 4, 7
Kagame, Paul 288
Kampala Capital City Authority (KCCA) 352

Karamoja sub-regions 85
Kenya African National Union (KANU) 41, 46, 55
Kenyatta, Jomo 41, 54, 281
Kibaki, Mwai 46, 55
Kikuyu (Ky)
  community 37, 46, 58
  grievances 40
  lineages 52
Kimathi, Dedan 34, 41
Kony, Joseph 71, 72, 74, 75, 77, 78, 183
labour
  disputes 365
Labour
  Courts 365
land
  administration 94, 95, 97, 101, 103, 107, 112, 113, 123, 124, 127-130, 132, 144, 145, 169, 174, 192
  allocation 20, 94, 98, 109, 115, 117, 120, 125, 131, 139, 145, 149
  court administration 95
  developments 94, 99, 100
  dispute resolution(s) 174, 185, 191, 199, 210, 380
  disputes xvi, xvii, 19, 94, 95, 99-104, 108, 110, 118, 121, 124, 127, 128, 132, 140, 155, 158, 161, 181, 182, 184, 185, 190, 191-197, 200, 201, 202, 204, 206-213, 316, 381, 383
  dispute settlement 140
  governance 94, 95, 96, 97, 99, 100, 101, 102, 103, 104, 105, 106, 108, 109, 110, 112, 120, 125, 128, 130, 131
  information systems 95, 105, 111
  inheritance 114, 116, 117
  justice systems 23
  laws 95, 103, 104, 108, 109, 110, 113, 114, 120, 121, 122, 123, 125, 129, 130, 131, 132, 145, 146, 175, 213
  management control 102
  rights xvi, xvii, xxi, 24, 26, 86, 94, 102, 111, 112, 114, 115, 118, 119, 138-144, 146,-152, 155-161, 163, 164, 165, 168-175, 182, 185, 187, 189, 193-196, 204, 207, 210,-214, 381
Land
  Acquisition Act 1967 121, 122, 125
  Act 1998 (Ug) 191
  Act 1999 (TZ) 94, 114, 115, 121-125, 136, 142
  Amendment Act of 2010 (Ug) 170
  Equity Movement 166, 195, 212
  registration 98, 99, 104, 118
land administration 94, 95, 97, 101, 103, 107, 112, 113, 123, 124, 127-130, 132, 144, 145, 169, 174, 192
Land grabbing/forcible acquisition 197, 208
language groups 157
Leasehold land tenure system 188
legal
  aid services 212, 366, 373
  pluralism 14, 24, 28, 204, 205, 206, 207, 208, 217, 219
Legal
  Aid Project (Ug) 191, 212
  Aid Providers 212, 373
  Justice 283

livelihoods interventions 257
Local Council Courts
  Act, 2006 (LCCA) 383
Local council courts (Ug) 18, 142, 149, 151, 153, 155-157, 159-161, 168, 169, 170, 174, 175, 182, 201, 203, 204, 209, 213, 215, 381, 383, 384
Local Defence Units (LDUs) 336
local police 336, 367
Lord's Resistance Army (LRA) 12, 67, 70, 71, 74, 75, 77, 78, 84, 183, 184, 196, 197
lower-level workers 289
low-income groups 3
Lukwiya, Raska 77
Mailo land system (Ug) 188
mama kits 238, 239, 242
mass communication 80
maternal health care xviii, 231, 243, 245, 246
maternal health needs 246
Maternal ill-health 230
Maternal mortality/maternal deaths 243
maternity care services 230
Mato Oput 72
Mau Mau (Ky) vi, xiv, xv, 23, 32, 33, 34, 35, 37, 38, 40, 41, 42, 45, 46, 47, 48, 49, 50, 51, 52, 53, 54, 57, 58, 59, 60, 61, 380
  movement 40, 48, 53
  veterans 23, 32, 34, 59
medical midwives 232
mental abilities 251
mental health 257
mental impairment 273
Millennium Development Goal (MDG) 229, 230
mob action 326, 328, 330
Mob violence/justice xx, xxi, 13, 17, 25, 322-335, 337-352, 354, 355, 381
Moi, Arap Daniel (President) 44
mortgage payments 173
mother-to-child HIV/AIDS transmission 225
mulerwa. *See* TBAs
multiparty politics 39
Mungiki
  revolt 58
  violence 55
  women 45
  youth movement 46
Nakivale refugee settlement (Ug) 255
Nakulabye market 345
National land policy 1995 (TZ) 99, 115, 135
National Land Policy 2013 210
Nation Resistance Movement (NRM) 77, 153, 342, 344, 379
neo-natal care 226
neo-traditional institutions 22
New Public Management (NPM) 294
non-custodial sentencing 19
non-formal justice systems 14, 15
Non-governmental organisations (NGOs) xv, xxi, 23, 62, 66, 171, 208, 360
Northern Uganda media club (NU-MEC) 65, 66, 67, 68
Northern Uganda Media Club (NU-MEC) 65
Norwegian Refugee Council (NRC) 184, 190, 191

obstetric complications 243
Odhiambo, Okot 77
Ombudsman (Rw & BR) 20, 370, 376
Ongwen, Dominic 78
Organic Land Law 2005 144
organisational culture 301
Otti, Vincent 78
Owino market 339, 341, 342, 345, 346, 347, 349, 350
ownership disputes 158
patrilineal inheritance 163
patrimonial leadership 42
Peaceful resolution(s) 361, 362
personal liberty 10, 21
personal security 251, 372
Persons with Disabilities (PWDs) 251
persons with special needs (PSNs) 252, 263, 264
petty theft 332
physical capability 250
Physical disabilities/physical impairment 260, 266
political affiliations 159
political crisis. *See* political instability
political federation 360, 361, 363
political instability 255
political intimidation 38
political militia 38
Political Participation 177
political tensions 81
political violence xiv, 34, 42
Post-conflict – development xvii, 89
post-conflict land justice 205
Post-Conflict Societies 219
post-election violence (Ky) 22, 33, 55, 340
Post-election violence (Ky) 340
post-natal stages 224
post-war
  recovery 89
  situation(s) 68, 85
post-war Amuru 190
post-war communities 82, 206
post-war justice 62
Post-war (Northern Uganda) vii, xv, 9, 12, 68, 70, 85, 89, 181, 182, 190, 194, 204, 206, 381
Poverty Reduction 134, 177, 359
Poverty Reduction Strategy Plans (PRSP) 359
power relations 41
power-sharing 76
Primary courts (Rw) 294, 307
professional malpractice 13
property rights 109, 115, 181, 188, 190, 192, 195, 206
psychological rehabilitation 276
public affairs management 294
public agenda 83
public distrust 331
public opinion 81
public property 97, 110
Public sector reforms (Rw) 294
public servants 9, 21, 129, 130, 298
punitive justice 88
radio Télévision Libre des Mille Collines (RTLM) 81
recognitional justice 37
refugee leaders xix, 251, 261, 264, 266, 267, 269, 276, 277
refugee protection 23
refugee rights 23
refugee settlements 254, 264, 267, 274, 277, 280
Refugees with disabilities (RWDS)

275, 278
refugee welfare committees (RWCS) 260, 266
regional peace 362
religious cult(s) 42, 52
reproductive health advice 244
Resistance councils (RCs)/local councils (LCs) 140, 152, 179, 336
restorative justice 63, 64, 74, 79, 88
Rural Uganda Land Alliance 171
Rwandan genocide (1994) 81, 297
Rwandan judicial reforms 289, 294, 295, 297
Rwandan Judiciary Annual Report 2010 288
Rwandan Patriotic Front (RPF) 297
same-sex relationships 378
sanitation improvement 268
security information 362
settlement activities 252
settlements
 Kiryandongo 254
 Kyangwali 254
sexually transmitted infections 234, 244
sexual minorities 22
sexual orientation 251, 378
sexual violence 12, 88, 329
skills upgrading 257
social barriers 256
social bonds 346, 351, 381
Social Development vi, vii, xii, 2, 10, 18, 21, 140, 151, 171, 279, 365
social divisions 81
social justice xiv, xv, xxi, 1-10, 12-14, 17, 19, 22-26, 28, 32, 35, 37, 41, 42, 43, 47, 56, 57, 63, 64, 89, 99, 101, 131, 141, 145, 168, 223, 232, 250,-253, 256, 258, 260, 261, 264, 266, 267, 268, 274-277, 324, 331, 358, 359, 360, 361, 364, 369, 372, 377-382
social justice-oriented reforms 14
social land rights 102
social problems 3, 13
social protection vi, 16, 21, 358, 359, 360, 365, 375
social protection systems 21
social realities 76
social relations 73, 83
social rights 12
social stigma 256
social structures 80
Social Work ii, vii, 354
societal attitudes 260
socio-economic development 147, 361, 369
socio-economic disparities 48
spiritual beliefs 47
street-level bureaucrats 25, 284, 285, 286, 290, 291, 292, 295, 300, 301, 302, 303, 304, 305, 314, 315, 316, 317
structural inequalities 3
Subsistence agriculture/farming 139, 140, 157
Succession Act (Ug) 151, 152, 163
Sustainable Development 133, 180, 218, 219
systematic injustices 87
Systemic social justice 5
territorial conflicts 76
Toro agreement (1900) 188
Traditional Beliefs 248
Traditional Birth Attendants (TBAs) xviii, 222

traditional institutions 15, 20, 22, 204, 208
traditional leaders 191, 192, 196, 209, 211, 212
traditional midwives. *See* TBA
traditional values 37, 43
transitional justice vii, xv, 12, 19, 20, 21, 22, 27, 65, 71, 79
transitional politics 42
tribal conflict 255
Uganda constitution 1995 224
Uganda Human Rights Commission (UHRC) 192
Uganda Land Alliance (ULA) 191
Uganda Land Commission 183
Uganda law society (ULS) 212
Uganda Police Force (UPF) 335
UN-Habitat 101, 102, 103, 136, 149
United Nations High Commission for Refugees (UNHCR) 184
Universal Declaration of Human Rights (UDHR) 186
universal land rights 189
Universal primary education (UPE) 245
Urban Governance Index (UGI) 102
urban land governance 105, 110, 120
urban Mbeya xvi, 94, 95, 96, 100, 103, 113, 115, 117, 121, 123, 129, 130, 170, 381
urban slums 258
victim-centred justice 88, 380
Village land act 1999, (TZ) 94, 114, 115, 121, 123, 124, 125, 136, 142
village land councils (TZ) 126
Village land councils (TZ) 98
Village Land Councils (TZ) 143
vulnerable persons 202, 366
vulnerable refugee groups 257
war crimes 64, 72, 75, 77, 78, 79, 86
war crime trials 72, 74, 86
water source management 268
women's empowerment 174
Women's refugee commission (2010) 258
World Bank (WB) 76, 92, 101, 102, 103, 133, 134, 136, 167, 178, 179, 219, 279, 359
World Health Organisation (WHO) 274, 281, 331, 357
World Vision 222
World War II 81

www.ingramcontent.com/pod-product-compliance
Lightning Source LLC
LaVergne TN
LVHW052024200926
848481LV00005B/1576
9789970258871